ROCKS AND HARD PLACES

Antarctica is the coldest, windiest, highest and driest continent on earth.

ROCKS AND HARD PLACES

Alex Harris

A South African's journey to the highest mountain on every continent

First published in 2004 by Struik Publishers
(a division of New Holland Publishing
(South Africa) (Pty) Ltd)
New Holland Publishing is a member of Johnnic Communications Ltd

London • Cape Town • Sydney • Auckland

Cornelis Struik House, 80 McKenzie Street, Cape Town 8001

ISBN 1 86872 871 4

1 3 5 7 9 10 8 6 4 2

Publishing Manager: Dominique le Roux
Managing Editor: Lesley Hay-Whitton
Editor: Michelle Coburn
Designer: Sian Marshall
Proofreader: Tessa Kennedy

Reproduction by Hirt & Carter Cape (Pty) Ltd
Printed and bound in Hong Kong by Sing Cheong Printing Company Limited

Additional photographs for this book were supplied by the following:
Matthew Holt: Chairlifts on Elbrus (pp28 to 29); **Neil Griffin:** Alex Harris and Sean Disney meet Sir Edmund Hillary (p87);
Mike Hodges: Carstensz summit ridge (p147); **Discovery Health:** video stills (pp189 to 195);
Struik Image Library, Daryl and Sharna Balfour: Amboseli National Elephant Park, Kenya (pp92 to 93);
Brit Harris: portrait of Alex Harris, inside back flap. Thanks to **George Mallory II** for supplying his photo on p71.
Front Cover Image: Joby Ogwyn reaches the summit of Mount Vinson, photo by Alex Harris.
Back Cover Image: Hercules landing on ice at Patriot Hills, Antarctica, photo by Alex Harris.

Visit us at **www.struik.co.za**

Log on to our photographic website
www.imagesofafrica.co.za for an
African experience.

To Brit, the unknown hero in my life.

Contents

Sean Disney and Sean Wisedale near the top of the Khumbu Icefall, Everest.

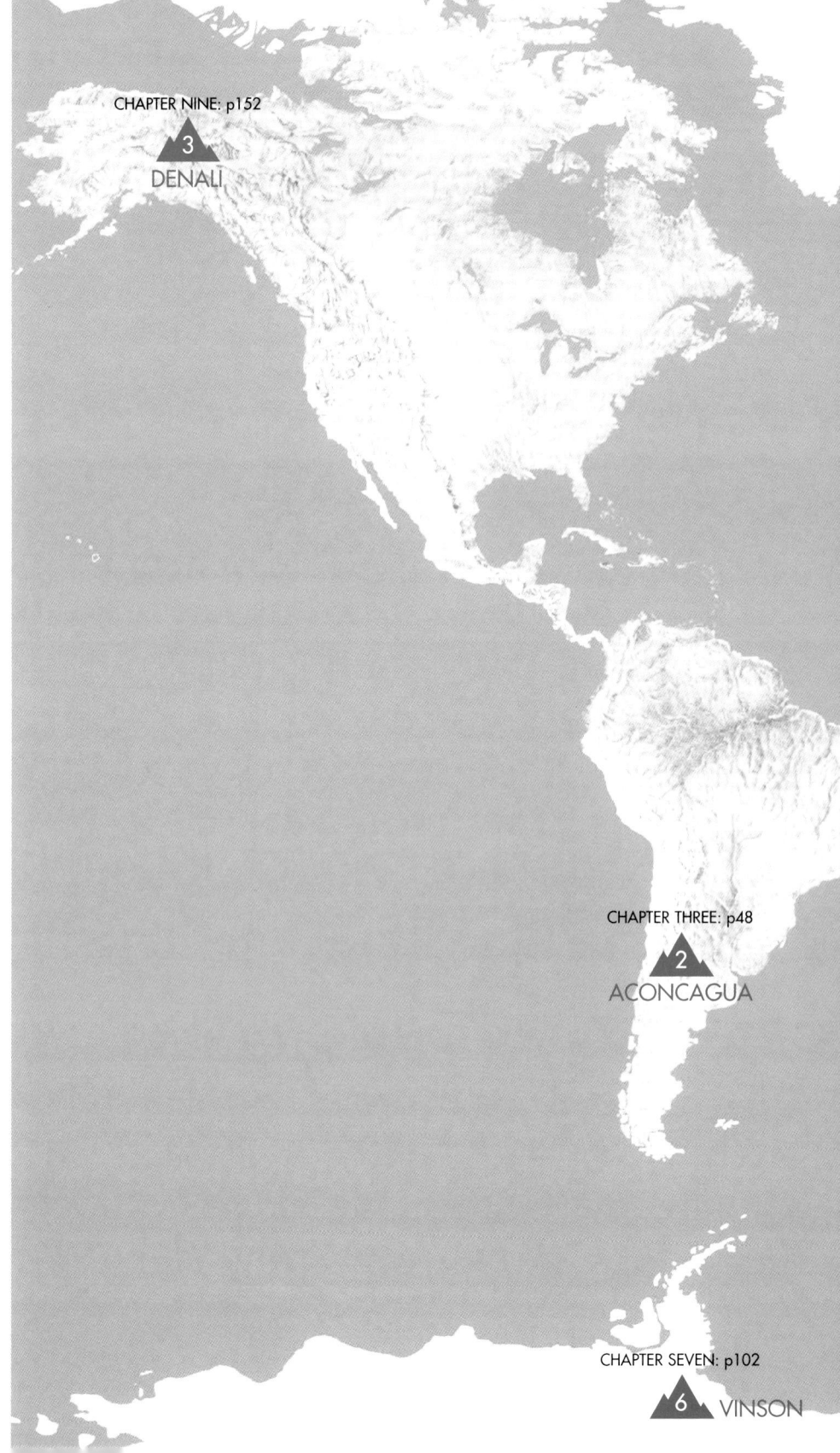

The Seven Summits

The highest mountain on each continent in height order:

EVEREST
8 850 metres (29 035 feet)
Tibet/Nepal, Asia

ACONCAGUA
6 959 metres (22 834 feet)
Argentina, South America

DENALI (Mount McKinley)
6 194 metres (20 320 feet)
Alaska, North America

KILIMANJARO
5 895 metres (19 340 feet)
Tanzania, Africa

ELBRUS
5 642 metres (18 510 feet)
Russia, Europe

MOUNT VINSON
4 897 metres (16 066 feet)
Antarctica

CARSTENSZ PYRAMID
4 884 metres (16 023 feet)
Indonesia, Australasia

Source: Encyclopaedia Britannica

CHAPTER NINE: p152
3 DENALI

CHAPTER THREE: p48
2 ACONCAGUA

CHAPTER SEVEN: p102
6 VINSON

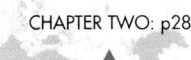

Foreword

Sometimes in life, nature throws up an opportunity to meet an extraordinary person in unusual circumstances. Such was my experience in meeting Alex Harris.

It was on the slopes of the highest mountain in Antarctica with the ambient temperature inside our small two-metre by two-metre tent at −20°C. Outside, the wind was howling at over 100 kilometres an hour and the temperature was touching −40°C. In such an icy and uncomfortable setting, nervously sheltering from the gigantic storm raging outside on Mount Vinson, I got to know a very interesting person.

Over a 48-hour period, during which sleep came only sporadically, Alex attempted to calm frayed nerves by conducting discussions on subjects ranging from Einstein's Theory of Relativity, to whether God actually spoke to Moses on Mount Sinai, to how to make millions marketing certain products on E-Bay's worldwide consumer network. His inquiring mind had led him to give thought to these (and many more!) subjects and each one was pursued with an intelligence and purpose that commanded much respect.

As a result of his adventurer's need to understand the universe in which we live, Alex was able to talk with absolute authority on this diverse range of subjects for those 48 hours − of course making him a perfect climbing partner!

In addition, his calm demeanour in such adverse conditions showed that, as a high altitude mountain climber, he ranks up there with the best in the world. Not many high altitude climbers can still boast 10 toes and 10 fingers after spending nearly 15 years scaling the highest peaks in the world. This is as much testimony to his natural climbing skills, as it is to his desire to preserve his health so that he can fulfil his life in many other avenues.

In many respects, getting to know Alex is like climbing a high mountain − every time you crest a hill expecting it to be the end of the climb, a new peak presents itself and, although the climber is fatigued, the new challenge is irresistible!

Lawrence Seeff
August 2003

'There is a place where the African plains cease their flat wandering and rise sharply to the sky. A place where the dust turns to ice and brown becomes white, and the elephants can lift their heads and know this is Africa.'
— Alex Harris

CHAPTER ONE
Glittering Peak

I can't remember exactly when I first thought about climbing Kilimanjaro. I know it was some time in that first year after school when no-one really knew what they wanted to do with their lives. Most of my friends had gone to university and said they were certain about their chosen careers. But I didn't believe them. If they were only half as confused as I was, then they didn't have a clue.

I was bobbing around like a fish in a tank waiting to be fed. So it could have been one of any number of things that inspired me – a picture or even a television programme – I can't really say. But I remember that climbing Kilimanjaro was something I really wanted to do. Deep down inside me this thing was growing out of control. There was nothing I could do to stop it. I just had to climb Africa's highest mountain.

But I knew diddly squat about climbing mountains. I had only recently joined the Mountain Club of South Africa (MCSA). I knew what a rope was and could just manage to pronounce 'karabiner'. Knowledge about exactly how all these pieces of equipment worked together would come with time. For now it didn't matter. My mind was made up. I was going to climb Kilimanjaro and that was that.

So, how does a young guy fresh out of school go about climbing one of the world's largest free-standing volcanoes? Well, when you're young and ignorant you tend not to think about things that really are quite important. What I did realize was that this was something I shouldn't do alone. Enter Robin.

Robin Walshaw was one of those guys who seemed to know exactly what they wanted to do with their lives. He had a couple of months to muck around before he committed four years of his life to discovering everything a person might want to know about computers. He was bright but definitely not a geek and you could still bend his arm to do something fun, adventurous or crazy.

'What did you say?' Robin asked incredulously.

'Kilimanjaro,' I replied.

'You mean that great big volcano in Kenya?'

'Well actually it's in Tanzania but yeah, that's the one.'

'You're nuts.'

We were pushing our bicycles along a busy street just after sunset. I can't remember exactly what it was, but we had just finished doing something harebrained that had left one of our bikes immobile. This happened a lot of the time, leaving both of us moping along and one of us in pain. And it was always my fault, or so Robin had everyone believe.

Robin was a stubborn bloke filled with that fiery English patriotism that can be so frustrating to others. He was born in Yorkshire and his family had moved to South Africa when he was still a child. Deep down he loved Africa but he couldn't help letting you know just how great the British Empire was. On occasion, his large head would fill up with that fiery Anglo blood and glow royally. There were times when I could've sworn I caught a glimpse of the Union Jack emblazoned on his forehead and I would want to bop him one. But generally, we got on very well.

Robin looked at me for the first time along this section of the road.

'What do we know about climbing anyway?' he asked.

'What a stupid question,' I thought.

'What's your point?' I replied.

'Well isn't it 6 000 metres high, or something?'

'It's less than that. It's about 5 800 or 5 900 metres.'

'Great. I feel much better. And exactly how high have you been?'

This kind of talk annoyed the hell out of me. But, then again, Robin and I often frustrated each other.

'Look, it's a volcano. You don't need to use ropes or anything. It's just a bit high.'

'A bit high! You're nuts!'

But that was that. A seed had been sown and I couldn't ignore it.

Robin spent weeks deliberating before finally confessing that his parents thought it was a foolish idea. Of course it was. Yes, he knew it would be fun but his parents had said 'no'. Remember, we had recently finished school, so our parents still took it upon themselves to make sure we didn't do anything foolish. I guess mine were more lenient than Robin's.

D-day arrived and no amount of arm-twisting could persuade Robin to join me. A part of me felt sad because he really wanted to go and I knew how much fun it would be if he did. 'Next time!' I said. Man, how prophetic that would turn out to be.

Back in 1989, South Africans weren't allowed anywhere near Tanzania. Rumours abounded about how some young South African had been caught on one of the Tanzanian islands. Last anyone knew he was rotting away in a tin jail in the middle of nowhere. Poor kid. Yup, the politics were pretty screwed up back then. But when you're young and naïve you don't understand all that complicated stuff. All I knew was that I couldn't get into Tanzania and that it was a big problem. But I was smart – or at least Mom had been.

Shortly before I was born, my mother had thought it prudent to let the momentous occasion of my entry into the world happen somewhere else – Portugal, to be specific. Somewhere back in her lineage, her family had produced wine in a valley in Portugal. How thoughtful of them. So, I had a Portuguese passport. This would later get me into more trouble than I could possibly imagine. But, for now, I had it sussed. I would just trot along with my two passports and, when the time came, I would proudly display my foreign passport. Boy, would those border guards be impressed!

Africa is a big place. In fact, there are a great number of valleys between my home, in a small suburb of Johannesburg, and the plains that suffer under the weight of Kilimanjaro. My plan was simple. I would fly to Malawi, known as the Warm Heart of Africa, and then take a bus up to the Tanzanian border. Once across the border, I would use local transport to Moshi, a small town at the foot of Kili. I would then organize the porters I needed and climb the mountain. Once down, I would simply reverse the trip, perhaps even taking the time to swim in Lake Malawi on the way back. The plan seemed perfect. What could go wrong?

As for gear, that base was also covered. Someone had once told me that Kilimanjaro was quite cold. They seemed to know what they were talking about, so I packed a jersey. My mom thought it would be colder, so I packed another.

'But you've never even been there! How would you know how cold it's going to be?' I protested.

'Just take it,' she said.

'I've got enough clothes. How am I supposed to carry all this stuff anyway?'

'Oh for crying out loud, will you just take the jersey?'

'Okay, okay! Jeepers, it's not you who has to lug all this stuff up there, you know.'

'I'm sure you will be fine.'

Yeah, so was I. Except that my bag had now grown from the size of a small kit bag, to the size of one of those backbreaking bags you see the Special Forces carrying around in war movies. Seriously, how was I going to carry all this stuff? Someone had told me 'they' liked clothes 'up there'. Perfect. I'd just give away all my spare T-shirts as I made my way through Africa.

Three hours in a plane and I was in

Lilongwe, the commercial capital of Malawi. But I wasn't too keen to see the sights. I was a young man on a mission and wanted to get going. However, I did have to spend a night in a youth hostel, which I soon discovered was a very good thing.

I had a five am bus booked for the next day, so thought I would eat a small snack and then hit the sack. I walked down to the hostel's small lounge and sat down opposite a Chinese guy. Well, I guess he could also have been from Hong Kong, Singapore or Taiwan. However he was definitely from the East, way East. He seemed older than me, but was still a reasonably young lad.

'Howzit going!' I stretched out my hand.

'Good, good.' We shook hands.

'I'm Alex from South Africa.'

'Ah, South Africa.' He seemed impressed. Wait until I told him what I was going to do.

'You go diving in the lake?' he asked.

This was the part of the conversation I was really looking forward to.

'No, I am going to climb Kilimanjaro!' I blurted out. As far as I was concerned, I had climbed it already.

'Ah, Kilimanjaro!' he exclaimed. He was obviously very impressed.

'Do you know of Kilimanjaro?' I asked. It seemed like a reasonable question.

'Yes, I climb it!'

'What?' I said. 'You're also going to climb it?'

'No, I climb it two weeks ago.'

'You've climbed it already? All the way to the top?'

My Chinese friend smiled. 'Yes, to top.'

I was stumped. Bowled over. Hit for a six by a man from the East. Here was someone who had climbed Kilimanjaro all the way to the top and he didn't even look like a mountain climber. This was going to be a piece of cake.

I spent the next hour bugging my new friend with questions about the mountain. How long did it take? How cold was it? What kind of clothes did he have? These were questions I should have asked a long time before that but they had never seemed important. Now I was beginning to see exactly how important they were.

He dug through his belongings and pulled out a business card belonging to the Tanzanian company he had used to organize the logistics of his ascent. He showed it to me. I was impressed. It carried the name of the company, which I can't remember, and a stylized picture of Kilimanjaro. The mountain looked just as I had imagined it: easy slopes and a big, round top.

I said good night to my Chinese friend and retired. I now had more of a plan. I knew how long it would take to climb Kilimanjaro. I knew how cold it would be and I knew exactly what clothes I had in that great, big bag of mine.

Some of the worst moments of my life, the really agonizing ones, have been spent on buses. Long trips, hot trips, bumpy trips – they have all been on

buses. To get to the northern part of Malawi, the very tip that shared a border with Tanzania, I had to go on a bus trip, and a long one at that – 18 hours of agony. There was no way around it. I could travel by boat but that would take days and I had more important things to do.

Discomfort takes on a whole new meaning when you're travelling on a bus that's meant to carry 50 people but has been filled with 100 passengers and some chickens. Padded seats don't exist, nor does air-conditioning. Toilet? Forget it. I sat in the front of the bus and got as comfortable as I could. This was going to be hell – or character building, as I would often be told on many similar journeys in years to come.

The first few hours of the trip were fine. It was dark and cool outside. The heat of Africa was hidden for the moment and my mind drifted. What would Kilimanjaro look like when I saw it for the first time? Would it tower as high into the sky as it did in my mind?

Hours later, I woke up with a throbbing head. I'd been trying so desperately to sleep that I'd propped my head on the bar in front of me, only to have it bashed about on the bumpy road. It was impossible to tell how long we'd been driving for, but it felt like forever. And now it was hot.

Towards the middle of the day, the bus veered off the main road and sped in the wrong direction. I was vaguely aware that this wasn't the right way but no-one else seemed to care, so I ignored the unannounced detour. The bus continued for close to an hour before it ground to a halt in a small village in the middle of nowhere. The door opened and a man climbed aboard. One man. Not a whole village, just one lonely guy. He didn't even have a bag with him. The bus turned around and sped back to the main road. 'Jeepers,' I thought, 'what the heck was that all about?'

I was too tired to be angry but made a mental note to blow my fuse at some point in the future.

'The Warm Heart of Africa'

should instead read 'The Blistering Butt of Africa'. I was a wreck when the bus rolled into Kaporo, about 30 kilometres (19 miles) from the Tanzanian border. I couldn't walk straight for several minutes and hobbled about, rubbing my head and trying as hard as I could to stretch my legs. I had about an hour before sunset and it wasn't far to the border so I asked around for a ride on one of the local taxis. I soon found myself jammed into a taxi with four other people and feeling like I'd commandeered a Land Rover Discovery.

We soon reached the village that formed the border post at the northern tip of Malawi. It consisted of nothing more than a few dusty shacks and a gate. Chickens pecked around in the dirt and the usual mangy dogs moped and whined for scraps. It was bleak.

I climbed out of the taxi and scanned the surrounding area. What now? The sun was about to set and the border had been closed for a while. I would have to wait until morning before entering Tanzania. I asked some people what travellers generally did when they arrived after dark. All I got in reply were shrugs and blank stares. Several people pointed 'that way', so I went that way. But there was nothing there. Then I saw a couple of backpackers. 'Great,' I thought. 'They'll know exactly what to do.' I approached them, introduced myself and was surprised to find they were from Australia. Wow, that far from home! And I had thought *I* was out of *my* comfort zone.

The Australians, James and Keri, had found a spot to set up camp and were only too happy for me to join them. They were also heading across the border the next day, although they weren't being quite as adventurous as I was. Kilimanjaro wasn't mentioned, although they did say something about Lake Victoria. I also didn't reveal too much about my intentions. I told them I was thinking about climbing the mountain, depending on the cost and other factors involved. What a lie! I knew damn well exactly what I wanted to do. Why was I being so hesitant? Maybe I wasn't too keen to meet anyone else who had sauntered up Kilimanjaro. Hey, this was my first great adventure, and a dangerous one it was.

During the course of the evening we got onto the subject of the border post and the political hostilities between South Africa and Tanzania. It was a fascinating but scary conversation. Earlier in the day I'd happened to glance across at a man sitting next to me on the bus from hell. He had been looking at his bright yellow Tanzanian passport. In the middle of the page, in bold letters, had been the remarkable words:

'VALID FOR ALL COUNTRIES EXCEPT SOUTH AFRICA.' What? The words leapt from the page and struck me a blow! How could that be? It was ridiculous!

The rigours of the journey had soon made me forget the incident. But I was now reminded of it. James and Keri were telling me that it would be impossible for them to travel to Tanzania if they had visited South Africa within the previous few months.

'That's crazy!' I said.

'Oh it gets worse than that,' said James.

'Why?'

'Well, regardless of what passport you have, if your

stamps aren't in order, you don't get in either.'

'What do you mean?' I was a little concerned.

'If you don't have correct entry stamps, they won't let you into the country.'

'Are they that serious?'

'Yeah mate, that's all those bloody buggers do at the post.'

'Shit!'

'Why, what's the problem?'

'Well, I'm travelling on two passports.'

'Good for you, mate.'

'*Ja*, but the problem is that I landed on my South African passport and the bloody entry stamp is in that one.'

'Oh shit!' James understood. 'Yeah that's going to be a problem.'

'What do you think I can do?'

'Well there's not much you can do. I wouldn't even think about bribing them because these buggers have been known to be tough asses.'

I looked down at my passport. How could I have been such a lunk-head after everything I'd gone through to get to this point?

'Let's have a look at it.'

I tossed it across the fire and James flipped through the pages. 'Look, sometimes they're pretty lenient or aren't paying too much attention. Maybe you'll get lucky.'

I thought I was a lucky kind of guy. My tension level dropped a bit.

Our bags were packed early the next morning and we were ready to catch the first lift into Tanzania. The Malawian side was so relaxed that we'd all managed to have our passports stamped the night before. All we needed was a thumb out and a ride through the gate.

ABOVE AND TOP: People disbelieved the first reports that there was snow on the highest mountain in Africa, thinking it was impossible for this to occur near the equator.

We set off, masking our faces from the growing pall of dust. The trees on either side of the road were red with the stuff. Either it hadn't rained for a while, or the roads were permanently so dusty that there was always a cloud waiting to settle on everything. But the dust couldn't conceal the beauty of the landscape – the thick jungle stretching right up to the hills.

And then there it was, the Songwe River and a small bridge crossing into Tanzania, with a border post on either side. The truck rattled across the bridge and ground to a halt on the other side. Technically, we were in Tanzania. All I had to do was convince the buggers to let me stay.

We piled out and walked up to the first of three small huts. There was a rickety sign hanging from the door that read 'Immigration'. The second hut was labelled 'Customs', and the third 'Health'. I wondered how many I would get through. It was decided that James and Keri would go first because all their documents were in order. If I could learn anything from them, great. If not, I wouldn't be jeopardizing their entry into Tanzania.

I shuffled around outside, occasionally glancing up at the huts. They seemed to be taking an awfully long time. The Songwe followed its tired path just a short distance from the road. We were still quite close to Lake Malawi, which was probably five or six kilometres (three or four miles) away, so there was no white water, just the tired brown of a river that had run its course. The bush looked the same as it did on the Malawian side – covered in

Taking a break on the saddle between Kibo and Mawenzi.

Where it all begins: the entrance gate to the Kilimanjaro National Park.

thick red dust from the ground to the tops of the trees. And, as always, there was the obligatory chicken scratching in the dirt.

At last it was my turn. The Australians had made it to Customs and my moment of truth had arrived. Showdown time! All or nothing! I casually wandered up to the hut and stepped inside but, if I'd been any bigger, part of me would have been left standing in the street, that's how small this shack was. A wooden counter separated me from an armed guard. I proudly handed him my Portuguese passport. It felt like all I could do was smile and nod – the kind of silly nodding you do when you've been really stupid and know you can't hide it. I could barely conceal my apprehension. This was my dream and I wasn't prepared to have it swept aside by some arbitrary guard who apparently had nothing better to do than give innocent people a hard time.

I kept quiet. He started flipping through my passport, glancing up at me every now and then. How long would it take before he realized there was no stamp? Maybe he wouldn't see it at all. Would he really care? 'When did you land?' Great, that lasted long!

'Two days ago. Why?' Act dumb, the manual said.

'Where's your stamp?'

'Which stamp?' Now I was pushing it.

'Where's your stamp into Malawi?'

'Oh, that one.'

This was the part I'd rehearsed, the part where I spun him a yarn about also being a Canadian citizen. I'd landed with my Canadian passport but it was stolen when I was mugged – a reasonable explanation. I didn't have time to report the theft to the police because I wanted to climb Africa's highest mountain. You know, Kilimanjaro – it's in your country. And, well, here I am with my Portuguese passport because I'm one of those very interesting travellers who have two nationalities. What a crock of shit! The guy's never going to buy this.

The guard continued flipping through my passport, asking me an occasional question. I answered some of them smartly and others I really screwed up. This interrogation went on for about an hour. I wasn't making any headway but, then again, neither was he. I was still there, on the other side of his filthy counter, trying desperately to convince him to let me into his country.

Then it occurred to me that he might just be waiting for me to make him an offer he couldn't refuse. Sod that! I had just as much right to get into his country as anyone else. I sure wasn't going to bribe him in order to do it. I didn't make the offer. He didn't budge. I was getting desperate but still wasn't going to pay him. He eventually told me to leave. I refused. I had come halfway around the world to climb his mountain and I wasn't going anywhere. It did feel like I'd come from the farthest reaches of the planet to climb this mountain. And for some reason this felt strangely important.

We'd reached a stalemate, except he had the rifle and we were on his turf. He stepped outside and left me leaning on the counter – wondering, hoping. Ten minutes later he returned and again told me to leave. This time he was serious. No more games. I needed to get the hell out of there, or else there'd be serious consequences. I made one last plea but it fell on deaf ears. He called his friend, who didn't muck around with pleasantries but got right down to the bully. Pointing his rifle at me, he motioned for me to step outside. Fine, I thought. If you're going to play hardball then so be it.

ABOVE: *Kilimanjaro was always at the back of my mind when I was a kid: I used to think it was unbelievably high and definitely something that only adults should tackle.*

BELOW: *Daybreak on the rim of Kilimanjaro's crater.*

I stepped out of the hut. He muttered something and pointed his rifle to the other side of the bridge. That was where I needed to head – and now! I turned and gazed up the road that led into the interior, and the realization of my dreams. It looked like all the other dusty roads I'd seen on my journey. But this one was different. This one led to a place I longed for, and I felt I would never see it again.

I started walking back across the Songwe River into Malawi. Halfway across the bridge, I broke down and cried. I was so angry, so livid, that the only thing I could do was cry big, gushing sobs. It was over just like that. Some prick had put an end to my dreams, my destiny. Did he even know who I was, or care? It bugged me how someone seemingly insignificant could change the destiny of another person.

I reached the other side of the bridge, still in tears. I noticed a small clearing and a few huts that I hadn't seen earlier. Four or five old men sat in a circle on some logs, passing the time in the heat of the day. How strange I must have looked to them – a weeping figure crossing the bridge.

'Why is he crying?' they must have thought. 'What could possibly have meant so much to him, that he has now lost?'

One of the men stood up and motioned for me to sit with them. A kind gesture, but what would I say? They asked what had happened to upset me, but I could hardly speak. I tried to explain but my lungs were still trying to recover after my bawling fit. I made some horrible noises and wiped snot from my face. Then I sat down.

I soon got my breath back and gave them a shortened version of the story. They just nodded as I went along, muttering a word here and there. After a while one of the men said he could row me across the Songwe River for ten tambala, the equivalent of about five South African cents. It was a good idea for all of five seconds. Then I remembered the South African stuck somewhere in jail, rotting away. I wasn't keen to get to know him. I stood up and walked off. I didn't even say goodbye to the old men.

I was still mad, and would be for months. In fact, deep down, there is still a part of me that would like to let that guard have it – every angry mouthful. Still, I guess he was just doing his job. And hey, that's Africa.

'Always, and more especially on mountains, have I watched daybreak with deep awe. It is an age-old miracle which repeats itself again and again, every day the same and every day different. It is the hour of Genesis.'
— Felice Benuzzi,
No Picnic on Mt Kenya

24

OPPOSITE TOP: *Looking across the snow-covered crater.*

OPPOSITE BELOW: *Mawenzi Peak stands out as a shadow against the rising sun.*

ABOVE: *It's estimated that Kilimanjaro's spectacular glaciers will have completely disappeared by 2020.*

LEFT: *About to reach the crater in the cold light of dawn.*

BELOW: *A section of the last few remaining permanent pieces of ice on Kilimanjaro.*

OPPOSITE: *The campsites hidden in the forests form one of the many attractions of the Machame Route.*

THE MOUNTAIN GUIDE:
Elbrus

- **ALSO KNOWN AS:** Mingi-Tau, meaning 'Resembling 1 000 mountains', because of its size.

- **HEIGHT:** 5 642 metres (18 510 feet).

- **FIRST ASCENT:** 1874 by A. Moore, F. Gardiner, F. Grove and H. Walker.

- **LOCATION:** The Caucasus, Russia.

- **POINT OF INTEREST:** A twin-peaked volcano (extinct).

In 1874 guide Akia Sottaev summited with the Grove Expedition. He was 85 at the time, and was the first person to have summited both the East and West Peaks.

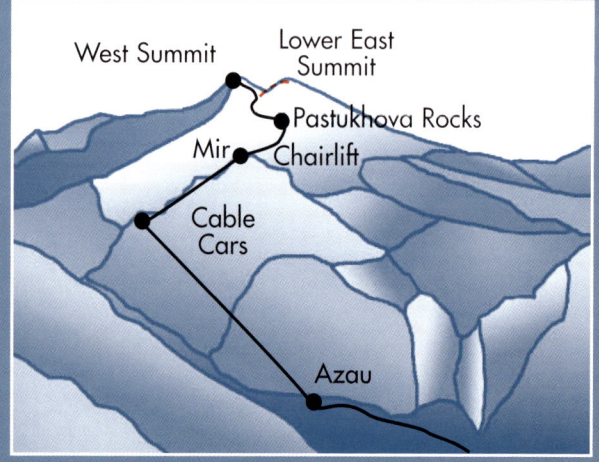

A ski lift assists climbers on Elbrus by taking them up to 4 000 metres (13 123 feet) before they have to start climbing.

LEFT: *Learning the ropes in Russia.*

ABOVE: *Gaining some ice experience in the Bezengi Valley before moving on to Elbrus.*

Elbrus consists mostly of snow slopes and the odd steep section.

CHAPTER TWO

High Drama

'*V drygoe komnate okno ni atkruvaitsa*', or in English: The window in the other room doesn't open. This very useful sentence happened to be the first bit of Russian I learnt. I was sure it would come in handy while I discovered the joys and difficulties of travelling in Russia. It was 1992 and, as apartheid came to an end, South Africans accustomed to international isolation were being allowed into Russia for the first time. Political, social and economic changes were taking effect in this giant country, the curtains were slowly opening and we were among the few who were daring to step inside.

It all began as an exchange programme between the Mountain Club of South Africa and one of the many Russian federation clubs. The Russians would host our climbers, and we would return their hospitality at some stage in the future.

The club decided I was an up-and-coming young climber who deserved to go on the first exchange. I'm not sure why, because at the time I hadn't climbed anything significant. Maybe all my dreaming was paying off at last. Hey, it was a chance to climb some big mountains. How could I say no?

The Russian club in question thought the Caucasus mountain range would be a good place to visit. It was accessible – not too high, but technical enough to make it fun – or at least that's what we were told.

Including all the states that were once members of the former Soviet Union, the region has more than five mountain ranges that leave their mark on any map, some of them reaching as high as 7 500 metres (24 606 feet). At 5 642 metres (18 510 feet), Elbrus stands the tallest in the Caucasus.

It is a beautiful volcano that towers above the range, close to the Black Sea. The group was excited at the thought of just getting near it.

We didn't do too much thinking for ourselves in those early days of travelling in Russia and left most of that up to our hosts, generally because we had no other choice. Politically, Russia was a pretty sensitive place in 1992, and so was South Africa. We could only travel in Russia if we were officially invited, which we were, and then continuously 'looked after' by our hosts – Tola, Valodya and Vova. The constant 'looking after' was the part that wore us down. It wasn't long before we felt like children on a school field trip. Someone was always keeping an eye on us. I'm sure they meant well. They just didn't know much about looking after a bunch of South Africans. The following should give you some idea of what it was like: 'Greg, are you keen for a Coke?'

We were stuck in a town called Mineralnye Vody, which means 'mineral water', but don't assume there was heaps of it about. The place was a dump. We were on our way south from Moscow, heading towards the Caucasus, and had a day to spend sorting things out.

'What about Tola?' was Greg's response. Tola was a host who was particularly watchful.

'He'll be fine. We'll only take 10 minutes.'

We shuffled down the stairs and into the streets of Vody. Five minutes later we had bought a couple of Cokes and were about to head back when a white Lada pulled up next to us. Out jumped Tola.

'Alex, Greg, where you go?'

'We just went to get a Coke,' Greg replied.

'But you had Coke yesterday!'

Greg and I looked at each other.

'Please, gentlemen. It is foolish to go alone.'

'What are you talking about? We've only been gone for 10 minutes.'

'Come. We go back.' Tola was motioning for us to get into the car.

That was it then. We were allowed to have one Coke every two days.

Our many questions would get few answers in the coming days. At best, we would end up more confused. The word 'Mafia' came up often. That's why we couldn't walk about alone – the Mafia would get us, or rob us, or do something nasty. We never did see any members of the Mafia but we slowly grew intolerant of the Russians' suffocating attentiveness.

We arrived in the Bezengi Valley two days later, and were impressed by its incredible beauty. It was headed by the Bezengi Wall – eight kilometres (five miles) long, with peaks soaring to over 5 000 metres (16 404 feet). None of them looked easy. This would be our base for a couple of weeks, serving as both a training ground and an opportunity to do some serious ice climbing – exactly how serious this was going to be, would depend entirely on us.

The camp was filled with monstrous mess halls and tin huts, a legacy from the former Soviet Union. It was in these very halls that many of Russia's most famous mountaineers had started their climbing careers. Higher up in the valley, they had honed the skills that kept them alive on some of the world's highest peaks, including Everest.

We would soon find out that this was not a place for beginners, which is what most of us were. At 21, I was by far the youngest in the group – a complete novice with only a couple of years of rock climbing experience in South Africa behind me. Next were Darryl Margetts and Martin Seegers, middle-aged climbing partners who were seriously good on rock. They had also done an ice course in the Alps. Greg Devine was in the same league: a good rock climber but hoping to get some ice experience. Topping the group of South Africans were Germans Ulrike Kiefer and Hermann Vogl, who were older than the rest of us and had heaps of climbing experience between the two of them.

We spent the first few days settling in and relaxing, poring over maps and photos of various routes and trying to decide what would be a reasonable proposition.

> Gestola towered at the head of the valley – a peak so striking in its symmetry that it closely resembled the pyramids at Giza. It would arrest and hold my gaze, no matter where else in the valley I was intending to look. Wouldn't it be awesome to climb that thing?

For now, though, we had to be content with pottering around the lower valleys, honing the basic skills that would be essential later. When we mentioned Gestola as a goal, the Russians agreed. But there was some work to be done beforehand.

After a few days of climbing on the snout of the glacier, we moved further up the valley. Gestola grew in the sky above us. It was even more impressive now that we were closer to it but was by no means the highest in the valley. Famous peaks like Shkhara and Dykh Tau were a good few hundred metres higher, but they were out of our league and we thought they didn't look nearly as impressive.

The group set up camp at the point where the valley split both east and west, a position that looked precarious but was relatively sheltered and gave us grandstand views of the odd avalanche crashing down the mountain. It also felt good to be away from the monotony of Base Camp.

The plan was to climb a 'little' peak called Sella – small compared to the giants around, but it was still 4 300 metres (14 107 feet) high. This was the first time on ice for most of us, and boy was it fun! It was a perfect day for the job, and we set out to climb slowly up a 400-metre (1 312-foot) face of sparkling snow. But, after barely 50 metres (164 feet), I dropped one of my mittens. There it went, tumbling down the face and settling on the glacier. Shit! That thing cost me 500 bucks! The weather was good so I didn't have to worry about my hands. But climbing with one glove was still a pain.

We topped out on Sella at midday. My first South African first! No-one from my country had ever done this before. Not a single cloud hindered our view of the sweep of the Bezengi Wall. And there, a few kilometres away, stood Gestola. We were ready.

The rest of the day was spent abseiling down the other side of Sella and then walking, bum-sliding and falling our way down the glacier to camp. While everyone settled down for a late afternoon rest, I disappeared up the glacier to retrieve my glove – all on my own! How the clouds of ignorance hide the view of reality. I don't know which was worse: me setting off alone on a glacier, or the others letting me go. But retrieve my glove I did, nervously stepping from one crevasse to another.

In the morning we were ready to move across the valley and climb Gestola. Before we left we questioned a Russian party about the difficulty of the route. The only worrying thing they had to say was that bad weather was coming, and lots of it. A cold front was heading towards us from the Black Sea at high speed. We asked how long it would take to reach us. Two days. Maybe more, maybe less. Great, just what we needed – snow for the next few days.

We discussed all our options. No-one could be 100

percent sure but we all agreed that we could probably climb the peak before the storm hit us. What did I think? Well, I wasn't really thinking. Not about the serious stuff anyway. I just wanted to make sure I didn't get left behind. Hey, there was a peak to bag. Another South African first. And that's what it was all about, wasn't it?

Darryl disagreed. He was wise – the only one amongst us. His reasoning was: why rush and risk getting caught in the storm when we still had a couple of weeks to give it a go? So why weren't the rest of us thinking clearly?

Darryl stayed behind and the rest of us set off. It took most of that day to hike across the valley to the base of the west side. We were now in a corner of the Bezengi Wall that was surrounded by ice cliffs on either side. The energy of the group was go, go, go; and we still weren't thinking rationally.

Gestola wasn't too technical but it was a complex climb nevertheless. The route would involve climbing and hiking up to the pass to access the Bezengi Wall. Then we would begin the traverse. First we would climb Lyalver, which was a fair-sized peak in its own right, and then we would descend the other side and climb an intervening peak. And, finally, we would ascend Gestola. All this would be on ice and rock. Once on top of Gestola, we would have to reverse the journey to get down the pass and safely back to camp.

Accommodation on Elbrus consists of the 'Coke cans', barrel-like huts that each sleep four people.

Sella gave me my first taste of ice.

first on deep snow, and then on ice. The ice sections were great fun but extremely slow going. They were tricky and involved moving around rocky outcrops at regular intervals. Then it was just rock. For some reason I don't remember much of this section on the journey up, but the downward trip would be forever imprinted on my mind.

It was mid-morning when we summited Lyalver and we were all jubilant. This merry bunch of South Africans had bagged another first. We whipped out the flag and took several photos, just in case we didn't have time on the way down. What a view! The Caucasus were slowly opening up around us, and for the first time we could see just how complicated our chosen route was. Gestola still seemed miles away, and so much higher than we were.

We slowly descended Lyalver's other side. It wasn't nearly as steep as it had been on the climb up, but we were now right next to the ridge. The fall down the Bezengi Wall was staggeringly sheer and every now and again we got far too close to the edge for comfort. At last we arrived in the small neck between Lyalver and the next peak. This was the first flat area we had seen since leaving camp six hours before. We dumped our packs in the snow and flopped back, breathless. The air was thinning and, with it, our energy was slipping away.

It was during this break that I looked up and noticed the clouds. Not just one or two drifting about, but great streaks lurking everywhere. 'Good heavens,' I thought, 'where the hell did that lot come from?' They'd sprung on us out of nowhere and left me feeling startled and concerned. What else was going to take us by surprise? We picked up our packs and carried on climbing. Deep down I could feel a sense of foreboding but I guess, to a degree, we were all just following our Russian hosts. We were the students

Here's the strange part: We knew it would take us longer than a day because we had taken along tents and sleeping gear. We also knew the storm would be upon us within 18 hours. So why did we go at all? I still haven't figured that one out.

In the early hours of the morning we buried the stuff we'd decided to leave behind and set off on our journey, slowly following a trail of scree that zigzagged up the slope. It was quiet and the sky was clear. We reached the pass about an hour later and stared out west towards the Black Sea. It still looked clear, with no sign of the predicted storm.

The climb became more difficult from here on, so it was time for us to rope up. Slowly, we climbed higher, and they were the teachers. Don't question, just follow. That was the Russian way.

The route climbed diagonally outwards from the neck, avoiding the summit of the intervening peak. Slowly we traversed ever closer to Gestola, frustratingly hidden from view by the steep slopes of the intervening peak. And then suddenly there she was, rising magnificently out of nowhere. How close she now seemed.

Again we descended a short way into the neck before Gestola, and again we rested. We now had perhaps two hours to go before we reached the summit. It was just past midday. Surely we would achieve our goal?

From the neck up the final face was steep, so we had to use our ice axes. It was late in the afternoon when we finally reached the top of the pyramid we had been admiring ever since arriving in the valley. The group was tired but jubilant. This was a peak, high and proper. It was becoming a happy ritual: pulling out the flag, posing, and taking photos. It was all part of the mountaineering experience and we were rightly chuffed. Way below we could see the site where we had camped. It was miles away.

We didn't stay on the summit of

Gestola for long – just enough time to take a few pics and have a snack. But that was it. The clouds were now starting to thicken ominously, filling every inch of sky. It wasn't necessary for anyone to speak. We all silently knew the seriousness of the situation. The group had a long way to go and not much time in which to do it. Vova, who always had a worried expression on his face, went about placing an anchor in the ice and one by one we set off on the descent. Metre after painstaking metre, we abseiled down the ice and snow.

Looking across at the summit of Lyalver, the scene of the tragic storm.

When we were all safely in the neck between Gestola and the intervening peak, we carefully discussed our options. There were few. The day had run its course and it would be impossible to get all the way down in the fading light. We had to camp, and this neck seemed to be as good a place as any.

We'd pitched the tents within minutes and huddled together inside them. Greg began the task of melting snow and boiling water, both for a hot drink and to cook what little food we had. The rest of us lay there quietly, feeling tired and very concerned. We would definitely be caught in the storm; it was just a matter of when it would hit. How bad would it be? And how long would it last? These were the questions playing at the backs of our minds, nagging for answers. No-one had much to say.

Then it started. Light snowfall at first, gradually becoming heavier. Then it eased up unexpectedly and the atmosphere became quiet. The silence was unnerving.

And that's when the crackling began. At first it was just an occasional buzz, so subtle we could hardly hear it. But then the buzzing turned into crackling and whipping and we sat up straight. Now we were paying attention.

'What was that?' Martin asked the question that was on all our minds, and yet we all knew the answer. It was lightning. We were about to be caught in the middle of an electric storm high up in the Caucasus. I looked across at Greg and Martin, and their eyes revealed a sense of helplessness that I, too, could feel. With a feeling of apathy, I resigned myself to whatever fate was in

the clouds. This was it. The crackling got louder. Vova said we should collapse our poles.

'Why?' someone asked. Because, a few years ago, nine people died in their tent in exactly this spot, was the answer. We weren't going to argue with him. Within seconds, the poles were collapsed and the tent settled on our stiff bodies. No-one dared move – not that this would have made any difference. Things were only going to get worse, and lying in the flattened tent was both disorienting and suffocating.

It was impossible to tell how long this went on for, but at some point we agreed that we had to continue, as we had no doubt that things were only going to get worse. We set off, moving slowly. Visibility had decreased dramatically but it was still light. Maybe it was the next day. I guess it must have been, although it was difficult to say. But the electricity was still crackling around us, searching for something, or someone, to touch. Snow was being whipped around by the wind and simply trying to talk was a mission. We pressed on, huddled close together, but still on our ropes. Being tied together was more than a physical bond that would save us if we fell; it was also an emotional bond. Knowing that you were tied to someone just made the awfulness of the storm seem less threatening.

Slowly, we wound our way back up the peak with no name. Then back down into that first gap. We rested for a few seconds before continuing our exhausting journey. There were seven of us, tied to three ropes, each fighting our own fight as the storm intensified. I can't remember who was in the front but I knew that Valodya was right at the back, tied to Martin. Then it was me, tied to Greg, who was somewhere in front of me. Visibility was now so bad I could see barely 10 metres (32 feet) ahead, which at times meant that Greg disappeared altogether. We had to get back over Lyalver, which now seemed insurmountable. I tried not to think about it because the idea terrified me.

Martin and I stuck close together, offering words of encouragement now and again. Halfway up Lyalver's slope, Tola shouted for us to stop. We all got down and crouched in the lee of a rocky outcrop. He also ordered us to toss our ice axes, which we did. There we sat for 10 minutes, cowering as the lightning picked up. It was awful. And yet I had completely resigned myself to the wisdom of the older members in the group, those who were more experienced. Surely they should know what to do?

The sky was now a moody black. It was still daytime, but thick, dark cloud had almost turned the sky to night. Then everyone was moving again, picking up their ice axes and heading up the slope. Why? I thought. What was the point of us stopping in the first place? The storm was just as bad as it had been earlier. Why had we even left our campsite? But the luxury of asking questions had long been stolen from me. Now I just had to follow. We were nearing the summit of Lyalver.

'What was your worst epic?' I asked Martin.

'You mean other than this?'

He was still strong. Good, I thought.

'Ja, other than this.'

'Blouberg. With Darryl.'

'What happened there?'

Blouberg is a notoriously difficult cliff face in South Africa's Limpopo Province.

Martin thought awhile.

'We were caught out late on the wall. By the time we got up it was dark, and no-one knew the way down. We then missioned for hours trying to find our way through The Maze. But that doesn't come near to this.'

We carried on climbing, one slow step after another up the face. I turned again to Martin.

'Well, just take it one step at a time. 'What a stupid thing to say,' I thought. But that's what I said.

Before we knew it, we were on the summit of Lyalver – the same spot where we had taken those ecstatic photos the day before. How quickly things had changed in such a short period of time. I noticed that the others had already descended the other side and had disappeared from view. Only Greg stood waiting on the edge for his turn. I sat on the far side of the summit, watching him and keeping the rope tight in case he fell. God knows, I would have been able to do very little if he had fallen. But I was doing what I could. I was going by the book.

Then Greg was gone, descending the far side. Now it was my turn to go. I hurried across the summit and crouched on the other side, followed by Martin and Valodya. The three of us huddled together, stuck in the maelstrom. The lightning had got so bad that it felt like we were in the middle of a science experiment. The air was thick with static. I didn't know it at that moment, but I look back now and realize the air was thick with something else. Death.

At this point I was shit scared. I had never been a fan of lightning but hadn't been so close to the damn stuff before. Here, it was everywhere and it was the worst sound I had ever heard – like giant elastic bands twanging around a static-filled room. It's a sound I never want to hear again.

I had my ice axe plunged into the snow and was practically lying on the thing. I turned and looked at Martin. He was crouching, but at least he was down. He was braver than I was. Then I looked at Valodya. My God, he's standing! Is he nuts?

I remember thinking I should tell him to get the fuck down. But he was older, far more experienced and much wiser. I said nothing. Then my rope moved and finally I took the first step downwards. Martin stayed close behind. The ridge was narrow and exposed and I wondered how the hell I was going to get down it. We hadn't gone two steps when I felt Martin's hand on my back.

'Alex, my rope's gone tight.'

'What?' The storm had got so loud that I had to shout.

'I said my rope's gone tight.'

'What does that mean?' I asked.

'I don't know, but I have to go back up.'

'Shit. Well, get off there as soon as you can.'

Martin turned and vanished.

At this point my rope wasn't moving, so I turned and stuffed my head into a crevice, along with my ice axe. Anything to get it out of harm's way – that's how vulnerable I felt. I could hear lightning arcing and smashing into the mountain all around me. Shit, I wanted to stay in this crack forever; or at least until the world calmed down. Then I heard shouting, lots of it, and in Russian. I didn't want to turn and look around. But then I heard my name. I looked down. Tola was shouting up at Valodya on the summit, who was shouting back at him. Then Greg was yelling. Then Tola was shouting at me.

'Alex. You must go up.'

You've got to be nuts, I thought.

'I can't go up.'

Why the hell did he want me to go up?

'Please. You must.'

'I can't. You're crazy!'

'Please. Martin sick. You must go.'

'What do you mean he's sick?'

There was no answer, only more shouting in Russian. Then Tola was climbing past me. 'Alex, you go down,' he shouted.

I looked down at Greg, who was slowly descending. Finally, I thought, I can get out of this godforsaken place.

I began climbing, taking one careful and deliberate step after another. I realized that, if I slipped, there was no way in hell Greg would be able to hold me. We would both go hurtling down to the glacier thousands of feet below. I thought about looking back but decided against it. The truth was, I was so scared I felt nauseous. In the back of my mind I wondered how Martin could be sick. I knew he couldn't have any kind of altitude sickness because he had acclimatized well. I decided he was also nauseous, just like me. Surely Tola and Valodya would be able to help him?

I arrived at a vertical part of the ridge where the others had set up an abseil rope. Until then we'd been climbing and sliding down – desperate stuff in the storm but there wasn't any other way. I clipped onto the rope and swung myself over the edge, glad for a little security for the first time in what seemed like ages. The rope went down for maybe six metres (19 feet) and I landed on a flat section of the ridge. I noticed that Ulrike and Vova had cleared away part of the ridge and had put up one of the tents.

Greg was standing next to me, still clipped to the rope. He wanted to know what was going on but I had no answers. I was tired and fed up. I just wanted to rest. Somewhere above us were Martin, Tola and Valodya. Why were they taking so long?

Then we heard screaming. Someone was yelling in pain, but who was it? There was nothing we could do but wait and continue clearing the snow.

When we looked up we could just make out the shapes of two people above us. Tola seemed to be lowering Valodya, who was screaming in agony. But there was no sign of Martin.

'Where's Martin?' Greg shouted up at the others.

No-one responded. Valodya was shrieking with even the smallest move, as he was painstakingly lowered towards us.

Greg was growing impatient. 'Tola, where's Martin?' There was still no reply. Every time Valodya screamed, I winced. How could someone be in so much pain?

Tola came over the edge and landed next to us. 'What's happened to Martin?'

Greg seemed to be doing all the talking. Tola ignored him. Then Greg lost it.

'Tola, what the fuck has happened to Martin?'

'Martin die!'

'What?'

Tola's words made no sense, and yet I understood him. He said it again. 'Martin die!'

I started crying, bawling again like I had that time on the bridge. But this time it hurt and I can't say why. Was I sad? Sure I was. But the acute senselessness of the last few hours hurt, and it hurt badly. Martin was dead.

We spent the next 18 hours curled up in two tiny shelters suspended on a ridge. I was on one side with my butt hanging in space. There was nothing under me. Those 18 hours still stand as the worst night of my life.

A few seconds after Martin and I had started moving off the summit, Valodya had been struck by lightning. The strike had caught him on the back and exited his knee. He had been alive and conscious but his insides had been burnt up. He'd pulled Martin's rope tight as he'd fallen over. That's when Martin had turned to me and said he had to go back up. As he'd reached the top, he'd seen Valodya lying on the summit, barely alive. He'd moved to help him and had been struck on the head by a lightning bolt, which had travelled through his entire body and exited through his boot. The doctors told us later that Martin was killed instantly.

Despite this, Tola had tried CPR for about 45 minutes after climbing back up to the summit.

I looked across at Valodya, who was lying next to me. He was barely awake. Every time anyone moved and touched him, even slightly, he screamed. He would be in intense pain for the next two days, and then we would never hear from him again.

The storm carried on for the whole of the next day, making rescue impossible. We spent that long, lonely night suspended somewhere in that dark sky. I didn't care if we got hit again. I just lay there, too tired to think. A packet of raisins mixed with chunks of salted fat served as our dinner before we started the descent.

The situation was desperate. For hour after hour we lowered Valodya, moaning and screaming, down the face. Late on the second day, almost on cue, the clouds cleared and we were shown the final way into camp. It was over.

Darryl was waiting on the porch when I got back to our hut at Base Camp. He had heard the news via one of the Russian radios and had then spent the next two nights tossing and turning, worrying about the rest of us. I had to tell him exactly what had happened. He had been Martin's closest friend and they had climbed together through the best and the worst of it. It all seemed so needless and avoidable. Yet, in his mature way, he seemed to take the news quite well.

When the others arrived, we spent time talking about things past, and things to come. I drove into town with Darryl and we flew back in a helicopter to retrieve Martin's body. The Russians assisted Valodya to a small clinic somewhere, and we didn't see him again. Did he survive after being taken to hospital? I don't know.

No-one felt like doing much anymore, and certainly not in this valley. It all seemed too difficult and dangerous now. But our feelings quickly changed when Elbrus was mentioned. It wasn't far away and wasn't at all technical. After all, it was a volcano, and it happened to be Europe's highest peak. Darryl said that Martin had wanted to climb Elbrus, so that decided it: we would climb Europe's highest mountain, if not for ourselves, then for Martin.

The next week was strange. Our mood was one of reserved excitement. We were not totally convinced that we should still be climbing. As we spent the day driving to the Elbrus Valley, some of the group discussed the option of bailing altogether and heading back home. In the end, Greg and Darryl did just that. They didn't feel it made sense for them to carry on climbing when they were still mourning Martin's death. In a way, I envied them. They could just bail when they wanted to, yet I still felt pressure to hang around and perform and climb. I was young and fit, I had no excuse to run, and a part of me still wanted to go bagging peaks and making first South African ascents. Wow! Imagine being the first South Africans up Europe's highest mountain! We would be famous. My mind was still clouded by the ignorance of youth.

Our group was now down to Ulrike and Hermann, Vova, Tola, and Sergei – who had replaced Valodya on the team – and then me. We took those first few days slowly, hiking up easy valleys and camping where it was safe.

I grew weary of trying to answer questions. The 'window in the other room' sentence I'd learnt at the start of the trip had grown wholly inadequate to answer the range of questions that were being thrown at me, questions like: 'Wasn't there anything you could've done for Martin?' I didn't have the answers. Shit, what did I know? Ask the others!

Each night we stared at the gentle slopes of Elbrus guarding the valley. It looked peaceful in the soft pink light of evening. The weather was good; the skies were clear. This might be just what the doctor ordered: a spring-cleaning of the soul. We decided to set off in the morning. Besides, we had run out of rations and were living off mushrooms picked from the forests. It was time to move.

We left for the cable station early that morning. The cable car was a short cut to about 4 000 metres (13 123 feet), eliminating a really grotty section of the lower slopes of Elbrus that consisted of piles of crumbling lava and shale. Dirty and desperate stuff. Our hosts assured us that we wouldn't want to hike anywhere near it.

From 3 700 metres (12 139 feet), we took ski lifts to the 4 000-metre mark. The 'hotel' had recently burnt down and we would have to stay in the 'Coke cans', which were small can-shaped huts that each accommodated four people. They were tiny but adequate for our needs. We settled down for a few hours of rest until someone called us at midnight, and we started the tiring process of gearing up and drinking something warm. I hadn't slept and had that pseudo drunken feeling you often get in the mountains. You haven't had a thing to drink but feel as if you've got a whopping hangover. Boy, would I get more of those in the years to come.

We piled onto a snowplough and thundered away up the slope. How cool, I thought.
'Can this thing go all the way to the top?' I asked.
'If you have enough dollar!' was the reply.
'How much dollar?' I guess I was feeling lazy.
'Too much!'
We carried on bumping and grinding up the snow. At 4 700 metres (15 419 feet) , the plough ground to a

My name had now become Sasha, Russian for Alexander. I was now 'officially' Russian and this would mean hugely discounted rates on the mountain. Ulrike had become Ulrikiana, or something like that. All we had to do was nod and say 'Da' ('Yes') whenever we heard our names.

'Sasha, ny pashli!' (саша, ну пошли)

'Da.' (Да.)

You get the idea. If it didn't work, no-one really cared at this point. Not much more could go wrong.

саша, НУ ПОШЛИ!

halt and we climbed out. The joyride was over. Now the real fun would start.

Slowly, and in a long line, we kicked our way towards the neck.

> Elbrus was a twin-peaked mountain whose summits were only 12 metres (39 feet) apart, vertically. From the valley, it had seemed like one beautiful cone-shaped volcano.

We didn't realize how different the mountain would look as we began to traverse round and into the neck. It was also far bigger than we had thought. We climbed for hours, digging our crampons into the frozen snow.

At daybreak I found myself experiencing the worst headache of my life. This one was definitely occupying the number one spot in cranial pounders. It felt like I had used my head to stop a runaway snowplough, and had succeeded. I thought my head was going to explode. Sergei gave me a pill and said I would be fine. I swallowed it and then took the time to look around. We were somewhere in the col – the lowest point on the ridge connecting the two peaks. Dawn had arrived and soft shades of pink and red were dancing over the cold, grey slopes. Wow, it was pretty. We turned and headed up the final slope onto the summit cone.

I summited about an hour later. Ulrike and Hermann had arrived shortly before me and already had a flag unfurled. The view was spectacular. The Caucasus stretched forever towards the Caspian Sea. The soft hues of early dawn had faded but it was still a special moment. There was a bust of some Russian hero and a few other odds and ends on top of the mountain. In the distance, I could make out Shkhara

in the Bezengi Valley. I couldn't see Lyalver but knew exactly where it was. The sky looked so clear, it was hard to imagine how different it had all been on that recent fateful day.

The others soon started bustling around, getting ready to leave. My head was still pounding and I was happy to head down. It had taken us less than 24 hours to climb Elbrus, with little time for acclimatization. The adjustments our bodies had undergone in the Bezengi Valley had quickly been lost in the Tjerskol Valley, while we were soul searching and resting. Now I was paying the price. I was feeling nauseous when we got back to the col. I swallowed another pill and turned down an offer to scramble up the other summit. You're crazy, I thought. Why the heck would I want to do that?

As we sped down the slopes back to the Coke cans, my headache slowly waned and it had completely disappeared by the time we reached the bottom of the valley. Sasha was feeling perky again. Hey, I had a bloody good reason to feel better. We had just climbed Europe's highest mountain and were the first South Africans to have done so.

That night we celebrated the way the Russians do when they've just climbed a mountain: drink lots of vodka; make loud noises and salutations in foreign languages; then drink more vodka. This carried on for most of the evening. Things got rowdy but they were still under control. At some point I turned to Sergei and told him my folks would be proud that I had climbed to Europe's highest point.

'Nearly top,' he said.

'What do you mean?' Sure, I had had my share of vodka, but what was he talking about?

'You climb East Summit.' Sergei was smiling and waving his glass about.

'Yeah, so? We climbed the East Summit, the highest summit.'

'No! Not highest. West Summit is highest.' Sergei was still smiling. I wasn't.

'What are you talking about? Surely we climbed the higher of the two summits. Why would we go up the lower one?' I was sobering up fast.

'Alex, Alex, you are still young.'

'Sergei, you can't be serious?' Surely he was joking.

I left it at that, assuming he'd had too much vodka, and retired late that night with the rest of the crew. I was still elated in the morning. I had a bit of a headache but that didn't dampen my spirits. Then I remembered my conversation with Sergei the night before. I told the others what he'd said and they replied that he was talking nonsense.

Then someone had a bright idea and pulled out a map and satellite picture of Elbrus. Quickly, we spread the chart on a table and squinted at the figures written in bold. It was true. We had climbed the wrong summit. No amount of turning the map around or upside down could change the fact that we had climbed the East Summit of Elbrus and any self-respecting mountaineer knows that the highest summit is the west one. Boy did that hurt! When we confronted our hosts, they just shrugged and said 'next time'. Sure there would be a next time. But that didn't squash the urge to bash them over their heads.

RIGHT: *Later, when I did finally climb the West Summit of Elbrus, it was with Robin Walshaw. I guess I finally managed to twist his arm!*

That first trip to Russia wasn't about climbing mountains. It was about growing up. I spent the next six months living in Germany doing odd jobs and making friends. But I thought about Russia most of the time. I remembered Martin and that dark day. And I thought about life and death. I lost count of the number of nights I woke in a cold sweat, with the awful, crackling sound of lightning haunting me. It made no sense to me: why had I been spared and he hadn't? My mind was filled with the images of those few days. And when I thought about mountaineering, it was all bad.

I almost threw in the towel. I remember sitting in a bar with some German friends, talking about it and saying that I never wanted to climb again. And that was being honest. Part of me never wanted to see a mountain again. Right then, I just needed to rest and give up thinking and feeling. But I knew that I had been given another day and I had to go out and live it. It wouldn't do to ponder 'what-ifs'.

THE MOUNTAIN GUIDE:
Aconcagua

- ALSO KNOWN AS: Cerro Aconcagua ('Cerro' meaning 'hill').

- HEIGHT: 6 959 metres (22 834 feet).

- FIRST ASCENT: 14 January 1897 by M. Zurbriggen.

- LOCATION: The Andes, Argentina.

- POINT OF INTEREST: Given its name by the Incas, Aconcagua means 'Stone Sentinel'.

  This is the highest summit in the western hemisphere. Its peak is in Mendoza province in northwestern Argentina, but its western flanks build up from the coastal lowlands of Chile, just north of Santiago.

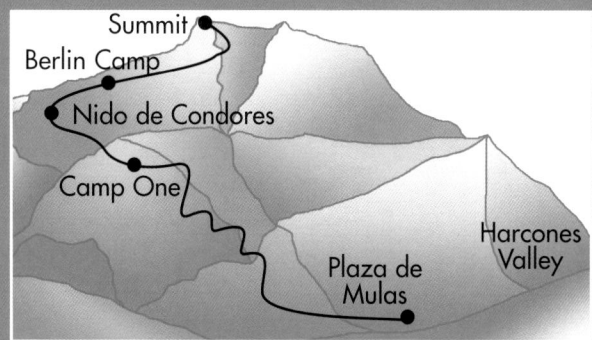

The intimidating South Face of Aconcagua.

CHAPTER THREE
Stone Sentinel

By the start of 1993, at the age of 21, I had still only climbed one of the Seven Summits – Kilimanjaro. Yes, I did eventually get up it – at the end of 1992 with Greg Devine and Darryl Margetts. Russia had been a pretty hectic experience for all of us and a leisurely stroll up Kili had been just what we'd needed when we returned to South Africa.

As for Robin Walshaw, he and I were spending more and more time rock climbing in the kloofs of the Magaliesberg but I still couldn't bend his arm to climb a big peak. This was where Sean Disney entered the picture.

Sean and I had first met in the South African Air Force in 1991. I had just finished my duties as a physical training instructor, he had worked in the mess corps and we were both stationed at Pretoria's Waterkloof Air Force base to see out the last few months of our national service. I had been climbing for a couple of years and Sean had just discovered the sport. We clicked immediately. Tall, with ruffled hair, broad shoulders and dark eyes peeking through his glasses, Sean looked like a mountaineer, or at least someone who was soon to become one.

Sean and I would climb most of the Seven Summits together, although back then, in Waterkloof's cleanly swept mess halls, neither of us had any idea about where on the planet our friendship would end up taking us.

In 1993 I began planning a second season in Russia and I persuaded Sean to join me. I hadn't yet learnt all the lessons that I would out of Mother Russia and it was another opportunity that I couldn't turn down. At the end of the trip, as with the previous Russian expedition, I decided to live with my friends in Germany for a while and talked Sean into joining me.

Sean was in the same position I had been in the year before: dead keen to climb internationally, even if it was in Russia. We were both in a similar place – neither of us had any idea what we really wanted to do with our lives. I had thought about becoming a pilot, but soon became disillusioned by my spell in the Air Force. Military life definitely wasn't for me. As for Sean, he had absolutely no idea. Anything was game. Germany sounded ideal: no commitments, new friends, exciting women and good money – and maybe, somewhere in all of that, the chance to find out what it was we really wanted in life.

We set up our digs on the third storey of a small block of flats in Bonn. The flat belonged to an old lady whom we hardly saw. But we were good tenants who worked for most of the day, razzled the town with our mates at night, and generally kept out of her way. As far as work went, we didn't do anything too serious. We were there to earn some dough, so anything went – from painting to construction to computer assembly. We didn't mind. As long as we were earning Deutschmarks, we were happy.

One thing we couldn't take, though, was the winter. It was dreadful. Thick grey clouds would brood in the sky for weeks at a time. As November approached, a light drizzle would add to the gloom and temperatures would drop dramatically. It was miserable. Day in and day out we would tell our friends of this place called Africa, a place where the sun shone all day, every day. 'So geht das leben' they would say. That's life. I never realized how much I needed the sun until I spent two winters in Germany. I would long for it like you long for a favourite dish when you've been stuck in a tent for weeks on end, and all you've been eating is freeze-dried rations that taste like cardboard.

Sometime during those six months, Sean and I sat around a table and pulled out an atlas. That bug was biting again. We wanted to go climbing – somewhere far away and something big, but it couldn't be too hectic. Those were the criteria. When you've got a bit of an imagination, lots of time, and a good atlas, you can come up with a lot of options. But the one that we kept returning to was Aconcagua, South America's highest mountain.

A couple of years previously, at more or less the same time as my aborted Kilimanjaro attempt, Ivan Battison and I had decided we wanted to climb Aconcagua. Again, the choice had been made impulsively. Ivan was a friend I'd grown up with in the neighbourhood. We had gone out and bought ourselves brand new ice axes, then taken one good look at a photo of the South Face and given it up as a bad idea. But another seed had been sown. A few years down the line and a couple of expeditions under the belt, and the idea of climbing another of the Seven didn't seem that far-fetched.

By November of 1993 we had managed to save up the money required for the trip – roughly 1 000 dollars each – and had taken enough leave. We had also been training in a local gym for the previous few weeks. Hey, we were serious about this. We were going to get up this thing, no matter what. Our friends thought we were crazy. Yeah, join the queue. So did most of the people we knew. They were still our friends, though, so we thought it would be a good idea to throw a party the night before we left, in honour of two great mountaineers. Back then, any reason to throw a party was good enough.

They arrived in their numbers. Two South Africans who climbed mountains in Russia were considered interesting people and we had made many friends in our six months in Germany. I would drink in the early days of my career as a climber – not all the time but enough, on occasion, to get out of hand. This was one such occasion. Everyone drank and everyone got out of hand. Vodka, German beer, you name it. By 10 pm everyone was on a first name basis. By 11 pm they were all trashed, myself included.

Gradually, every item of our furniture was squeezed through the window and tossed with disdain into the street below. This included our prize possession: a cane chair we had found in that very street, dumped by our neighbour months before. It was now unceremoniously returned from whence it came. Once the contents of our sitting-room were on the street, the fridge was next on the list, and so it went until we had nothing left in the flat. I recall one awful moment when Sean picked up my prized Russian guitar (actually it was a piece of crap but I loved it anyway), and smashed it into 100 pieces against the wall. Then he threw the biggest pieces out of the window and into the street. Sean was also trashed.

Most of our mates had left by two am. Those who remained were the faithful rabble – people you could count on for anything, but they weren't always well-behaved. I don't remember much of the next couple of hours, only that someone desperately needed a crap and, considering that our third storey window was being used for everything else, why not? The said person managed to squeeze his butt out of a small window way above the street, and let rip. I can remember much laughter and some desperate clutching on the windowsill.

By morning our little corner had become the centre of attention in the neighbourhood. Hordes of people stood around staring in disbelief at the pile of junk strewn across the street. Someone pointed at the toilet paper stuck high up on our neighbour's wall, and there were

oohhs and aahhs. Someone else pointed out the soiled awning directly below the window, and there were gasps. This type of thing didn't happen in this neighbourhood. As for us, well, we couldn't remember who the guilty party was, although most think it was me. As I said, I don't remember much about the early hours of that morning.

The next day Sean and I boarded a plane bound for Chile. We had pounding headaches and unsettled stomachs, but we were in high spirits. Our plan was to climb the highest mountain in South America and all systems were go. We were fit, we had the right gear, but, more importantly, we had the right attitude. We were going to take our time no matter how long we needed. And we weren't going to let any dickhead scare us off!

A day later we touched down on a hot strip in Santiago, Chile's capital. Through a friend of a friend, we managed to find a place to crash for a couple of days before we headed out. It was a beautiful house in a posh northern suburb, built high on a hill overlooking the sprawling city. The streets were filled with lush trees and the place was quiet – just what we needed. I always feel like a complete wreck after a long flight and need a day or two to feel perky again. This spot was perfect.

Santiago impressed me. I had underestimated the conveniences and 'high-techness' of the city. It had malls just like at home, some even bigger. Hey, it even had a metro. Two days was all we spent in the city before we got on a bus headed northeast towards the Argentine border. It would be two weeks before we had access to the luxuries of the big city again.

As with all big mountains, one needs a permit to climb Aconcagua. This you get in Mendoza, a town in

Argentina. You're probably wondering if I'm getting my logistics messed up. Why am I flying to Santiago in Chile when I need to go to Mendoza in Argentina? Well, Aconcagua lies just inside the border between Argentina and Chile. Santiago is only 150 kilometres (93 miles) from the border, so it makes sense to fly in there and then bus it to the border. Once at the border, you still have to make your way to Mendoza which is another 80 kilometres (50 miles) away. There was no point in both of us going all the way to Mendoza, only to come back to Punta del Inca, just inside the border, to start the climb. So we picked straws. Sean got the short straw. This was only the beginning. In the next decade Sean would pick many a short straw.

Punta del Inca is a small frontier town just inside Argentina. It is difficult to imagine why it exists because there's not much there, other than a few mineral springs and a hotel. But if you want to climb Aconcagua, this is where you start. The bus pulled into Punta and I jumped off. Sean carried on to Mendoza to sort out the permit. I would wait for him and we would meet up the next day. Punta del Inca was a lonely and dusty place, with only the main road from the border passing through it. Here and there a small side street headed off nowhere. A river ran parallel to the main road, just a short distance away. It lay in a steep ravine so was hidden from view most of the time. But it was noisy and dirty, carrying with it the debris from the high Andes.

I walked along, wondering how to pass the time and where I would spend the night. A few hundred metres beyond the hotel, I passed a police post. I went inside and asked if they would mind if I camped in their yard. They didn't. I had a place for the night and it wasn't going to cost me anything. Anyway, Sean had all the cash so I didn't really have any option. I pitched the

The slopes of Aconcagua are, for the most part, dry and windswept.

Aconcagua lies roughly in the middle of the Andean range. It towers a massive 6 959 metres (22 834 feet) above the Pacific Ocean and is a great hulk of a mountain. It's even more intimidating when viewed from the south. The South Face drops three kilometres (1.86 miles) from the summit and is one of the biggest faces in the world – enough to send any mountaineer packing, no matter how experienced he, or she, is. But we'd chosen a route around the side and up one of the easier slopes – the route first used to climb the mountain. On a normal day it should be a doddle but the mountain gets its fair share of high winds and freezing temperatures. Most people are surprised when they hear how many people have been killed up there, and we weren't planning to take any chances.

Punta del Inca has a natural 'jacuzzi' that makes the rigours of the climb all seem worth it.

tent, stashed my gear and then headed off to see what the town had to offer.

A freezing cold wind blew down the valley, adding to my feeling of isolation. I knew that Aconcagua was very close to the town, but, although I was already at 2 700 metres (8 858 feet), I still couldn't see the mountain because it was hidden behind a hill at the head of the valley. The area was dry and semi-desert-like, without any bushes or trees to offer any shade. The only colours in the surrounding landscape were the browns and reds of the surrounding hills. I wandered around for a while before heading down to the impressive sulphur springs, which sprang out of the earth in hot jets. They made a great place to bathe but I decided to delay the experience until after we'd climbed the mountain. It made sense to have something to look forward to. I headed back to my tent. It was getting dark and the chill was getting worse.

Sean arrived with the permit the next morning. His foray to the parks office had been successful but he had somehow managed to spend all our money. All of it! 'What do you mean it's all gone? That's impossible.' I stared at him in disbelief.
'I'm telling you it's gone.'
'Well, what the hell have you been doing?'
Sean stared back through his thick glasses.
'I don't know, it's just gone.'
'Did you get mugged or something?'
'No. I couldn't find a place to stay so I had to check into a hotel.'
'Well, why the hell couldn't you camp like I did?'
I was pissed off that I had spent a frigid night to save money but Sean had blown all our cash in one fell swoop. It was pointless arguing. It was done and from now on we would have to live off our rations.

We set off an hour later with our massive packs. They were stretched to the absolute limit and must have weighed nearly 30 kilograms (66 pounds) each. The problem was that we had our heavy double ice boots stuffed into the bags, as they would only be used higher up the mountain. Those first few hours were painful. We left the town on foot and within the first kilometre had taken a wrong turn. We reached a bridge spanning the river and weren't sure if we should leave the road and follow the river, or head on straight. Follow the river we did, and it was a big mistake. We spent the next three hours mucking about on the wrong side of the bank, trying to figure out how we could cross it. Finally we got back to the right side, but at the cost of wetting pretty much everything we had.

Great start! We couldn't even see the mountain and we were already making an epic of it.

Things brightened up when we found the path again. It turned out that the road would've been a much better option and would've saved us hours. At length, we got to the crest of the valley, the point at which it split and our path would turn northwards, towards Aconcagua. This was the moment we had been waiting for – our first glimpse of the peak. We turned to our right, crested a short knoll and there it was, the South Face of Aconcagua. Wow! It reared 3 000 metres (9 842 feet) above the valley in which we were standing.
'Shit dude, look at that sucker!' Sean was definitely on the money.
'Wooooweee! That's wild!' I was struck by how steep it looked.
'Man, we're going to get our butts whipped!'

'You reckon?'

We both just stood there for a while, carrying on like groupies.

'Do we get anywhere near that face?' Sean was sounding concerned.

'Naa, we head around to the left of it and then come up the back, pretty much between the two summits.'

'You mean that low point in the ridge?' Sean was pointing up into the sky, somewhere near the summit.

'Yeah, that's it. And then we're going to head up straight to the summit.'

'Which one is the summit?'

It was a good question. From the low point in the summit ridge, a slope headed both left and right up to the North and South Summits. From where we stood, it was impossible to tell which was higher. There was only about 50 metres (164 feet) in it anyway, but that's not a mistake you want to make on summit day.

'I think it's the right one.' I was pretty confident it was.

'Are you sure?' Sean wasn't as confident.

'Yeah, I think so. But we can check on the map later.'

We continued plodding. Slowly, we left the valley of Punta del Inca behind. The mountain slopes surrounding us were dry and crumbly, and nowhere was there a trace of green. We walked for four hours before the path we were on fell steeply to the river. Soon we clambered over some giant boulders and arrived at Confluencia, where two rivers came together in a brown explosion of turbulent water. One tumbled from the foot of the South Face and the other fell from high up the valley. It was the latter one that we would follow. But tonight we would camp next to tufts of lush green scrub. There were also some birds chittering about, hopping from rock to rock and inspecting exactly who was disturbing their paradise. They helped us forget about the struggle ahead.

We set off in the morning, leaving the green of Confluencia behind. Before long, we crested a hill and arrived at the entrance to the great valley that leads to Base Camp. The valley stretched as far as the eye could see. On either side, steep peaks gazed down at our slow progress. There was a chilly wind blowing down and we were walking directly into it. It would be a tough day. We laboured alongside a stream for hour after hour, crossing it now and then. When we needed rest, we took shelter behind a boulder or crouched in a gully. The sun was high and ran its course unhindered by clouds, and yet it was still cold – a biting cold that found its way through our many layers.

By late afternoon the broad valley had given way to a steep slope of tumbling ice and rock gullies. We left the flatness behind and picked a route upwards. It was too late to make it all the way to Plaza de Mulas, so we hiked on until we found the first flat spot, up against some ice. It was a dirty place for camping, but it would do. The small stream that ran alongside the ice was a murky brown and was thick with silt.

'What do you think?' I was wary of continuing. It was late and I was buggered.

'It's a crap spot but what are our options?'

'Well, we could leave our stuff here and push on a bit longer.'

'No, this is fine. It's for one night.'

It was decided then: we would spend one more night out before reaching Base Camp.

We arrived at Plaza de Mulas before noon the next day. It lay at 4 300 metres (14 107 feet) and was a truly dramatic place. On the one side, the Northwest Face rose steeply up to the Northern Summit. Behind it, at the head of the valley, Cuernos towered 5 400 metres (17 716 feet) above sea level. It was more than a kilometre lower than Aconcagua but still looked very high and steep. On the far side, there was another peak of over 5 000 metres (16 404 feet). At the foot of this peak stood the Plaza de Mulas Refugia, a monstrous hut that claimed to be the world's highest hotel. We doubted it, but on subsequent trips I would find out that they made the best ham and cheese lomitos anywhere. A short way along the rock field we could see a few scattered tents. It was still late November and the season was just beginning. By January the camp would grow to more than 100 tents. We were glad for the solitude.

We busied ourselves over the next

few days with the task of setting up Base Camp. This involved more than just pitching one tent. We strung up our South African flag between our tent and a rock, proudly announcing to all from whence we had come. We also went on hikes during the day. This was not only to keep us busy, but also to help us acclimatize. As you climb higher, the air gets thinner and you have to adapt slowly to it. It's easier to do this during the day when you are active, so we made sure we kept our schedule filled with daily sorties up the scree slope. But there are only so many times you can do this before you go crazy and by the third night we had decided to head up to a higher camp.

The next day was clear, boding well for our climb up the slope. There wasn't anything technical for us to do but we would be very exposed higher up on the mountain and there were also the threats presented by being at a high altitude.

Sean also hadn't been that high before and certainly neither of us had ever climbed above 6 000 metres (19 685 feet). Would we acclimatize, or would we succumb to altitude sickness and have to retreat? These were questions that only experience would enable us to answer. We were about to get ours.

Go slow! Those are the two words you will hear time and again if you ever get to climb a mountain. Above us stretched a scree slope to beat all scree slopes. It must have been all of three kilometres (1.86 miles) in length, and zigzagged a mad pattern ever higher. We started briskly but soon slowed down. The path followed the line of least resistance but still consisted of loose shale and small rocks, making it easy to lose your balance and stumble a few paces backwards. Our packs weren't nearly as heavy as they had been when we'd trudged up the valley, but they were still a burden. They swayed to and fro like drunkards, and threatened to topple us. We rested often, and more so as we got higher. It was a tiring day and we were never rewarded with a view of our destination.

> Always, the top seemed to be 'just there', but always it eluded us. There was still another rise, and another slope, on and on.

By late afternoon, Sean and I had arrived at 5 000 metres (16 404 feet). We were tired and still had no idea how much further it was to the next main camp – Nido de Condores, or the Nest of the Condors. But we knew we wouldn't get there in a single push, so looked around for a place to camp and discovered a few spots that had been used before. The crest we were on had a stunning view but was also seriously exposed. It was situated at the precise area where the steep scree slope slackened off and bent backwards into a small glacier.

The glacier rose to a short knoll, and above it somewhere was Nido. This was a place to spend one night, and no more. We shuddered to think what it would be like to be caught here in a storm.

Minutes later, we had pitched our tent as best we could. It was a tent borrowed from Axel, one of our German friends – the kind that German lovers would pitch on the banks of the Rhine. By no means was it to be used on a hill or mountain of any sort. We had just signed up at the School of Mountain Lessons and were about to learn a big one!

As the sun vanished, a red strip of light raced across the sky, covering the peaks in a last faint glow. It was cold. It wasn't long before the wind picked up, just a breeze at first but it quickly became menacing. Our lovers' tent swayed and buckled under the probing tugs. The wind was like an enemy exploring the weaknesses of his foe and we could feel the corners of the tent creaking and stretching. We soon realized that we would have to reinforce the ropes with rocks, so decided to brave it outside. Sean and I were amazed at how much louder the wind had sounded from inside the tent. That gave us little comfort though, as we knew the night was young and things would only get worse.

By midnight the wind had reached gale-force, or so it seemed. We had our backs to the sides of the tent, desperately trying to hold it up. This wasn't a battle we could afford to lose. If the tent went, we would go with it – right down to Base Camp. That night seemed to stretch on forever. But somewhere in the early hours of the morning I woke up and realized that I had in fact slept, and that the wind had died down. Sean was still sound asleep so I buried myself in my bag and drifted off again.

We were in high spirits when we set off for Nido. The sky was clear and it would be a short day.

'Dude, what were you thinking getting that tent?' Sean broke the silence of the early morning.

'What are you talking about?'

'That thing's going to be the death of us.'

'Yes, so? It wasn't my idea.'

'Sure it was.'

'No ways. I seem to remember telling you it wouldn't be strong enough.'

'What!'

We carried on like this, back and forth, for ages. Neither of us wanted to claim responsibility for the lovers' tent, which we were now pretty sure would be our downfall on the mountain. That it had survived the previous night spoke wonders for German engineering, but how long would it last?

From our camp at 5 000 metres (16 404 feet), the route crossed a small ice field. It was similar to a glacier but technically it wasn't one. You couldn't fall into a crevasse because there weren't any. But it was still ice and required us having to put on our crampons for the first time. By noon we had arrived at Nido and set about trying to find a suitable spot. We had been warned that this was one of the windiest places on the mountain. Nido was an immense plateau scarred with giant boulders. It looked like the surface of Mars but was the colour of the moon. It was desolate – not the kind of place where you lie outside basking in the sunshine.

We dumped our packs and wandered around checking out the real estate. The good thing about being on the mountain this early in the season was that we had first choice of all the campsites.

Reaching Aconcagua's Base Camp involves a long, gruelling walk.

Nido stretched for hundreds of metres in length but it was only about 200 metres (656 feet) wide. At that point, the mountain seemed to drop off forever, with steep slopes disappearing into a formless valley. We decided to camp somewhere near the upper slope, just in case.

That night was as windy as the previous one, but this time we were more sheltered. Although we could hear the wind tugging away outside, the tent held. Sleep came swiftly, without the worry of being blown away, and we were feeling very optimistic when we considered our options the next morning. Sean and I had seen one or two small parties about, but the masses would only arrive in a month's time. It felt lonely but that just added to the excitement, as we had to decide for ourselves when to move and when to stay; where to camp, and for how long.

It felt good to be independent, weighing everything up and then acting upon it. This was what big mountains were about. In a sense we were still winging it, what with our lovers' tent and all that, but we felt we were at the right place, with the right experience, trying to do the right thing. That made the difference.

Most parties spend a day or two acclimatizing at Nido. We figured that, since we were still feeling good and the weather was settled, why not keep going? This was a strategy that would work for us time and again in the years to come. It was a tricky game to play – balancing up the weather and how good one felt, and then going for it. The risk of failure was always there but on some days there were other risks to think about as well – like avalanches or rock falls – things we could do very little about.

From Nido, the route followed a lazy zigzag up a short slope. Berlin was the next camp at 5 850 metres (19 192 feet), so, in terms of the vertical distance we had to cover, it was a short day.

The hike took two or three hours and it was therefore something of a rest day for us. We didn't set out until way after noon because we didn't want to reach Berlin too early and then just hang around. The two of us took it easy up the slope, arriving in the late afternoon. The camp, including the small hut, was empty. In fact, using the word 'hut' was a compliment because it was so small that even hobbits would have had to crouch inside it. But it provided shelter, and it was already standing, requiring no effort from us.

We dumped our gear outside and crawled inside with only the necessary items. This included our sleeping gear and a pot or two for cooking. I felt strangely fatigued as I crawled about, so tried not to overdo things. We were close to 6 000 metres (19 685 feet), which meant that any exertion required five times the amount of energy that it would back home. Even the little things demanded huge effort. Filling a pot with ice was like playing three squash games on the trot, leaving you huffing and puffing. Rest was the key. Try not to do too much and, if you do have to do something, make sure you do it slowly.

I lay back in the small space and stared blankly at the roof of the hut. I was happy to be resting. We hadn't yet done anything technical but we had been working hard every single day and I was tired. The space we were in was dark, apart from the small doorway of light telling us it was still day. The gas stove hissed in the middle of the floor as it tried to boil some water. Sean lay on the other side. Quiet.

Suddenly I was aware that my head was pounding. Soon I was extremely nauseous. It scared me that it had managed to sneak up on me quietly, just like that. I started breathing more deeply in an effort to make the feeling go away but it wasn't long before I felt even worse. I dug around in my bag for a Disprin and quickly swallowed it with some water, certain that it would help. But it didn't. I was now getting worried. This wasn't a normal altitude headache; this was a brain-numbing throb. Then I thought about the stove and it slowly occurred to me that we were probably poisoning ourselves and the hut was turning into a death trap. In a flash I was up and crawling outside, mumbling a warning to Sean about the air in the hut. He muttered back but didn't budge.

Outside, the cold air was like a slap to the face. But it was fresh and I breathed in deeply, feeling like I had been set free. I spent the next five minutes concentrating on my breathing, almost hyperventilating. Slowly the headache disappeared and my breathing slowed down. Then the pain was gone and I was left lying on the cold gravel of the slope. Night had long since come to the valleys far below us but up here the light lingered for longer, playing tricks on our senses. Then it raced away for one last time across the slope and was gone. A deep cold filled the Berlin camp and I crawled back to the hut.

Sean had placed the stove outside the hut and was still sleeping within. It was a cramped night but we managed to rest. We knew we had been silly with the stove. Later we heard that two young Swiss guys had died doing exactly what we had done. Death by carbon monoxide poisoning came swiftly, but its path was insidious. We would be far more careful in the future.

The next morning was cold and a chilly breeze blew. Thin clouds drifted far overhead but most of the sky was clear. We had been hoping to leave camp at about five am but it was too cold in those early hours. When we did finally leave the silence of that small hut, it was well past eight am. Now we would have to move.

The route continued from Berlin at an easy angle, closely following a ridge. Away to our right stretched the vast *canaletta* – a scree slope so wide and high that it made all those we had ever been on seem like garden paths. The *canaletta* dropped from the gap between the two summits, plunging three kilometres (1.86 miles) down to Base Camp. It was an uninterrupted highway of loose rock and shale. We had read much about the *canaletta* and how it would turn back the most determined parties, but tried not to think about it too much. We would eventually have to cross it, but only a very small section higher up the mountain. For now, it remained a spectacle far off to our right.

After two or three hours of mindless trudging, the path left the ridge and crossed a small scoop. Sean and I were now at about 6 300 metres (20 669 feet), a new altitude record for both of us. Every step from here on up was record-breaking stuff. It was still bitterly cold and I decided I had to stop for a while and desperately try to warm my feet. I sat in the lee of a boulder and went about the painful business of rubbing them. Across the scoop lay the weathered remains of the Independencia hut. I marvelled at why anyone would want to build a hut in such a lonely and hostile place. I could not imagine a day when the elements would make this area seem welcoming. It was permanently bleak.

Minutes later, we were on the move again. Once across the scoop, the path zigzagged up a small snow field and then back towards the ridge. When we got to the ridge we slumped on our packs and rested. The *canaletta* seemed so close, and so much bigger than it had earlier. From here onwards, the trail left the ridge and made a great traverse into the heart of the *canaletta*. It then rose up towards the summit ridge. The traverse looked immense, a stony path rising imperceptibly upwards without interruption. Halfway along the traverse we could make out a pinnacle of sorts. It seemed a good place to rest and we agreed this would be our next stop.

'Howzit going?' I asked. Sean was looking strong.

'I'm all right hey, and you?'

'I'm good!'

'How are your feet?'

'They're still cold but they're better,' I replied.

'What do you think the weather is doing?'

I raised my eyes and scanned the sky.

'I think it's going to hold.'

'Let's make for that pinnacle and then eat something.'

It was important to have these small attainable goals. The terrain and the task at hand were too big and monotonous to comprehend all at once. Broken down into manageable sections and accompanied with treats like rest or food, the whole thing seemed more 'do-able'. I could not imagine doing it any other way.

We donned our packs and slowly set off towards the *canaletta*. Sean and I were now exposed to the full force of the wind for the first time, as we had been sheltered from the worst of it behind the ridge. It was blowing at about 30 or 40 kilometres (19 to 25 miles) an hour. Doesn't sound like much, but when the ambient temperature was already as low as −15°C (5°F), it suddenly got a lot colder – too cold to stop and chat or admire the scenery. We just plodded along, one step after another. Every now and then I would look up to treat myself to a glance at how much closer the pinnacle was. But if I looked too early there would be no difference, and I would be disappointed. These were the games we played in our minds as the dull hues of the slope and the dryness of the rock slowly drifted by. Like a dawn that just won't come after a cold night, so the pinnacle kept its distance.

At last we were there. In the context of this great mountain, we were no closer to the top. But we had achieved another small goal and the rewards were rest and some food, and that was far more rewarding than any gain in ground. The pinnacle was really a thin outcrop of rock that stood about five metres (16 feet) tall; not too wide, but wide enough for two people to get behind and take shelter from the wind. We threw our packs down and lay back against the slope.

All too soon it was time to carry on hiking. The sky was still clear but the wind tugged at us. We left the shelter of the pinnacle and moved slowly upwards. After an hour we had traversed into the heart of the *canaletta*. It was time to head directly upwards. I stopped to lean on my ski pole and stared up at the gap between the two summits. We were close but we were now well over 6 700 metres (21 981 feet), making it an effort just to breathe. As we climbed ever higher, we had to stop every few steps and breathe like people who had just swum 10 lengths under water. That was just to get our breath back. When we were on the move, we couldn't stop huffing and puffing as we struggled ahead. It was hard to say how long this section took and impossible to think of anything other than the next step. Our surroundings seemed irrelevant. We had become beings with one, focused purpose: taking the next step. No talking, no looking, no nothing. Just step.

It came as a bit of a shock when we arrived at the summit ridge. We looked to our left and our right, sussing out both the North and South Summits. I remembered our conversation ages earlier when we had first seen the mountain. I wished I had paid more attention from a distance when it had been easier to see which of the two peaks seemed higher. Now we were too close to tell.

Sean looked at me blankly. 'So, which is it?'

I looked down towards the South Face but it was hidden. A thick wall of cloud seemed to bubble up from its depths and rise straight up above the ridge. It was held back by the wind that had been bugging us the whole day – a wall of murky white.

'I still think it's the left one,' I said.

'Well, you had better be sure. If it's wrong, we're going to be stuffed.'

Sean was right. The summits were too far apart to allow us the luxury of heading up the wrong one first. If we botched it, well, that would be that.

'It's definitely this one.' I turned and started up the last section of ridge, hoping more than ever that I had made the right call.

The path now traced a line that was just inside the ridge. It was dizzying stuff. A stumble too far to the right would end up being the express route down Aconcagua's South Face. But at some point I realized we were definitely going to make it, no matter what. This filled me with a renewed energy and I increased the pace. Sean also sensed that we were close and upped his tempo.

A few minutes after five o'clock on a windy, lonely afternoon, Sean Disney and I climbed up a large boulder and found ourselves on the roof of South America. The metal cross marking the summit confirmed that we had climbed another of the Seven Summits – my second.

To the north and south, the Andes seemed to stretch forever. Away to the west, we thought we could make out the Pacific Ocean, grey and distant. No matter where we looked, the world seemed to curve away. It was beautiful and lonely, but it was right.

I turned to Sean and we hugged. At this very moment we were the highest people in the world outside of Asia. This was where we were meant to be. We took some photos and then left. Our time was up.

We had been given just a few moments in that special place, but it was enough. It gave us a view of the world we had never seen and a view of ourselves we had always suspected. I had been right — we'd been called to this.

We'd been
called to this

THE MOUNTAIN GUIDE:
Everest, North Face

- **ALSO KNOWN AS:** Peak 15, the name given to Everest by British surveyors in the 1800s. In Tibet Everest is called Chomolungma (Mother of the Universe).

- **HEIGHT:** 8 850 metres (29 035 feet).

- **FIRST ASCENT:** 25 May 1960 by Wang Fu-chou and Chu Yin-hua.

- **LOCATION:** The Himalayas, on the border between Nepal and Tibet.

- **POINT OF INTEREST:** Named after the former Surveyor General of India in the mid-1800s, Sir George Everest.

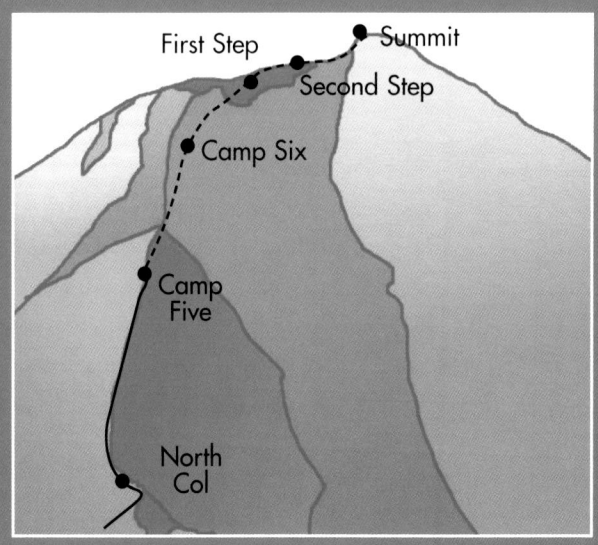

Everest's impenetrable ice and rock form the border between Tibet and Nepal.

CHAPTER FOUR

Peak 15

My appetite for climbing grew considerably over the next few years. I would spend more and more of my time rock–climbing in the hills, and this fed the desire to move on to even bigger mountains. The concept of the Seven Summits hadn't yet completely formed in my mind, but there was an underlying sense that what we were doing was more than just fun – a distant, appealing idea that there was a lot more to it than just climbing. This would all change in the middle of 1995. This was the year that a few of us started seriously talking about Everest for the first time.

By this stage I had been a member of the Mountain Club for a few years and had made some good friends. One of them was a man called Russ Dodding. An immigrant from the UK, Russ had been climbing for many years and was capable of doing routes far harder than I could manage. He had a reputation for being a safe, sensible climber, and his manner was mild and easygoing.

Rumour had it that a section of the club had managed to secure a permit to climb Everest from the northern side. At the beginning of 1995 no South African had yet climbed Everest, so this was a pretty big thing. Russ phoned me up and asked if we could meet.

'How are you doing, lad?' Russ still had a noticeable accent. 'Here's the deal. Have you heard about the Magaliesberg sections permit for Everest?'

'A little bit, but mostly rumour.'

'Well it's true, and they want me to be part of it.' Russ was smiling.

'Awesome!' I was genuinely pleased for Russ. He was the kind of guy who deserved to be invited on a trip up a big peak.

'Yeah, well, there's one problem.'

'What, money?' This was always the problem.

'Well, no. They are hoping to get the trip sponsored. The problem is I can't make it.'

'Why?'

'The timing's not great and I doubt I can get that kind of time off.'

'Jeepers, that's a bummer.' I thought Russ was being crazy, but I also knew that, if he said no, then his reasons were legitimate.

'Anyway,' he said, 'that's why I wanted to see you.'

My heart jumped in my chest. Could he be thinking what I was thinking? Surely not. I was still too young and inexperienced.

'Do you want to take my place?'

There it was. Just like that, Everest entered my life. One simple question and the wheels of an event that would change my life forever were set in motion.

I stared back at Russ. 'You're crazy! I don't have the experience to go to Everest!'

'Look, I have already spoken to Phillip, the leader, and he is happy with what you've done. You just need to give him a call.'

I didn't realize how much Everest had been lying dormant inside me until Russ popped the question. Now it sprang up suddenly like a Jack-in-the-box to demand my attention.

For the next few months I would speak to Phillip a lot, bugging him with endless questions about Everest It turned out that he didn't have a permit for Everest but had in fact applied for one. As he wanted to climb it from the northern side, he was doing most of his dealing with the Tibetan Mountaineering Association, or TMA.

At some point halfway through the year, though, Phillip phoned me up and said he had to pull out. It seemed work commitments were interfering with most of the team's plans, including those of the leader. Those who were still keen met one afternoon and thrashed out the issue. After two hours of heated debate, we decided we would still go, and I would be leader. I didn't realize then exactly what this would entail, or that I would be setting a record as the youngest person to lead a team to Everest. I was still on a learning curve. Yes, we lacked the experience to go to Everest. And yes, we were meant to go. There were powers at work that would conspire to get me there, but for reasons very different from those I was imagining.

The first thing we had to do was organize ourselves a permit. This I left up to Mark Campbell, an accountant who had a knack for taking on those really painful tasks, like liaising with bureaucratic government officials and negotiating permits. He seemed to relish the challenge of dealing with the frustrations involved, and he always got results. On a fateful day in October 1995, Mark called me up with a definite zing in his voice.

'Alex ...' He was drawing something out. I sensed that his labours had borne fruit and he was keen to get the most out of the moment.

'Ja, what's up?'

'We've got it!'

'Got what?' I was playing dumb. I knew he was going to love telling me about this.

'The permit dude! We've got the permit.'

'Are you serious?' Even though a part of me knew it was coming, the news still floored me when I heard it.

'Yup. Got it right here in my hand. It was faxed to my Dad.'

'That's incredible!' But, at the same time, part of me balked.

> We'd been given permission to climb Everest – a chance to be reborn, or die. We were no longer playing games and were now part of the big league, whether we were ready or not.

On paper, there was nothing much to it – just an A4 sheet divided into two halves and transcribed in landscape format. On the one half was written a whole bunch of Chinese, completely incomprehensible. On the other half it had the date, Chomolungma (Tibetan for 'Mother Goddess of the Earth'), in other words Everest, and the height, 8 850 metres (29 035 feet). Yup, it was official. It had cost six of us 3 500 rand each. A small price to pay.

One week later Mark phoned me again, this time sounding concerned.

'Alex, have you seen the paper?'

'Which one?' I had no idea what he was about to say.

'The *Sunday Times*.' His voice had a high pitch to it.

'No, why?'

'They are sponsoring an expedition to Everest.'

'What? You can't be serious? Led by whom?'

'Some British guy called Ian Woodall.'

'Who's he?'

Until this moment, none of us had ever heard of Ian Woodall but his name would make the headlines the following year for very controversial reasons.

'I've got no idea. But they are calling it the first South African expedition to Everest.'

'When are they planning to go?'

'In March.'

'Shit!'

This was a problem; a big problem. Our permit was for the post-monsoon season of 1996, in other words, September and October. The *Sunday Times* Expedition was scheduled to attempt Everest in the more traditional pre-monsoon season of 1996. That would make it in April and May, a full four months before us.

This had one major drawback. We were planning to use the tag of 'first South African expedition' as a drawcard to attract sponsors. If the *Sunday Times* Expedition was going before us, we couldn't do this. And, if we couldn't get sponsors, we couldn't go to Everest. It was as simple as that. Once again, a ditch had been dug as an obstacle on our road to Chomolungma. And once again, things looked extremely uncertain. Mark quickly scheduled a meeting with Ian Woodall. Our options were running out but, if we could link up with their expedition, that might just solve things.

Late one afternoon a few days later, Greg Devine, Mark and I met Ian for the first time. He had brought along his deputy leader and photographer, Bruce Herrod, who was also British. We met at a sidewalk café in a busy section of Sandton, and quickly went through formalities. Both Ian and Bruce seemed knowledgeable and friendly but somewhat reserved. Little did any of us suspect the drama that would unfold four months later, leading ultimately to the death of Bruce Herrod.

Ian made it clear that his team had already been selected, although he would not disclose who the members were. He also made it clear that it was a signed and sealed contract with the *Sunday Times*. Under no circumstances could he change any of the particulars of the expedition, especially who was on the team. It was therefore going to be impossible for us to join him. We suggested a joint effort from both sides of the mountain, seeing as our permit was from Tibet. That, too, wasn't an option. As a last resort, we asked if we could be a back-up team in case anything happened to any of the climbers on his team. Again, the answer was no. We left feeling stumped.

The rest of November and December of 1995 was a pretty frustrating time for us. We weren't too sure of what to do or how to go about negotiating this new obstacle, and decided to wait a few months to see how things panned out. Then, in January 1996, something pivotal happened that would again put me back on the road to Everest.

Over the previous few years I had

settled down into a career of sorts. I still had no idea what I wanted to do in the long run, but I had found myself a job that, for the time being, gave me the best of both worlds. I was working for an English company called The Hospitality Group International. How I came by that job was fortuitous in itself. I had just returned from a climbing trip at the beginning of 1994 and was looking for work as usual. The very next Sunday I had gone out climbing with the Mountain Club and had met a young man named Stephan Meigh. Stephan had just arrived in South Africa to set up an office for THG International, as we called it. We happened to be teamed up on that Sunday, and, as we climbed up and down the cliffs of Magaliesberg, we seemed to hit it off immediately. Stephan said he was looking for sales-people and I needed a job. He hired me on the spot. No interview, nothing.

Stephan would become a good friend over the next few years and THG would fund my climbing expeditions. It was the type of job where you could make a heap of money if you worked hard. We had a simple arrangement: as long as I was making THG lots of money, I could disappear twice a year to climb some obscure peak in a corner of the planet.

By the time 1996 came along, I had quickly risen through the ranks of THG South Africa. In January of that year Stephan was replaced by someone else. But, more importantly, I was offered the opportunity to move to Hong Kong and become General Manager in that part of the world. This was a big step and would mean serious money – money that I hadn't dreamed of as a young climber trying to find his feet in the world. It would also mean at least three years of my life and a more serious commitment to my career. But what about Everest? Deep down I knew that both couldn't happen. It was one or the other.

I decided to take a few days off to think about it. I also met with Sean Disney and Anton Erasmus, who were both part of our Everest team. We had a long chat about the issue and one thing was very clear: if I was going to be leader of the Everest team, then I was going to play a major part in the planning and fundraising for the expedition. I had to make the choice. Anton and Sean weren't too concerned. If I decided to go to Hong Kong, well then, Everest would happen next year, or some other time in the future.

The other reason for our meeting was that the three of us, along with a young lady called Daniella Levitt, my girlfriend at the time, had been thinking about starting an adventure company. We realized the Everest trip might be a good platform to get things going, but of course that meant I would have to resign. In the end, I deliberated for a few more days and spoke to the people who were really close to me. My heart said 'Everest' but my pocket said 'Hong Kong'. I was already at the point where I was making a heap of cash, and I wasn't doing anything with it except funding climbing trips around the world. Hong Kong meant making four to five times what I was currently earning.

On Monday morning I walked into the office and handed in my resignation. My new boss was astounded. It was done. I had made one more decision that would point my compass directly at Everest. The fact that I was now available full-time to the Everest project didn't help matters. We still had to contend with the problem of sponsors, and the media monster of the *Sunday Times* Expedition was starting to roll. By the end of January 1996, we were realizing just how big a project it was. The idea of a South African standing on the summit of Everest for the first time was an appealing one, and it was starting to capture the imaginations of South Africans. But this was making our job all the more difficult.

The problem was that if the *Sunday Times* Expedition succeeded in putting someone on Everest, the best we could hope for was a second ascent although, technically, the first South African person to stand on Everest had done so in May of 1995 (*see box, top right*).

I remember the day that Russ had broken the news to me of Mallory's successful ascent. I was sad in a way because I had often dreamt of being the first South African on Everest's summit. But it was done and life went on. Sadly, this fact seemed to have been forgotten by those involved in the *Sunday Times* Expedition. Or they just didn't know it. Nonetheless, at best, we were

following where others had already walked. There wasn't much to offer our sponsors.

Things looked bleak when our team met at the beginning of February 1996. We still hadn't raised a cent and most of the media's attention had turned elsewhere. Once again we had one of those long sessions where we argued back and forth. The question of what to do was a tough one. At some point in the debate, someone proposed changing our permit to another of the 8 000-metre (26 246-feet) peaks. The advantage of this was that it would be much cheaper to get to, and of course we had a far greater chance of success. There was also the option of doing a first South African ascent of some or other peak although, truth be told, we weren't really sure that it was technically possible for us to do this. Again, we decided to wait.

As the pre-monsoon season on Everest got under way, early signs were that this was going to be no ordinary season. It seemed that both people and the mountain were doing crazy things. From the outset, the *Sunday Times* Expedition seemed to be troubled with team difficulties. People were resigning, others were being fired, and still others were left off the permit. And then, to cap things off, a storm settled over the high slopes of the mountain and brought with it a fury that had not been seen for decades. In one fateful night, eight people died on the slopes of Everest and the year would become the mountain's most fatal one.

In the early hours of a Saturday morning late in May 1996, Sean Disney kicked me awake. I had spent the night at his house and was lying ensconced in a sleeping bag on the floor. In the background I could just make out the tired but jubilant voice of Cathy O'Dowd. She had just reached the summit of Everest and had become the second South African to do so. It was done. We finally

In 1959, John and Jennifer Mallory had a son, whom they named George – grandson of the famous George Mallory who had disappeared high on Everest in 1924. The young George grew up in Pretoria and became an exceptional rock climber, before emigrating to Australia in 1989. His timing was good, for a few years later a large international expedition to Everest invited him along. They were hoping to climb Everest from the north side and commemorate the 71st anniversary of Mallory's disappearance. On a clear, warm day in May 1995, George Mallory II, grandson of the enigmatic Mallory, reached the summit of Everest and became the first South African-born person to stand on top of the world.

had a result. The *Sunday Times* Expedition had succeeded in placing someone on top. The time for procrastinating was over. We had to make up our minds – and fast.

That Monday, the team met as it had done virtually every Monday for the previous five months. Our options were few. We could make a first ascent of another 8 000-metre peak. But no-one was really keen to do this. We all felt that we would be selling our souls if we gave in and changed our goal. On paper, the best we could offer a sponsor was a third South African ascent. But how would we raise the money in the time left to us? That task alone seemed impossible.

At the end of it, one element of the whole protracted process stood out. As an entity, the *Sunday Times* Everest Expedition had botched it, no matter which way you looked at it. The three lead climbers had resigned, the doctor had been fired, and the leader and sponsor were involved in an acrimonious debate that would leave a shroud of controversy over the expedition. At the very

least, we felt we could do a better job. And we weren't about to let some strangers put an end to plans and dreams that had been years in the making. It was finally decided. God willing, we would be going to Everest in three months' time.

It is both a liberating and terrifying moment when you realize you have committed yourself to a single task.

Everest is no different. Yes, we could lose our lives, but most of the time that's not what we fear. We fear failing. We fear taking that step out onto a rickety bridge and feeling it collapse beneath us, leaving the masses standing on the banks saying 'I told you so'. We fear discovering that the reality falls far short of the dreams we have for ourselves. As a result, most of us are afraid to discover, and some of us won't even dream.

The day we made our final decision, things started happening. Sponsors started saying yes. Cheques started coming in and targets were being met. Our team had been finalized by the end of June: Sean Disney, Mark Campbell, Anton Erasmus, Robin Walshaw and I. Sean Wisedale, a film-maker, would join us shortly before we left. None of us had ever heard of him before but he had seen an article about us in the media and had phoned me up to ask if he could come along as our cameraman.

By this stage all five of us had resigned from our jobs. We were gambling everything. We used to joke that it would be easier to meet women once we had climbed Everest. We didn't think too much about the reality that we were all now unemployed, and that the next cheque any of us would earn would be 15 months away. For the time being, that didn't matter. For the next few months we would eat, sleep and drink Everest. Deep down, we knew that would be the only way for us to get there.

There were two things we couldn't change. First, our permit was from the Tibetan side, and, second, it was for the post-monsoon season of 1996. A fair number of people around us, media included, felt we were jumping on the Everest bandwagon and that we were asking for trouble. We grew tired of answering questions and justifying why we were going, especially considering what had happened on Everest during the stormy spring season, when a total of 15 climbers from various teams had died. Eventually, the media started ignoring us, which suited us fine. When we asked why, it turned out we weren't controversial enough. It seemed they'd had a field day covering the other South African expedition. Our team seemed like the Brady Bunch in comparison, and no-one wanted to write about the Brady Bunch.

The only difference between Everest and any of the other Seven Summits was that it required far more logistically. We initially figured that 600 kilograms (1 322 pounds) of equipment would suffice but this

figure quickly grew to two tons – the food alone weighed in at 600 kilograms. We were learning fast and had almost every base covered.

As for oxygen, we weren't taking any with us. This was for two reasons. One, we couldn't afford it. Right from the start we knew that luxuries like oxygen would be in short supply. Secondly, the team was divided on the ethical use of it. Some of us, myself included, had always wanted to try climbing Everest without it. It's not that we felt using oxygen would be outright cheating. We just wanted to test what God had given us – our own pair of lungs – while the rest of the team couldn't give a hoot how much oxygen they used. It was all fair game. No-one was right or wrong; this was just how you played it. We had yet to learn about the dangers of trying Everest without supplemental oxygen.

About a month before we left,

I fell in love. Now, as any self-respecting mountaineer will tell you, don't go dating girls before a big trip. Well, Seanne was different. I had recently broken up with my girlfriend of three years. Daniella was tired of too many trips away and she was thinking of going to live in the United States. Added to that, she was Jewish and I wasn't. The writing was on the wall and Everest was the catalyst. So I was single but I wasn't looking for a relationship. Hey, I was the leader of an Everest expedition and Sean Disney had told me time and again that, if I met someone, my mind would go to pot and, if that happened, well then the trip wouldn't happen.

On an ordinary Friday night I unsuspectingly went clubbing with my sister, who was a couple of years younger than me. This wasn't something I did often. In fact, I had long since given up clubbing and Sharon had to do some serious arm-twisting to get me to go out any more. But I capitulated and we ended up at some or other nightclub with loud music and lots of smoke. It just wasn't my scene. I was beginning to regret that I had come. Until Sharon introduced me to her friend, that is. Seanne and Sharon had grown up together but they hadn't seen much of each other since leaving school. I can vaguely recall her visiting my sister now and then when we were kids, but my main aim then had been to scare her off along with any other girls who showed up at our home. I would burp in their faces when they rang the bell. But on this night, when Sharon turned to me and said: 'Alex, do you remember my friend Seanne?' it was as if someone had pulled back the curtains and suddenly spring had found its way into a dark room. She was beautiful.

It was the gleam in her eyes and the smile on her face that held me captive for the entire evening. We spoke about much that night, but mostly about God and Christianity. I felt young and free again, like a kid on the first day of summer holidays. When I fall, I fall hard, but this time I was knocked flat. I was writing love songs in my head when I went home. Oh boy, my mind had gone to pot! What would the others say?

I decided to keep this latest development to myself, which was highly uncharacteristic. Man, I was bursting every day to tell someone about how I felt but I managed to keep it inside. The Friday night before the team left, we held an expedition party at the MCSA hall in Johannesburg. Everyone came: friends, family and even some sponsors. I stood up on the stage early in the evening to give a synopsis of what we were hoping to do. Then I introduced the team. After that my younger brother Mark took over as DJ and the party started. Some time later I made my way over to Seanne who was sitting on a mat up against the wall. Up till now I had been playing the host so I hadn't had much time for socializing. I had seen her maybe once in the month that had passed since we'd first met, and even then it was with my sister somewhere out on the town. But all the time I had wanted to talk to her, maybe spend some time with her. I was leaving for Everest in two days and could no longer contain my feelings. I had to open up to someone. I decided the two of us needed to talk.

The next day, we met under a tree in my garden. As is my way, I spilt my guts, telling her everything. She just stared blankly. My honesty had come as a shock to her. Then she said an interesting thing. She told me there could never be anything between us as long as things remained as they were. 'How's that?' I asked. She explained that, as long as she was a Christian and I wasn't, there could be no future for us. Her conviction intrigued me but I could sense something else. From the way she smiled at me, I was sure she felt something.

I was right. That night we went out and we kissed. By now I had fallen so hard that I felt anything was possible, including climbing Everest solo, without oxygen and in my underpants. But at the same time a deep void was forming inside me. I was about to leave for Everest and I wouldn't see her for at least two months. How would I cope? I continually assumed the worst – that she was just being nice and would wake up one morning wondering who that crazy guy at the party was, and then carry on as normal. But I couldn't do that. I was really falling for her, big time!

When the team left the next day, Seanne and I hugged each other and said goodbye. There were no expectations. I had to get down to business. Everest was calling.

CHAPTER FIVE

Chomolungma

Kathmandu is a part of the world that has never really understood what it means to rest. Both night and day, the colours and lights of the town vie for the attention of the unsuspecting traveller.

Rickshaws speed haphazardly up and down tiny streets on errands of huge importance, while cows stand idly by. Tiger balm pedlars ply their trade as if it's the cure for every ailment, nagging and pulling at your arm.

'Tiger balm! Tiger balm! Only ten rupees.'

'No thanks.'

'Okay, five rupees!'

'I said no. I don't need any bloody tiger balm.'

'One rupee.'

'Listen buddy, I said I ...'

'Okay, okay, I give you three for one rupee.'

And so it goes on until you're breathless and worn out. But it's an exciting place. Surprise lurks around every corner and dark alleys stretch in all directions, filled with every kind of shop imaginable. Kathmandu is like a giant ant farm. Yup, it's hard to catch your breath.

We arrived in late August as the monsoon was slowly winding down – two weeks later than we had planned. One of our sponsors, Air India, had cancelled a flight routing at the last minute, leaving us with the unexpected delay. It was frustrating. Every day we wasted was one day less to acclimatize.

As if that wasn't enough, we still had complications in our dealings with China. We were going to be the first South African climbing expedition into Tibet and, as it was occupied by China, most of our dealings were with Beijing. Unfortunately this process required two weeks of negotiating back and forth, all while we were getting to grips with Kathmandu.

Of course there was a positive side to this – we got to know Kathmandu really well. Robin and I have a habit on all these big trips. We stock up on a few tomes and spend the time reading in our tents. Then we swap books and repeat the process. After this, we argue about what we've both read.

This time I suggested that we read the Bible. We'd both being wanting to for years, and what better time than a 10-week expedition? Robin was an atheist and I was agnostic. He thought it was a good idea, only trying to find a Bible in Kathmandu was a bit like Neil Armstrong trying to find a climbing wall on the moon. But find one I did, in a tiny book shop, tucked away in a street in some obscure corner of the town. It was an old, tattered copy from the Bible Society of Nigeria. 'What kind of journey has this book been on?' I wondered. It was done. I was proud of my efforts and quickly started reading: the first page of Genesis 1:1, just like any other book.

The time in Kathmandu passed slowly. Anton, who was the only Christian amongst us, made the suggestion that I should simultaneously read the New Testament, as it would make more sense that way. This I did, although, as I flipped through the worn pages, the task seemed overwhelming. At some point in that unexpectedly long sojourn in Kathmandu, our agent told us the permission was finally in place. China had co-operated and we were on our way to Everest.

Geographically, Everest lies plumb on the border between Tibet and Nepal. The northern side belongs to Tibet and this was where we were heading. There were two ways to get there. You could fly to Lhasa and then truck it to Base Camp, or you could truck it all the way from Kathmandu. We chose the latter option as we felt it would help us to acclimatize. It was a five-day journey, which included various stops on the way.

One day after leaving Kathmandu, we ground to a halt. We had come across the first of several landslides. The monsoon had been a heavy one and the saturated slopes had given way in many places, with disastrous results. Most of the time a section of the hill would collapse and destroy part of the road. But sometimes the landslide would be so big that it would destroy an entire village.

The first of these was small, although it was big enough to halt us in our tracks for the night. It was dark when we climbed out of the truck and started wandering around. We were in a small village spread along the slope of a hill. It was warm but the ground was wet and muddy, and a light drizzle was falling. We were soon ushered into a low room in a house and were shown some beds. This would be our home for the night. It was dank and smelt like a herd of yaks had been its previous occupants. We joked cheerfully about the state of the place and the amount of money it was costing us.

An hour later, our driver called us to dinner. This was in a house next door and was in an even lower room. The average Nepalese person is only about 1.65 metres (five feet six inches) in height, and they had clearly never taken visitors into account when they'd built their dwellings. We were welcomed by the smell of Dahl Bhat stewing away. Sean Wisedale was capturing the scene with his Beta Cam. Soon the camera was thrust into my face.

'Alex, what are you eating there?' Wisedale was peering through the eyepiece.

'It's Dahl Bhat.'

'Just describe it for me.'

I had a mouth full of lentils and wasn't too keen to be interviewed.

'Well, it's basically a brew of lentils. Like a stew I guess. It's one of their staple meals.'

Wise moved on to the next person. It was a noisy evening in those small confines. There was lots of joking about and interpreting, but eventually we drifted back to the room for our first night in the foothills.

In the morning we moved out on foot. The road had been so badly damaged that it was impossible for the trucks to continue. Porters from the village were arranged to carry the bulk of our gear, so that we.only had to carry small packs containing our valuables. We walked for about a kilometre in the wetness of early morning, marvelling at how bad the road was. Great gullies had been ripped across it, making it dangerous to cross.

We stood on the side and watched youngsters of no more than 16 years carrying barrels weighing as much as 50 kilograms (110 pounds) and stepping gingerly across gaping sections of the road. We warned them that, if a barrel dropped, they should get out of the way and not try to save it. Far below, the raging madness of a swollen river swept downwards at frightening speed.

In the next few days we would cross two more landslides. One was so big that it had swept away part of a small village and killed about 60 people. Still further along the road, we crossed a section that had been turned into a waterfall. It looked like a smaller version of Niagara and it was scary to think that this had once been the main highway. In time, we arrived at Friendship Bridge, the border post to Tibet. We had heard much about the bureaucracy of the Chinese border police and knew it was quite possible that our expedition would end right here. We were excited, but nervous.

Friendship Bridge is located in the most spectacular setting. On the Nepalese side, the valley comes to a halt in a series of waterfalls. The Nepalese border post consists mostly of a few small shacks and a road with some bars and hotels along it. Not much to speak of. Then the bridge itself swings across a turbulent mass of white water and into a small village on the far side. It's not clear why this little village exists, because the main Chinese town is higher up the mountain. The bridge itself is stationed with grim-faced Chinese soldiers, most of whom are very young. They look barely old enough to carry a gun, let alone aim and shoot one. Once across the bridge, the road zigzags higher up the mountain for about six kilometres (almost four miles). And there, somehow balanced on the slopes on an impossibly steep mountain, is the frontier town of Zhangmu.

It is difficult to imagine a town more precarious in its setting. It seems it would need only the wrath of one angry soldier to upset the whole balance and send Zhangmu plunging down into some dark abyss. And yet it stands, balanced on a myriad trestles and poles, hugging the mountain for dear life. Zhangmu is a town where one treads lightly and sneezes with care.

The passport section went more smoothly than we'd anticipated. Our permission to enter Tibet was in order, but we had no filming permit. Added to that was a lack of permission to use a satellite phone, and someone had hidden a good stash of girlie magazines deep in one of the barrels. There was plenty of reason for the Chinese to send us packing, or, at worst, lock us up in some remote jail. But they seemed content just to glance into the back of the truck and, fortunately, the magazines remained undiscovered. The tailgate to the truck was closed and the soldier nodded. We could proceed. Welcome to Tibet.

We spent the rest of that day

checking into a Zhangmu hotel and exploring the town. But by morning we were eager to move on, as the town had turned out to be a grey and depressing place. The sun seemed to keep its distance and the town was always covered in cloud.

It was as we were leaving that the unexpected happened. As the truck turned a steep bend, it bumped over a big rock, sending shudders down the length of the vehicle.

In the same instant the engine blew a gasket and stalled. The truck rolled slowly backwards over the same rock and, as it bumped a second time, a guitar flew out of the back and landed directly behind one of the wheels. The truck seemed to teeter for a few seconds and then carried on rolling, only settling once it was squarely on the guitar.

We jumped out amazed at all the different noises we had heard. And that's when we saw it. The guitar was squashed under the wheel and protruding at a sickening angle. It had been turned into firewood. But whose was it? Only once we'd confirmed that it was Robin's did the rest of us break into uncontrollable laughter. Robin just stood shaking his head. Then he started muttering, and soon afterwards he was shouting about it being from Canada and made from spruce, or something. To top it off, it took a couple of hours to fix the engine, and for all this time the guitar thrust out its neck in despair. Occasionally Robin would walk over and stroke it, but not without muttering to himself.

By evening we were in Nyalam, which was at the top of the pass we had been following for three days. It was set at 3 700 metres (12 139 feet) and was on the verge of the Tibetan plateau. From here on in the landscape would be dry, barren and windswept. We only spent one night in Nyalam, and it was one night too many. It was a dirty place and we were constantly looking down at our shoes to check where we were stepping. It seemed as if the town had been gutted in ages past and had never properly healed.

From here, the pass snaked further into Tibet and onto the plateau. We were now at an altitude of around 4 300 metres (14 107 feet) and the thin air was beginning to tell. Ahead of us the road stretched for 5 000 kilometres (3 106 miles) into the heartland of China. Who knew what valleys and lakes the road would pass through on its endless journey? Our surroundings were dry, and brown hills ran steeply up the sides of the road. They were dotted with crumbling ruins telling ancient stories. Those few days spent passing through Tibet to Base Camp seem to have blended into one faded memory. Like the blur of the passing fields, the timeless rocks slipped by unnoticed. It was only when we crested the Pang La pass at 5 000 metres (16 404 feet) that an image would assail me, terrify me and then take me into its magical hold and keep me transfixed. It was our first view of Everest.

Up until now, the last defiant streaks of the monsoon clouds had hidden everything from view. We had joked on occasion that we weren't really in the Himalayas because we hadn't yet seen anything to make us believe it. But, when the truck stopped on that pass and we saw Everest for the first time, humour was replaced with awe. There could be no doubt about where we were. Like ants, we had crawled over a small knoll and stood gazing across at what was unmistakably the highest mountain in the world. My head was pounding.

The rest of the day was spent descending the pass and then making our way up a long valley until, finally, we turned a bend and arrived at Base Camp. Up on a slope to the left stood the Rongbuk Monastery, the highest in the world. Its crimson flags were the only splash of colour in the dull, grey landscape. Ahead of us, the tumbling moraine of ice and rock stretched for 12 kilometres (7.5 miles) to the foot of Everest. And there it stood at the head of the valley, claiming its place in the world as mother of all mountains. The North Face towered all of 3 500 metres (11 483 feet) in one magnificent sweep. On the left we could see the Northeast Ridge rising sharply upwards to join the North Ridge. Base Camp was a fine place to stand and look – but it was also terrifying.

Those first few days at Base Camp were

spent battling headaches and sorting out logistics. We had to decide what we were leaving behind and what would be going up to Advance Base Camp, or ABC. The mountain seemed quiet. There were only four other teams about and one group, the Indonesians, was already on the North Ridge.

On the morning of the fourth day I woke up to the sound of bells announcing the arrival of our team of yaks. It was time for us to head higher up the mountain. There were about 25 animals standing about with their long tattered hair and great big horns, a large bell hanging from each of their necks. Their eyes were wise and they carried with them a rancid smell accumulated over years of wandering the plains of Tibet.

When the packing was done, we set off in one long train. The yak herders smelt no different from their charges, and we joked about how long it had been since any of them had felt the freshness of water on their mud-caked skin. There were turquoise and red beads dangling from their matted hair and some of the men had long knives hanging from their waists. Some of the knives had finely worked sheaths in tin, and handles carved from yak horn.

We had not journeyed for more than three hours up the valley when the train ground to a halt amidst grunting yaks and moaning herders. Something had happened. I was up ahead, about 15 minutes from the main group, when a herder started shouting at me. I didn't have a clue what he was on about, but it was clear that something required my immediate attention. I turned around and headed back down the trail.

A little way back, the main bunch was huddled in one noisy clump, pointing and talking animatedly. One of the yaks had fallen down a steep bank but had somehow survived. The animal was lurking nearby, disgruntled but unharmed. However, its barrels had taken the brunt of the fall and had come loose. They went tumbling down the slope, strewing their contents everywhere before crashing into the river below.

We scrambled about the slope trying to retrieve what we could and also trying to identify which barrels had gone. When the maths had been done, there was good news and bad news. None of the barrels contained any of our personal gear, so we were all fine. But one of them had contained our emergency oxygen supply – all six cylinders of it. Two were retrieved from the slope but they were damaged beyond repair. There was nothing left. It was sobering news but all we could do was press on. We would just have to be more conservative in our strategy.

We took three days to hike the 18 kilometres (11 miles) up to ABC, giving our bodies a chance to adapt to the altitude. No amount of trying enabled us to communicate with the herders. They knew no English and could understand very few hand signals. We soon realized that they were on their own mission and weren't too interested in what we had to say or how fast we wanted to move. They were going to get our loads to ABC, and then they were off. But they were a sharp bunch and nothing escaped their eyes.

On the third evening, we were invited into one of their makeshift tents for dinner. We warily crawled inside, expecting the worst, as we were pretty sure that some or other part of a yak was on the menu. Imagine our surprise when they passed around plates of food that looked remarkably like our rations. Then someone noticed a packet in the corner. The buggers had stolen some of our food and had cooked the stuff. We protested and waved our arms about but it had no effect. That was just their way. We soon left them to the smell of their yak-dung fire, but the noise from their tent would carry on late into the night.

It was snowing lightly when we arrived at ABC the next afternoon, our home for the next six weeks. Out of the 51 days we would spend on the mountain, only 10 would be spent at Base Camp. Every other day was spent either at ABC or higher up the mountain. This wasn't the sort of place you would see on a travel agent's brochure. This place was bleak – like a giant deep-freeze.

At the head of the valley, the East Rongbuk Glacier falls steeply from the North Col. Up to the left, the Northeast Face rises two kilometres (just over a mile) to the famous pinnacles.

Behind us, Changste rose 7 500 metres (24 606 feet). We could just make out the summit of Everest peaking up behind the North Ridge. From Base Camp, we had left the main Rongbuk Glacier and hiked up a side valley all the way around to one of the hidden sides of Everest. This was the route that George Mallory and Andrew Irvine had followed back in 1924; a hidden route that sneaked up on the higher slopes of the mountain.

Once ABC had been established, the process of acclimatization would start all over again. Days were spent fighting nausea and pounding headaches. At the first sign of shallow breathing, doubt would creep in that any advance would be made higher than this camp. My worst period on the mountain was at ABC. For all of four days I would bang my head on my mat to try to numb the pain so that I could get some sleep. I was racked with headaches so bad at times that I would wait for the inevitable 'bang' as my head exploded. I was sure it would. During the day we would lie about trying to occupy ourselves and then crawl into our sleeping bags at night. It was a desperate time. No-one said much in those first few days at ABC. It was in these dark times that I would find God.

Up until this point I had only really spoken to Anton about God. Anton Erasmus was a character I wished I had known all my life. He was a crazy guy, but kind, with rugged good looks and a chiselled jaw. In my mind God had taken all the qualities that I imagined a good man to have, and had moulded them into Anton. Anton was fearless and would try anything. He genuinely and passionately lived each and every day as if it were his last. For him, there was no midday, only dawn and twilight. New possibilities and different adventures, full of colour and promise, existed everywhere. He was great fun.

I had first met Anton some years back when he phoned me out of the blue. He had heard I was organizing a trip to Mount Kenya and wanted to know if he could come along. 'Sure,' I said. From then on we had grown close and had many climbing adventures together.

Anton had been a committed Christian ever since I had known him. But his past was very different. I would hear tales from some of his older friends about what a misdirected, rowdy lad he had been. Stories about his drinking and partying were legendary. I had grown to know that same spark in Anton, but it now burnt with a very different purpose. His passion was for the Lord and life. I hadn't quite confessed to Anton about Seanne yet, but I had confided in him that something was happening. Deep down I think I knew. I had taken the risk to walk down the road of knowing God but I didn't want to admit it. I was almost afraid to. I was scared I would lose something.

The funny thing was that I would lose something, but it was the very thing that was holding me back. I had thousands of questions for Anton. Would I still be able to date girls if I became a Christian? These were reasonable questions for a young guy in the prime of his life. Anton didn't have all the answers, but he was sure God would. As the weeks went by, I found myself more and more drawn to the Bible and wanting to learn more about God. I knew that it was only a matter of time before I would have some or other epiphany. It came sooner than I had expected.

By the fourth day at ABC, I was filled with fear. Everest had already had the most fatal year in its history. Another four people would die while we shared the same mountain. We were making an attempt without Sherpas and oxygen, and the task ahead of us was huge. A weight heavier than any mountain I'd ever seen was dragging at my shoulders, and in the back of my mind a mantra repeated itself. It happened the day we left for Everest. I had the parents of these five young guys come up to me in tears and whisper into my ear: 'Bring my son back alive.' The weight of that responsibility was finally taking its toll on me. Truth is, I didn't think I could do it, and it was there, in that deep trough of self-doubt, that I finally decided to give in. I would give my life to God. That night, for the first time in my life, I really prayed. And not for the things that first come to mind, like 'get us to the top', and 'get us home again', but for something far simpler. I prayed for an answer. I wanted to know if there was a reason why I was coming to Everest and if God was behind it. Was He behind everything?

The night went quickly and when I woke, in the stillness of the early morning, I had my answer. I don't think many people hear a loud, audible Voice of God. I believe most just hear the still, quiet voice deep inside themselves. But when you hear it for the first time, it doesn't matter which it is, it is just as loud, just as frightening, but at the same time, just as calming. The words were simple. I was to stop worrying about death and the dangers on the mountain. We were going to get back alive. He would make sure of that.

In that moment I felt that the weight I had been carrying around for so long lifted suddenly and was gone. It was replaced by hope and a faith that anything was possible. The change from fear to peace was instant and remarkable. Every single bit of doubt that had been rotting away in my body was gone. I had found my Maker and it was humbling. And, in humility, there was hope.

The next day, we set off to climb the North Col for the first time. It was a 400-metre ice cliff that dropped off the North Ridge. We had heard much about the dangers of the North Col and how so many people had died there. For this reason it was decided that Sean Wisedale would stay behind. He had never climbed a mountain before and going above the North Col without the necessary experience wasn't a risk worth taking.

The snow that had welcomed us into ABC had stopped and the sky was a dark blue. I happened to be climbing with Anton that morning, and, as we headed towards the foot of the fixed ropes, I stopped him in his tracks.

'Anton, I want to become a Christian!'

'Cool.' That's all he said.

'I want to give my life to God on the summit.'

'Awesome.'

That was Anton's way. He would later tell me that he and a lot of other people back home had been praying for me for a long time. It seemed that my ticket had been called and I didn't really have a say in it. Later, we would argue about this for what seemed like ages.

For the time being, things looked rosy. Anton and I were increasingly convinced that it was our destiny to get to the summit of Everest and that God had brought us here for that purpose alone. Anton had even made a small wooden cross that he was going to leave on the summit. We would also share a tent on the North Col and start praying together.

As the expedition wore on, it was becoming clear that 1996 was going to be a frustrating time to be on Everest. The jet-stream winds arrived earlier than expected. Not that one can really predict these things,

The top of the East Rongbuk Glacier, where Advance Base Camp is situated.

but history can give you a pretty good idea of when they normally start. We had hoped they would only arrive in the middle of October. Truth is, they started blowing halfway through September and never really let up. One by one, all five expeditions would slowly retreat and then give up altogether as they were beaten back by the freezing winds.

Only the Indonesian team managed to reach the summit. They were an interesting bunch. The only actual Indonesians involved were a man and a

the mountain a month longer than we had. They were in the right place at the right time to catch that one early break in the wind.

By the end of the first week in October we were resting back in Base Camp. Every other team had left the mountain. Even in the busiest of times, there is a strange loneliness to Everest. Although there are people about and tents scattered here and there, one sometimes feels stranded and lost. Now the place felt like a remote moon on the fringes of our solar system.

The cold slopes surrounding Advance Base Camp.

woman, but they had a Sherpa contingent of 12 strong lads. Their *Sirdar*, or Sherpa leader, was a well-known climber called Kaji Sherpa. He was as tough as a yak and as stubborn as an ox. He had already climbed Everest four or five times and this time he would lead Clara Sumarwati all the way to the top. She became the first Indonesian person to climb Everest, and, although there was much speculation about whether or not they'd got up, in our minds they had made it. They also had the luxury of being on

Nothing moved. It was as if Everest had just been pushed up out of a formless land to claim its place in the clouds. We dared not leave the first print in its unspoilt sand, lest we incur some unspoken wrath. High up off the summit, the winds were blowing a white plume across the sky. Everest stood brooding, its patience running thin.

Four days of rest was all we could afford before we headed back up to ABC. What had earlier taken us three days to do, now took just six and a half hours. We

Struggling up the North Ridge in high winds.

had acclimatized and were fit. We knew that our break would have to come soon or we would just weaken again and never get up the mountain. By the time we got back up to the North Col, Sean Disney had contracted a cold. There was nothing he could do but go down again, as a cold on a mountain can quickly develop into the fatal condition of pulmonary oedema if left unchecked. For Sean, Everest was over. He left us and headed down the fixed ropes to ABC. Time was running out for the rest of us.

Earlier in the expedition, Disney, Anton and I had reached 7 300 metres (23 950 feet), some way up the North Ridge. Strong winds and freezing temperatures had forced us to leave our bags anchored to the ropes and return to the shelter of the North Col. I could see that point up on the ridge and marked it as my first stop.

When the long process of dressing was complete we set off, hoping the wind was gone. In the shelter of the North Col, it was impossible to tell how strongly the wind was blowing, if at all. This left us with a false sense of hope for those first five minutes. It was only when we had left the last protecting cliff of the col that the wind rushed upon us. It was no different from before. If anything, it was stronger.

83

One by one, we set off on our climb up the ridge. It was impossible to talk so we each plodded at our own pace, looking around now and again. In time, we spread out along the fixed ropes that led to the higher camp. The Sherpas of the Indonesian expedition had left a tent for us somewhere higher up the mountain. This would be our goal for the day. By the time I reached our previous high point, the wind was blowing at between 100 and a 150 kilometres an hour (62 to 93 miles). It took all my energy just to lean into it and not fall over. I stopped and leant on my ski pole, gasping for air. My neoprene face mask protected me from the wind but the right side of my face was still beginning to go numb. I ripped the mask off and shouted at the wind until my throat was hoarse. I begged it to stop, to let up for just two or three days so we could finish this thing. But it blew on, indifferent to who we were and why we were there.

I sat down in the snow next to the pack we had left earlier and looked back down the ridge. It was at this point that I noticed something was wrong. Anton was there. Robin was there and so was Mark, but what was it about them that concerned me? I just stared, trying to figure it out. At these altitudes one's cognitive abilities are impaired and thought processes are sluggish. Five minutes later, I knew. They were all heading back down to the North Col. They had finally given in to the wind.

My brain was suddenly filled with questions and scenarios, flooding with thoughts my mind couldn't deal with – like a bad traffic jam when you're late for a meeting. I sat and stared. I had made a number of rules on Everest, one of which was that no-one climbs above the North Col on their own.

I knew deep down that, for the rest of the team, enough was enough. I also knew that no amount of shouting or screaming on their part would have got my attention. The wind was too strong to allow me to hear anything and I guess it finally got to them. Maybe I was just being more stubborn than they were. But it still left me with some pressing decisions. Should I carry on, or should I turn around and head back? Should I break the rule that I had set?

The post-monsoon season on Everest is always a windy time. This was especially so in 1996.

I turned my head and looked up towards the summit. It was still a long way off. The North Ridge swept upwards to the site of Camp Five. Then the route turned to the right and headed diagonally up towards the site of Camp Six. How high could I go, I wondered, before I became too cold? The cold was already seeping in and the wind had numbed the right side of my body. I had to decide and I had to decide now. I looked back down and could just make out the others, moving along the final section into camp.

Up until this point I had always thought success and failure were pretty simple concepts, particularly in mountaineering. If you got up, you succeeded. If you didn't, you failed. It was as simple as that. Now, that reality was pressing on me. If I turned around and headed back, we would fail. We would let down all the people who had believed in us and supported us. We would let ourselves down. I stood up and braced myself against the wind. My feet were losing the battle against the cold and it was time to move. I took one last look upwards, and then turned and headed down. We would fail.

The wind never did improve. Anton and I remained on the North Col for a further five days, psyching ourselves up for another bid. But that break never came. Finally, we ran out of options and the decision to head down to ABC was an easy one. The end had come and it was time to go home. Our long battle had played itself out and we were the losers, vanquished with disdain by our place of destiny.

At least that's what we all thought for those first few weeks after the expedition. It was only when we arrived to a heroes' welcome at Johannesburg International Airport, that we began to think that we had done something special. Those close to us had sown a seed, but it would take months for it to bear fruit. For now, we were still weighed down by the bulk of Everest. The picture of its summit soared ever upwards in our minds, and in our bodies the toil of its slopes pulled and tugged at our bones. We were tired, right down to the very core. Drained. What we needed was rest, long days of spring and the promise of summer.

Leaving the safety of the North Col for the exposed North Ridge.

LEFT: *Sean Disney gapes at the immense sweep of Everest's North Face.*

ABOVE: *Sean Disney (right) and I meet Sir Edmund Hillary at Johannesburg International Airport in 1993.*

PAGE 88: *A series of landslides had turned what was once the main 'highway' between Tibet and Nepal into an extremely dangerous route.*

PAGE 89: *Getting to know our team of yaks and their herders was almost as difficult a task as climbing the mountain.*

OPPOSITE TOP: Sean Disney training for the big one.

OPPOSITE BOTTOM: Robin Walshaw before Everest, and after – looking noticeably older!

BELOW: Cameraman Sean Wisedale in action.

RIGHT: Mark Campbell, our trusty accountant, on Everest.

BELOW RIGHT: Anton Erasmus getting down to business on Everest.

THE MOUNTAIN GUIDE:
Kilimanjaro

- ALSO KNOWN AS: Oldoinyo Oibor (White Mountain) to the Masai and Kilima Njaro (Glittering Mountain) in Swahili.

- HEIGHT: 5 895 metres (19 340 feet).

- FIRST ASCENT: 1889 by H. Meyer, L. Purtscheller and Y. Louwa, a 16-year-old Tanzanian guide.

- LOCATION: Tanzania, Africa.

- POINT OF INTEREST: A dormant volcano consisting of three cones: Kibo, Mawenzi and Shira. Kilimanjaro is one of the world's highest free-standing mountains.

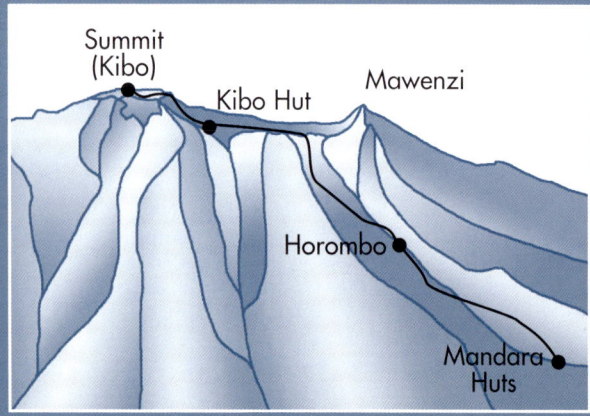

Summit (Kibo)

Mawenzi

Kibo Hut

Horombo

Mandara Huts

There is no mistaking the mountain that stands sentinel to the plains of Africa.

LEFT: The final 200 metres to the highest point in Africa.

BELOW: One of Adventure Dynamics' clients, Steven Bowden, gazes at the rising sun.

It has always been a privilege for me to watch people from normal walks of life take the last few steps and reach the Roof of Africa.

CHAPTER SIX

Roof of Africa

Spending 51 days on Everest without Sherpas and oxygen was both the best and the worst of times. In time I would realize that God certainly had a plan for me on that mountain, but it had little to do with the summit. I would also discover how to find the right balance between pursuit and retreat. Neither of these on their own will bring success, but together they provide the answers we seek. It is as hard to be humble as it is to be bold, but both are vital.

As for Seanne, we spent an intense month together before she realized I wasn't the one. But she would bring me to a church and help me find a spiritual home, and for that I am forever indebted to her. I don't know where she is now. Last I heard, she was teaching abroad. But, wherever she is, I am sure she is bringing joy to all who know her.

By the end of 1996 I was broke and unemployed. Everest had taken everything and given me life in return. But the practical side was that I still needed a career of sorts. Shortly after I had resigned earlier in the year, Anton had also left his employers, and together we'd started Adventure Dynamics. A few months later, Sean Disney had also left his job as a market researcher to join us.

Adventure Dynamics hadn't achieved much in the first few months of its existence because we'd been so busy trying to put the Everest trip together. We'd had great ideas for the company, but had known they would have to wait until after Everest.

It was slow going immediately after our return. We had no doubt that Everest had helped our reputations, although business definitely would have been better had we managed to summit. But, we made do with the little business we could get.

Leor Seeff, Lawrence's cousin, takes a break before taking the final few steps to the top of Kilimanjaro.

At the heart of it, we wanted to help people from the corporate world realize their own dreams. This started with guiding groups up some relatively easy mountains, but it quickly became more than just mountain climbing. Soon we were working with teams out in the hills of the Magaliesberg and helping them realize their potential. Speaking about our own adventures would, in time, also form part of the package. In December 1996 I took a small group to Aconcagua and made my second ascent.

As 1997 began, Adventure Dynamics looked for a corporate angle to get some leverage from the experience gained on Everest. Paul Booyens, a friend who worked at an insurance company, thought it would be a good idea if we spoke to some of his colleagues about our experiences. We said sure, and then spent days deliberating

over how much we should charge. We decided on a fee of R750, but in the backs of our minds we worried that it was too much.

Anton and I arrived on the appointed day and set up two bulky old slide machines and a CD player and put on a pretty good show. We still weren't slick but the story was good. It was genuine. All we did was share what it had been like as a team on Everest. It seemed there were interesting and relevant lessons we could share with corporates, and we were told afterwards that the talk had been worth far more than we had charged them. We met with speaking agents through the course of that year and refined the presentation. On the mountaineering side, we started advertising guided trips up Kilimanjaro and slowly started building up a steady client base.

It was good to get back to Kilimanjaro – my first love of the mountains. The guided trips with Adventure Dynamics were easy, but I often thought of the first time I finally got to stand on Africa's highest mountain. It was a small trip back in January 1999, just Greg Devine, Darryl Margetts and I. We weren't going to do anything fancy – just go there, sign up for the regular route, or the Coca-Cola Route, as it is sometimes called, and try and climb it. One of the more difficult hiking routes, the Machame Route, has been referred to as the Whisky Route and hence the easiest route, the Marangu, is known as the Coca-Cola Route, although I've no idea when or how these names came about. In a sense we were roughing it because we didn't have any porters with us (their absence has subsequently become unheard of when climbing Kilimanjaro). But hey, we were fit and raring for an adventure.

We followed the Marangu Route for five days, sleeping in a tent at night. Although this is the only route on Kilimanjaro with huts, we couldn't afford to use them. For the first two days, we hiked through some of the thickest jungle you are ever likely to see.

At times we would come across trees so grand it was hard to imagine that human eyes had ever seen them. They stood in silence in the cool light, their trunks twisting and turning in the undergrowth.

Speaking in these clearings was as shattering as breaking a piece of glass. We stood quietly and stared in awe. Moss hung everywhere, thick and green.

We moved from the jungle into an alpine zone of low bush and scrub. It was cooler now that we were at an altitude of 3 700 metres (12 139 feet), and what the environment lacked in jungle magnificence it made up for in scenic grandeur. We could now see out across the unmistakable flatness of Africa. It was December, the time of the rainy season, so the land was green and young. We could make out Kibo in the distance, the final crater of Kilimanjaro. It seemed so far away, almost like another mountain. We were but bugs on the bulk of a great mountain that proudly claimed its place on the continent.

Once we left the scrub zone behind us, we left all signs of life behind us too, and entered an area that could easily have been on Mars. The desert zone on Kilimanjaro is a dry, dusty, intimidating landscape. There are no plants, only soil and rock in varying shades of red and brown. It was here that, for the first time, we thought about the possibility of failure; of struggling in this barren landscape and not managing to summit.

But summit day arrived and we set off from the high camp at 4 750 metres (15 584 feet). It is 'tradition' on Kilimanjaro to leave at midnight and toil up the frozen slopes in the dead of night, arriving on the summit sometime around dawn, in time for the magnificent sunrise.

Well, most people are so buggered that they don't remember a thing from the top. It's only when they're looking at the photos back home that the memory of those few hours returns, and with it the fresh hues of that mighty vista of stars rising above Africa. I would be lying if I said my experience was any different. Yes, I had a headache and, yes, I was nauseous when I got up there.

> But, oh, that sun, rising
> like an orb from the very
> furnace in which God
> made the universe. On
> that morning it was ours,
> and ours alone. In fact,
> for a few moments it
> was mine, and it changed
> my life.

Kilimanjaro was the perfect climbing trip for Adventure Dynamics to guide. It was an extremely accessible mountain, being just a three-hour flight from Johannesburg, and it was also relatively safe to climb. We could pretty much guarantee our clients that nothing dangerous would happen to them, and most of them managed to summit successfully. We experienced a success rate of well over 90 percent. There was usually one person in a group of about 10 who didn't make it, but invariably that person had been ill prior to the trip. Kilimanjaro was also 'doable' for people who had never climbed a mountain before. Yes, it was tough going, but nothing that couldn't be conquered by sheer determination.

There were many South African tour operators who put together Kilimanjaro packages. Most of these were unguided trips, but they were still organized by reputable companies with good track records. The problem was that there were no companies offering trips to mountains higher or more challenging than Kilimanjaro. We found a good portion of our clients were phoning us up a few months after climbing Kilimanjaro to ask what else they could climb that was a little more difficult, or maybe slightly higher. Slowly,

we realized we were in a position to offer expertise to our client-base that they couldn't get elsewhere.

Adventure Dynamics started looking at maps and books about mountains, trying to figure out which peaks would be most appealing to our clients. They couldn't be just any mountains. They had to be worthy of paying large sums of money and travelling for days or weeks to far corners of the globe. People wanted war stories. They wanted to be able to say they had climbed this or that mountain, and then in the same breath say it was the highest in that country. But there weren't too many mountains like that. Most high mountains are too technical for your average beginner. This is where the Seven Summits journey took a pivotal turn.

We decided that some of the Seven could be easily guided, and they were interesting mountains that people knew about. Elbrus in Russia was arguably easier than Kilimanjaro, but it combined ice and snow, making an interesting challenge for those wanting to hone some basic skills. It was a good step up from Kili, being of similar height. Once a client had climbed those two, we recommended that they try Aconcagua. This was the next logical step. There were no difficulties involved, but there were small sections of ice and snow where the client would be able to test the skills they had developed on Elbrus. Of course the main challenge was the altitude. Clients would have been up to 5 900 metres (19 357 feet) on Kili, but no higher. Aconcagua was a great way to get close to 7 000 metres (22 965 feet) and see what it was like to be that high up.

For the select few who had done all three with us, we would have to be creative. We started looking at some of the other Seven. Denali in Alaska was out because only a select group of United States guiding companies had concessions to guide on its slopes. Everest was also out as that was just way out of our league. But Carstensz Pyramid in Indonesia and Mount Vinson in Antarctica were appealing. To add to that, no South African had ever climbed those two of the Seven Summits. It made sense to try to be the first, and imagine offering that opportunity to a client! Awesome!

But, as 1998 wore on, it became clear that it would be impossible to get to Carstensz Pyramid. It was situated on the island of New Guinea, but on the western side in the Indonesian province of Irian Jaya. It was a part of the world that constantly experienced ethnic upheaval. For our purposes, it was pretty much off-limits. For the time being we forgot about Carstensz Pyramid and turned our eyes southwards towards Antarctica.

Watching the sunrise from the top of Kilimanjaro is something everyone should do at least once in their lives.

THE MOUNTAIN GUIDE:
Mount Vinson

- **NAMED AFTER:** Carl G. Vinson, a Georgia Congressman and major supporter of US Antarctic exploration in the 20th century.

- **HEIGHT:** 4 897 metres (16 066 feet).

- **FIRST ASCENT:** In 1966 by the American Antarctic Mountaineering Expedition.

- **LOCATION:** Ellsworth Mountain Range, Antarctica.

- **POINT OF INTEREST:** Antarctica has been called the world's coldest desert. The interior receives less than three centimetres of snow a year, making it the driest continent on Earth.

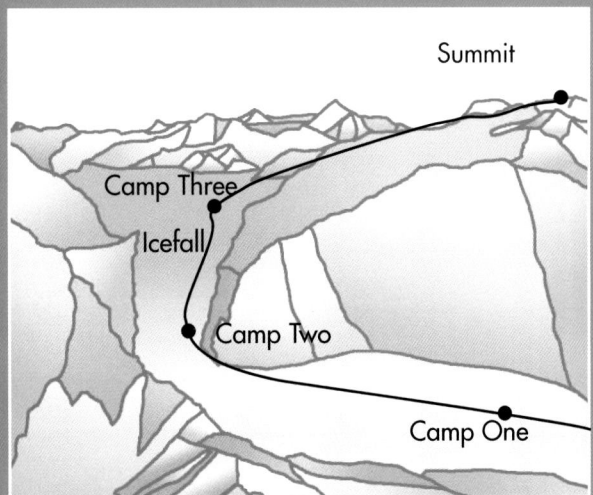

Starting the long sled haul towards Mount Vinson.

CHAPTER SEVEN

Cold Desert

Antarctica is probably one of the world's more difficult places to reach. Most of the people who visit the continent do so either as scientists working at one of the bases, or as tourists on ships passing the coastline. Either way, it is an expensive exercise.

The problem with Mount Vinson, Antarctica's highest mountain, is that it is located about 1 000 kilometres from the South Pole. This puts it slap bang in the middle of the continent and nowhere near the coastline. Logistically, trying to do this cheaply is like trying to build a rocket in your backyard and sending the family cat into a sub-orbital flight before landing it safely in the neighbourhood park. It just won't happen. Only one company makes it possible to get to Mount Vinson: Adventure Network International, or ANI.

ANI has a fascinating history. It was started by an aviation pioneer, Giles Kershaw, who recognized the need to service adventurers who wanted to fly into the interior of Antarctica and do a whole bunch of crazy things. Shortly after ANI was formed Giles was killed in a flying accident but his wife, Anne, then took over the company and slowly turned it into the only commercial operator to access the interior of the continent. But you can't just fly to Antarctica and land wherever you want to. It's a logistical nightmare. The right type of plane has to be used. Tons and tons of fuel has to be placed in safe areas along the flight route for back up. All in all, the costs of such an endeavour are prohibitively high, making it accessible to only a select few.

I had always wanted to get to Antarctica but had never been prepared to spend the 12 months at the South African research station. This is generally the length of commitment required because the cost involved is so high and it takes a long time to get there by ship. I had pretty much written it off as one of those places you can read about but never actually feel under your feet. But, slowly, the desire to visit this continent was growing out of control. We weren't too sure how we were going to pull it off but we knew we had to get there.

At first we thought about doing a combination of things, like climbing Mount Vinson and then walking unsupported to the South Pole. This had never been done before. We spent months pestering Anna about the costs of such an adventure, and then put a glossy brochure together. It promised sponsors the chance to take 'one step beyond', to go where no person had gone before. But we were asking people to pay one and a half million rand for the privilege.

As the months went by we had no joy raising sponsors and were becoming increasingly despondent. Slowly, we changed our plan. What if we just climbed the mountain, which was really the main goal? We looked through our client list for the individuals who had both the desire and the financial means to make it happen. Two stood out: Lawrence Seeff and Ruth Credo. Both had climbed Kilimanjaro and were keen to take the next step, and both were well established in the business world. Once they were convinced that Vinson was achievable and wouldn't be technically too difficult, they were in. But we still needed a third to make it happen.

A few months later, a friend called up out of the blue with the contact details for a guy called Roy Fouché. Having accompanied Ian Woodall on an unsuccessful expedition to the north side of Everest, he had returned disillusioned. However, he still wanted to do something special, and had the means to do so.

I phoned Roy up and we had a long chat. He was in. The idea of making the first South African ascent of one of the Seven Summits appealed to him – it was just the experience he had been looking for.

By December 1998, it hadn't yet sunk in that I was about to fly to Antarctica. We were so busy organizing logistics and negotiating prices with ANI, that we hadn't really had time to comprehend what was lying ahead.

If you take a map of the world and have a look at Antarctica, you will notice that the continent pretty much stretches from the left to the right of the map. Well, that's mostly because the map has been cut that way, but the point is that it is a big continent. Part of it reaches out towards South America, part of it stretches towards New Zealand, and some of it even faces South Africa. The part we were going to was the area near the Antarctic Peninsula, that strip that sticks way out into the ocean and seems to brush South America. To get there you have to fly to Chile, and then make your way down towards the southern tip, to a town called Punta Arenas.

Punta Arenas lies on the Straits of Magellan and overlooks the cold, turbulent waters. This windy town's claim to fame is that it has more brothels per capita than any other town in the world, no doubt to service countless sailors who have been stranded in atrocious weather. There is nothing inviting about the sea when you stand on the shores of Punta. The waters are dark and kick up an ominous froth in the wind. Even the beaches are harsh. There is no sand to be seen, only a rough gravel that cuts the feet. The sun sulks about and there is never a day when you feel it's safe to walk around in a T-shirt.

We spent the first few days settling in and busying ourselves with making sure we had everything we would need. Punta Arenas is really the start of the journey. ANI leases a giant four-engine Hercules for the summer months and then bases it in Punta. When the weather is perfect, the Hercules takes off and flies south for six and a half hours to a tiny strip of ice called Patriot Hills. But, in order to make that flight, a number of variables need to be in order. There can't be a crosswind of more than 15 knots (28 kilometres per hour). The snow at Patriot Hills can't exceed 15 centimetres (six inches). The visibility has to be this; the cloud cover has to be that. And it goes on and on. On most days four of five of the variables are fine, but, if one thing is wrong, the Hercules ain't going nowhere. Such is the fickle nature of Antarctic weather, the plane will only set out in perfect conditions. The Hercules never waits at Patriot Hills for longer than half an hour, and its engines cannot be turned off because it might be too cold for them ever to start again.

As the days went by, the news that the weather was still bad was exciting for us. We knew we were headed to a place that few people ever get to visit, and the hectic weather just reinforced this idea. But soon the days became a week and we started growing weary of repeatedly hearing the same news. The weather in Punta was good, so it was difficult for us to believe that it could be so bad elsewhere. But there was another more serious problem. Part of the reason Lawrence, Roy and Ruth were successful in business was that they had dedicated so much time to their careers. Two weeks away was pushing it. Any more and they ran the risk of complicating things back home. We had now been stuck in Punta Arenas for almost 10 days.

'How often do they fly in to Patriot Hills in a season?'

Lawrence had reached the end of his tether.

'Every two or three weeks, depending on weather of course. Why?'

'And how much does it cost them in fuel to do one trip?'

'No idea, but we have heard that, by the time a barrel of fuel gets to Patriot Hills, it's worth about 26 000 dollars.'

'Well, I think we're being had here.'

'What do you mean?'

'It just doesn't make economic sense to fly out there twice when you can do the trip once.'

'What are you saying?'

'I think they have a cut-off date and, if the weather hasn't improved by that date, they just wait for the next group to arrive and fly both out at the same time.'

'They can't do that,' I responded. Lawrence had a good point but I wasn't too sure if he was right.

'Why not?' he asked.

'It's too much of a risk. If they decide to wait until the weather is good, you could end up with a domino effect. I know the chances are small but it's still a risk.'

'I agree with Lawrence,' said Roy, a big burly chap who seemed built to deal with nonsense. 'I think they are stuffing us around and I'm running out of time fast.'

'Well, what do you suggest we do about it?'

'We confront them with it and find out what the story is.' Lawrence was still being sensible.

'Ja, and if they've been lying to us they're going to hear from my bloody lawyers.'

Roy wasn't only running out of time, he was running out of patience.

We all decided to head up to the ANI office and

confront them with this latest development. We knocked on the door and Rachel, the Operations Manager, ushered us inside. For the next hour, Lawrence and Roy bombarded her with questions. Ruth remained silent on the side, just observing the scene. Wisedale did what he does best: he filmed it all. It was a tough time. We had to be sensitive to our clients' needs because it was thanks to them that this was happening in the first place. But we also understood the rigours and logistics of adventure travel. Finally we left, but Lawrence and Roy still weren't convinced, despite ANI's assurance that the delay had nothing to do with economics, and everything to do with weather and safety conditions.

Christmas Day came and went and we were still stuck in Punta. We had been kicked out of one hotel for reasons that weren't quite true. They claimed we had broken two beds. We had certainly bust one, but that was by accident. They had also grown annoyed with Wisedale walking around at breakfast in his tasteless jocks and bare feet. Now we were holed up in a hotel further up the street, owned by two elderly ladies. We weren't too sure if they would be able to put up with our antics, but at this stage we didn't care.

As we carried our loads up the stairs to the first floor, I walked around checking the place out. That's when I noticed a small dog under a side-table in the passage. I called out to it but it ignored me. I walked up to the animal and crouched down warily. It looked like a dog that had spent its life being mistaken for a bitch on heat and being chased around, and it was fed-up with everything. I reached out to it cautiously. Still nothing. Then I gently stroked it on the side of its jaw. To my horror, it was rock-hard and fell over with a bang! I got the fright of my life. When my shock had subsided, I burst out laughing. The dog was stuffed.

There would be no end to the amusement that dog would provide. It turned out to be an old pet belonging to the two ladies. They had loved it so much that they had stuffed it after its death, and kept it right there for all to see. We took photos standing next to it, and placed it in the most ridiculous positions: on its nose, on its bum, on its side. We also threatened to blow it up after our second week in Punta had passed.

Day 15 and we finally got a call from

ANI to suit up. It was time to go. We pulled on our double boots and down jackets, and, in our ice and snow gear, we felt like astronauts preparing to go into outer space. We climbed aboard a bus and headed for the airport where we had to go through all the normal passport procedures. It was heaps of fun having our passports stamped and knowing that, rather than flying to another country, we were instead going to a territory controlled by 16 different nations. We climbed excitedly onto the Hercules and found ourselves a seat in the vast space of its cargo hold. This Hercules was slightly different because it had been fitted with airline seats to make the journey as comfortable as possible. It even had an air hostess.

The four great engines were soon drowning out all other sounds in the plane. I pulled my buckle tight and looked around. Roy had a big smile on his face and couldn't wait to crack open a beer. A couple of seats away from me was an American called Mike Hodges. He was a great bear of a guy, standing all of 1.93 metres (six foot four inches) tall. Amazingly, he had only arrived in Punta a few hours earlier and hadn't even left the airport before he was told he could climb aboard the Herc. Mike had been scheduled for a later trip than ours but our group had been stuck in Punta for so long that we were now flying out together. With a bump and a rumble the plane groaned into the sky and headed south. There was no turning back.

Hot air was slowly pumped through the plane from the front of the aircraft. The further south we flew, the lower the temperature fell. It was soon below freezing but a combination of the hot air and our suits kept us reasonably warm. Mike looked like a giant Michelin man in his 1.93-metre (six foot four) down suit and could barely fit into his seat. After about an hour, Faye, the air hostess, handed out fresh sandwiches and drinks.

About three hours into the flight, I moved up to one of the small porthole windows and stared down at the ocean 6 000 metres (19 685 feet) below us. I was amazed at what I saw. The ocean was filled with giant blocks of ice, some of them kilometres in diameter.

Looking down on them from that height was like staring into a bucket of ice at a party. The huge chunks were part of the Antarctic icepack that was slowly breaking up after being frozen in the continent's grip during the long winter. Now, with the onset of spring, the ice was thawing and slowly drifting north.

I settled back into my seat and tried to take a nap. I was nervous with excitement at the prospect of landing in the middle of nowhere in such a big plane. And the noise made it all the more frightening. There was so much happening and so much to see out of the window that it was impossible to sleep. We were soon nearing Patriot Hills and it was time to buckle up again.

A C130 Hercules is a beast of plane, with four giant engines to power it. The United States Air Force owns the only ones in the world that are equipped with skis for landing on snow. These regularly make the trip to

The dust-free air of Antarctica enables one to see clearly for more than 100 kilometres (62 miles).

the American base at the South Pole where they drop off tons of supplies. The Hercules we were in had wheels, just like any other plane, as we weren't going to land on snow but on ice, rock-hard blue ice.

Patriot Hills consists of a range of small hills that lie in a roughly east-west direction. This puts them straight across the path of the prevailing winds that come off the South Pole. As a result, the leeward side of the range has been scoured over millennia, creating a strip of blue ice about two and a half kilometres (1.5 miles) in length. It's by no means flat and undulates by a metre or two over its length, but it is possible for an aircraft like a Hercules to touch down and then skid to a halt as it grinds away over the ice. We had heard much about the landing and were all convinced it was the most dangerous part of the journey. We sat clenching our seats as Patriot Hills loomed.

The Herc circled as is normal flying practice before lining up on final approach. We could see the tiny dots of camp spread out over the snow about a kilometre from the 'runway', and, to the left, the Patriot Hills grew bigger and bigger. Mike turned to me for the first time in the flight: 'Are you a religious person?' he asked.

I get asked this question quite a lot, but this one took me by surprise.

'Yes, I am, why?'

'Well, now's a good time to start praying.'

I had only known Mike for a couple of hours so it was too soon to know if he was joking or not. I smiled and looked back out of the window.

Suddenly, one of the engineers ran down the stairs from the cockpit and disappeared towards the back of the plane. Seconds later he was followed by a second crew member. I turned and looked at Mike. He was as wide-eyed as I was. All of us were looking at each other, wondering what was up. The plane seemed poised to touch down. Again the two crew members rushed by pointing to the side of the plane, and then climbed the cockpit ladder and were gone. By now we were nervous, but still we didn't know what was wrong. Then the plane pulled up and banked sharply to the right. We had aborted the landing. But why? The weather seemed perfect.

The plane climbed steadily and slowly turned in a northerly direction. Moments later one of the crew came down and told us the bad news: one of the engines had had a throttle failure of sorts. Basically, it was impossible for it to throttle back and they had only realized this late on final approach. The engine would have to be shut down. This posed a serious problem because the Herc couldn't land on ice with only three engines running. It needed all four engines to control its skid after touching down. The only thing for it was to head all the way back to South America to try to sort out the problem.

We were heartbroken. Wisedale moved around the plane with his camera, trying to capture our thoughts and feelings. But there was nothing I could say. I just stared blankly back at him. I couldn't even shake my head. Six and a half hours later we were back in Punta Arenas. We had safely touched down on three engines but were too dazed to care. We moped back to the hotel and fell onto our beds, dead to the world. It had been a 13-hour emotional rollercoaster and none of us knew what the morning would bring.

The next day we walked back up the hill to the ANI office. Not surprisingly, no-one could tell us anything of use. They weren't sure how long it would take to fix the problem. There was even talk of flying out another Herc, which would take at least a week. We were crestfallen. They said they would keep us updated but for now we were restricted to the same 24-hour standby as before. It meant we couldn't leave Punta Arenas but had to pass the time in the town. We wandered back down to the centre of Punta. It was the same old story. We were sure that things unknown were conspiring against us. Unfortunately for Roy and Ruth, this was the end.

Without any definite timescale on the plane, it was impossible to predict how long this expedition was still going to take. It was day 15 and we still hadn't left Punta. We all sat down at lunch and thrashed out the various options. There weren't too many available. At the most, Roy and Ruth had only two weeks to spare. That had already been used up. Lawrence was pretty close to his limit as well. All three of them had pressing business engagements back home. It wasn't normal for them to be gone for more than a week at a time. We were now looking at a month and that was just too much. Roy and Ruth decided to head back as soon as possible. They would still have to negotiate with ANI about the vast amount of money they had paid. There was the possibility of obtaining a credit and returning at some point in the future, but, for the moment, nothing was certain. Lawrence, on the other hand, would think it over and let us know in the morning.

It was sad to see Roy and Ruth go. They had been vital in making this happen and now, because of unusual circumstances, they had to leave. As for the two Seans and me, we were in for the long haul. We were staying until we had got up this mountain, no matter how long it took.

By morning Lawrence had decided to hang around, but for no more than a few days. We passed the time as we always did in Punta: lunch at Lomit and drinks in the evening. Lomit was a diner of sorts that had a great atmosphere but sometimes served dodgy food, which was why Roy had nicknamed it 'Lomit's vomit comit'.

The phone rang at six the next morning.

'Hi, who's that?' asked the voice on the other end.

'It's Lawrence.'

'Morning, Lawrence, this is Faye. It's a go.'

'It's a go?'

'Yeah, pick up in one hour.'

Lawrence hung up and shouted down the hall: 'Boys, it's a go. Let's move it!'

Over the next few hours we went through the same procedures as before: suiting up, passport control, and then climbing aboard. They had managed to fix the problem and we were all set for go. It was day 17. We knew that, if it didn't happen now, it was never going to happen. There are only so many times you can keep motivating yourself and keeping up the enthusiasm. We had been nearing the end of our supply. If one more thing should go wrong, it would almost certainly be the last straw.

Six and a half hours later, we were once again lined up on final approach. Everyone was looking out of the windows, making sure the engines were all fine. Not that we could do much about it if anything did go wrong, but there was a sense of having been there before and that we could therefore master what was happening in the present. Deep down we felt we could have a positive effect if we kept an eye on things. Of course it was all nonsense, but we couldn't help looking at that engine.

Seconds later, we were down. The first bump was expected but the next few seconds were terrifying. As the Hercules hit the ice, it sped along at high speed, bumping and grinding. At each lurch we were sure we had pitched into a crevasse or lost a wheel. But this was all normal. Experiencing it for the first time, though, was like standing on the high diving board and everyone telling you to jump. Only difference was that, once you had jumped, there was another high board for you to brave, and another and another. The noise was awesome but we finally slowed down before turning and eventually coming to a halt. Cold air began to seep into the plane.

We unbuckled and stood up, anxious to get out. The ramp at the rear of the Hercules was slowly lowered and for the first time nothing stood between our eyes and the ice of Antarctica. We carefully made our way down the ramp and took our first steps. I thought about Neil Armstrong and how incredible his famous first step must have been. Ours felt similar in some small way. Yes, it was bright and endlessly white, but the thing I remember most about those first few steps was the cold.

That first breath of −7°C (19°F) air filling my lungs almost assaulted me and knocked me backwards. There was no question about where we were, and there was no question that this was not a place where humans dwelt.

There was no sign of life. Not even the sun could inspire. It formed a large circle low on the horizon, and it never disappeared.

We slid around on the ice without crampons for about 15 minutes, shouting and carrying on like kids. We fell over time and again but got up smiling and laughing. I could smell the cold and it was pure and untainted. It wasn't so much the ice or the snow, but the air. It hung there and wouldn't give in to our lungs willingly, but only with considerable effort. Soon, even our boyish efforts couldn't keep us warm and we had to get moving. Camp was over a kilometre away and we had the choice of riding on a skidoo, a kind of snowmobile, or walking. We chose to walk.

Behind us, we left Patriot Hills covered in shadow. We were now on snow so the going was much easier. In every direction, as far as the eye could see, the snow stretched, flat and unhindered. The colours of camp soon came into view and before long we were walking into the mess tent.

The camp of Patriot Hills only exists in the summer months. It is put up by ANI early in the season, and remains there till sometime in January, serving as a base for all kinds of adventurers. People would fly in and then take another flight to the South Pole. Others would move on to see the colonies of Emperor Penguins. There were even some people who were walking to the South Pole. The mix of people based at Patriot was quite varied, and their ages ranged from young adventurers, like ourselves, to retired folk who were keen on spending their hard-earned money flying to remote parts of the world.

For our group, Patriot Hills was simply a stopover. Mount Vinson still lay about an hour's flight away. But from here we would be getting onto a smaller plane. A twin-engine Otter was far more suited to these conditions and, as it was equipped with skis, it could land pretty much anywhere in Antarctica. Most people played the waiting game at Patriot, passing the time watching the weather. But we were lucky when we touched down. It seemed a good spell had arrived and the weather was clear right up to Mount Vinson. Steve Pinfield, the camp director, welcomed us but told us to remain ready as it was likely we would fly within the hour.

OPPOSITE LEFT: *Jaime Vinals became the first Guatemalan to complete the Seven Summits.*

LEFT: *The view from the top of Patriot Hills, looking towards the South Pole.*

BELOW: *The moment the American Joby Ogwyn arrived at the summit of Mount Vinson, he became the youngest person to complete the Seven Summits.*

The mess tent was a real weather haven. A big rectangular shape with curved sides, it was just about as weatherproof as a tent could be. It had to be, as the winds in Antarctica would often blow at gale-force speeds. But, for now, things were calm and it was warm inside. The tent had a kitchen area at the back where fresh food was cooked daily. As a result, the pleasant aroma of fresh bread would waft around the tent. We sat at one of the tables and helped ourselves to some hot drinks. There were even packs of wine on the shelves, and I couldn't help thinking this was a far cry from Robert Scott's day.

Steve informed us within the hour that we were pressing on. The weather breaks come so seldom that you have to be ready to take advantage of them as soon as they appear. While we would have loved to continue enjoying the warmth of the mess tent, we had to embark on the next leg of our journey. Our gear had already been moved to the small airstrip just outside the camp where two Twin-Otters stood next to each other, one slowly roaring into life. We were given a quick safety briefing about the emergency procedures, during which we were informed that the emergency supplies were duplicated in both the nose and tail of the plane. This was in the event of the plane breaking up during a crash landing. There were complete survival systems at both ends. We laughed at the thought of fighting over who got the nose and who got the tail, but this was the reality of flying in Antarctica.

It was colder inside the Otter than it had been in the Herc, but we were assured that, once we were airborne, hot air would soon fill the plane. We pulled out of camp and left 'civilization' behind us. We were finally heading to Mount Vinson.

The flight was unbelievable. It turned out that the landscape wasn't as flat as we had expected. Small hills and peaks dotted the place everywhere. On numerous occasions we flew over the most pyramidal peaks I have ever seen. They looked as though they had been wrought by the skilled hand of a sculptor. We crossed over many small ranges, and, at each pass, a sea of crevasses swept out in a great tide to the flatness beyond. No-one had ever been anywhere down there. It was incredible to think how many places still waited for the touch of human hands and the gaze of human eyes. Slowly, in the distance, a shape began taking form. It was the Ellsworth mountain range – the biggest in Antarctica and home to Vinson.

We all pressed our heads up between the cockpit seats to try to get a view, jostling to catch the first sighting of the peak we had come to climb. The range was covered in cloud, with just a few peaks sticking out here and there. It was impossible to distinguish where one ridge ended and another started. However our pilot, Bob Albus, seemed to know exactly what was what. He had done this many times before and knew all the ridges and routes. Soon we came low over a neck between two peaks, banked sharply and were lining up on final approach. The runway was just visible below. It was a stretch of snow marked by black rubbish bags that had been weighted down with snow. Nothing more. Seconds later, we touched down in a white whirl. We were there.

Base Camp at Mount Vinson

consisted of one communications tent and the resident ANI guide's sleeping tent. That was it. There were no comforts in this place, only the deep cold that you find in the secluded valleys of Antarctica.

This was a place where you trod with care; where you stuck to the sunlit areas and kept away from the shadows. We were now amongst the most remotely located humans on the planet. Help was days away, assuming the weather was perfect.

The Herc that had brought us to Patriot Hills only stayed for an hour before flying back to South America. It was too cold for it to wait in Antarctica. But it would keep flying people in, and hopefully, once we had climbed Vinson, we could time it right so that we could catch a flight out. The Otter, on the other hand, would wait for us here – our only lifeline to the outside world. In fact, we were so remote that Bob wasn't allowed to do anything while he waited for us. He could only lounge around and read. He was the one person who could fly us out of trouble and, if anything happened to him, that would be that. This fact drove home the point of how careful we had to be.

We cleared the runway and huddled around in a small group.

'What do you guys think?' I asked.

'Well, what are our options?'

'We could set up camp here and just rest a day. Or we could move on.'

'How much colder do you think it's going to get?' Wisedale wanted to know.

Apart from the mission we all had to go through, added to his was the task of filming it all.

'Dave reckons we should stay out of the shadows and only move when it's light,' I replied.

Dave Hahn was the ANI guide who manned Base Camp. He would be guiding Mike Hodges up Vinson.

'What, you mean pick a route around the shadows?'

'No. Basically our nights become the times that we are covered in shadow, regardless of what time that is. We then move whenever the sun is on us.'

'You reckon it's going to make that much of a difference?' Sean butted in.

'Dave reckons 20 degrees.'

'Wow. Well, that's me decided.'

The others agreed with him. The temperature was already about −10°C (14°F). To move when it was −25°C (−13°F) and −30°C (−22°F) was crazy. Our nights would become the times that the sun disappeared behind a peak and covered us in shadow.

It was late in the afternoon but the sun was still on us so we decided to carry on. Lawrence left all the decision-making up to us. This was a new world for him, a strange place very different from the world he knew. But he was coping well and was both mentally and physically strong. From here on we would be carrying all our stuff, and that meant we would each have to pull a small sled. The sled was really just a large, flat, plastic tray similar to the things kids use to fly down sand dunes. They easily carried 50 kilograms (110 pounds) and made relatively light work of transporting these kinds of loads. Of course we still had our packs on, stuffed with a good 15 to 20 kilos (33 to 44 pounds) each. Once our sleds were packed and roped up, we slowly wound our way out of camp.

We had landed on the foot of the Branscomb Glacier that fell from high up off Vinson. We could just see the tip of Vinson sticking out at the head of the valley. It looked close but that appearance was misleading, for our route followed the Branscomb all the way around its base. Then it climbed a headwall and finally swung back towards Vinson before heading directly towards its summit. If the weather held, it would be four or five days before we would reach the top.

I was roped to Lawrence and the two Seans were tied to each other, although Wisedale felt confident enough to unrope now and then and get ahead so he could film us passing him. The terrain steepened steadily as we climbed out of the dip where Base Camp lay. We found it difficult to regulate our warmth as we walked. When the sun was on us it was a good −10°C (14°F), and our bodies soon heated up and felt quite warm. The problem came when the sun vanished behind a cloud. Then the temperature would plummet. Even a small wisp of vapour that only slightly blocked the sun made it cold enough for us to stop and put on another layer. The sky was filled with many small clumps of cloud, each of which obscured the sun for 10 to 15 minutes at a time before it warmed up again. And so we went, battling to try to keep a constant temperature. Eventually we had an array of tops tucked under the pull straps on our sleds. This way they were easily accessible and we could change them in seconds.

As Base Camp disappeared

behind us, we climbed a short hill and made our way up to the head of the valley. The route then curved round to the left, hugging the face that led straight up to Vinson's summit. This wasn't a place to hang around, as giant chunks of ice hung precariously way up above us. But, despite this, it is true that Vinson is far safer than most mountains. Antarctica gets very little annual precipitation and the snow build-up is therefore minimal. Most of the ice faces have been compacted over time and they rarely come crashing down. But we still weren't about to tempt fate. It was nearing time to set up camp and we stopped for a short break. Wisedale pulled out the camera for one of those impromptu interviews that he enjoyed conducting.

'What do you think of the conditions so far?'

'Pretty good, although it's been a tough battle to try to dress right.'

'Okay, so what's the plan from here?'

'Well, we need to find a place to camp.'

'And what's wrong with right here?' Wisedale knew the answer to this but he was asking for the viewers' sake.

'Well, at the moment we're directly beneath this icefall.' I pointed high up to the face of ice suspended beneath the summit of Vinson. Wisedale's camera followed my finger. 'Even though that stuff is pretty stable, we probably won't have a good night's sleep wondering if it just might fall.'

'So what do you suggest?'

'Well, I think we should carry on for half an hour or so and try to find a spot that's sheltered from the wind.'

The thing we feared most out here was the wind. It blew like no other place on the planet. A slight breeze had already picked up without us realizing it, and this was having a dramatic effect on the temperature.

'Guys, I think we should move.'

While Wisedale and I had been bantering about on camera, Sean Disney had been looking back and watching the weather. It was starting to close in. We packed up the stove, finished our drinks and pressed on.

Soon the sun was hidden behind the clouds and it had become bitterly cold – too cold to walk using the ski poles. Within minutes my hands were drained of blood from the action of gripping the handles and I had to let them hang by my sides until my fingers had regained some of their warmth. It was time to stop. We had cleared the icefall but we moved about 100 metres (328 feet) away from the face, just in case. We didn't want to go too far because this would mean contending with the glacier and all its hidden crevasses, so we pitched the tents as fast as possible and put little effort into our snow walls. This would almost become our downfall, especially for the two Seans, who seldom put much work into theirs. Snow walls offer protection by breaking the force of the wind, but they have to be big in order to be effective. We were too tired to build anything bigger than a metre high.

An hour later we were safely in our tents boiling water when the wind started. A wind that starts as a breeze and builds up its strength is very different from a gale that suddenly arrives. The first catches you unawares in an insidious way. You know it's blowing but it never seems that hard and, by the time you realize it's grown into a howl, it's too late. We had been aware of the wind tugging and banging outside, seeking a weakness in the tents, but all the time we thought it would pass. Then it dawned on us that it had now been blowing for nearly four hours and the intensity had slowly increased. Lawrence and I jumped outside and frantically tried to strengthen our snow wall. It was just a pile of snow piled roughly in the shape of a wall between our tent and the direction the wind was blowing from. But it had to be made of solid blocks. Anything else and the wall would disintegrate into fine powder snow which would find its way into everything.

After six hours the situation had become desperate. What little wall the Seans had put up was gone and their tent was taking the full brunt of the wind's fury. Lawrence and I were only marginally better off. It

sounded like a freight train was tearing by only centimetres from our tent, and it just kept going and going and going. We had our backs to the windward side trying to brace the tent, but all the time we expected it to go. We played the scene over and over again in our minds so we would know exactly what to do if it did get whipped away.

I heard one of the Seans shouting through the drone of the wind.

'Alex!'

'Ja.'

'Our tent's abawaya ... blowayn yay ...'

I couldn't make out what the heck he was saying and wasn't too keen to stick my head outside. Again, he shouted something.

> Quickly I unzipped and stuck my head out into the maelstrom.
> 'What's happening?' They were only five metres (16 feet) away but I was struggling to see them.
> 'Our tent's about to blow away. It's torn everywhere.'
> 'What about your guy ropes?'
> 'They're all gone. We're not going to last another five minutes.'

'Hang on a sec, let me get hold of Base Camp.' We had the radios ready for the evening call.

'Base Camp, Base Camp, Base Camp. This is the South African expedition at Camp One. Do you read? Over.'

'Yeah, go ahead Camp One.' Dave Hahn's voice came over clearly.

'Dave we're being pummelled by 100-kilometre-an-hour winds up here. What's the status at Base Camp?'

'Uh, copy that. We're pretty calm over here. I've got a good idea of what you boys are experiencing. The Russians have got the same stuff up at Two.' A Russian expedition consisting of only two climbers was a day ahead of us.

'Dave, that's good news. We might lose a tent soon and if that happens two of us will bail and head back down.'

'Yeah, no problem. You'll probably find that the wind dies down once you turn the bend just past the icefall.'

Dave had made 13 ascents of Vinson and knew the mountain better than anyone.

'Copy that. We'll keep in touch.'

'Uh, roger that Camp One. Base Camp standing by.'

The radio went silent and my mind went back to the scream of the wind.

'Alex!'

I stuck my head out of the tent again.

'It's going. We're heading back down.'

'Okay. How are you guys feeling?'

'We're fine. We just want to get the heck out of here.'

'Right, here's the deal. You guys can crash with us till it's gone, or you can head back down to BC. Dave reckons it's quiet down there and you should be out of the worst of it when you turn the bend.'

The two Seans were outside sorting out their packs. In one nasty blast, the tent was wrenched free and swept up the side of the mountain. It was gone within seconds and there was no trace that it had ever been pitched. The two Seans donned their packs and disappeared. I envied them in a way. Their fate was clear. They would mission for an hour or two and then would be safely back at Base Camp. Our fate had yet to be decided.

The wind raged for another 20 hours before disappearing as suddenly as it had arrived. Lawrence turned to me, looking haggard.

'What do you think?'

'Well, we've survived, which is a good start.'

'What about the others?'

'Look, once they realize the weather has cleared it'll take them a couple of hours to get back. I say we just wait for them.'

We climbed out of the tent and looked around. It was stunning. The skies had cleared, leaving a deep, clear air hanging over the mountains. Our wall had held. We spent the next few hours sorting out stuff in the tent and trying to dry sleeping bags in the relative warmth of the sun. Before long the two Seans appeared on the rise.

'Howzit going, boys?'

They looked none the worse for wear and seemed quite chirpy.

'Did you guys survive?'

'You can't believe it. Just as you turn the corner on the other side of the icefall, it's dead calm.'

'Amazing, hey?'

'We've organized a spare tent from Dave.'

'Are you guys ready to press on or do you want to rest a while?'

'No, we're cool. We just want to dry out some of the camera stuff.'

We spent the next two hours lazing about while Wisedale stripped his cameras. His two digital video cameras had gone down in the storm. Even the big Betacam, or Chubby as it was affectionately called, had taken strain. Once he'd put them back together again, only Chubby worked. Wisedale muttered something about having to carry it all the way up the mountain, and then we pushed on.

The Branscomb Glacier climbed imperceptibly upwards from Camp One. This was going to be a short day – no more than two or three hours – and it was kind of thought of as a rest day. Our vertical gain was very little, so there wasn't a lot to be done. We were now making our way along the relative flatness of the glacier, keeping the bulk of Vinson to our right. At the head of the valley, the Branscomb made a sharp bend to the right and ended abruptly in the headwall. Camp Two was situated on the side of the slopes a short way back from the headwall. We arrived shortly after the Russians had returned from the summit after a crazy bid. During the wind storm that had bogged us down, they had decided to move on from Camp Two, skip Camp Three and, in a mammoth effort, top out in a white-out. We thought they were insane but Misha Malakov, famous Russian hero, according to him, thought differently.

'Misha, congratulations on the summit. Wasn't the weather bad?'

'Lawrence, in mountains there is no bad weather; only bad attitude.'

We laughed. It brought back memories of my numerous visits to their country. That was their way. No complaining, just dogged determination.

We tried questioning the Russians on the route but they couldn't tell us much. It had been a white-out for most of the way and they couldn't remember any distinguishing features.

We settled in for a cold night. Camp Two was set right next to a small peak on the slopes of Vinson. It caught the shadow early and remained enshrouded for ages.

As a result, the cold there seemed different – deeper and more intense. A metal spoon left lying in the tent and forgotten about would instantly freeze to the skin if you tried to pick it up. If you were hasty in trying to pull it away, it would just tear a layer of skin off and you would be left with a bleeding finger. The wise thing to do was hold it for a while and let your hand slowly heat the spoon. When it had warmed enough, it would slide away without causing harm. But this was not something I always remembered to do and on numerous occasions I had the spoon in a gloved hand and would move it to my mouth, only to have it stick to one of my lips. We had to remember that the tents were not places for dilly-dallying, and we had to go about the chores of cooking and heating water with great care and deliberation.

Another unique aspect of climbing in Antarctica was the task of going to the toilet. Because of the continent's low precipitation, anything that was spilt or left on the snow would stay there for ages, sometimes even decades. For this reason there was a designated 'pee hole' at each camp. This was just a yellow-orange hole in the snow where countless adventurers had taken a leak over the previous years. It was a big no-no to go and pee somewhere else, thereby creating a new pee hole. We had been briefed on a number of occasions that we had to use the same pee holes and this was not negotiable. And, as for a crap, well, that's where things became interesting. No solid waste was allowed to be left in Antarctica, so each person had to crap in a black dustbin bag. Once this had frozen into a nice manageable turd, the packet had to be rolled up and put into a dry bag, which was made of thick plastic that could be sealed. This bag was then tied to one of the sleds and dragged behind us as we made our way up Vinson. Normally the person who crapped the most ended up

ABOVE LEFT: *Moving up the last slopes to the summit.*

ABOVE RIGHT: *Lawrence Seeff, Sean Disney and Sean Wisedale climbing the headwall.*

carrying the bag, and, with my fast metabolism, most times this ended up being me. I would often protest that I was being unfairly penalized, but the others would hear nothing of it. And so, like an ass resigned to its fate of pulling a cart, I pulled with stoic indifference.

We stayed in the tents long into the next day as we waited for the sun to break over the headwall and chase away the shadows. The difference was remarkable. I could almost sense the heat dripping down from high above and filling our small valley. Only then could you think about unzipping the tent and starting the day. Everyone was still going strong. The altitude

hadn't yet posed a problem, although it would soon become one.

The top of Vinson is about 100 metres short of 5 000 metres (16 404 feet). This is misleading though, because the pressure at these latitudes is far less than at the equator. Most people believe the earth to be perfectly spherical, when in fact it's an oblate spheroid. That's just a fancy way of saying that the earth is slightly squashed from the top down, so there is less atmospheric pressure at the poles than there is at the equator. This means that if you're dealing with two mountains of the same height, one at the pole and one at the equator, the one at the pole will pose the greater altitude problem because of its lower pressure. We were treating Vinson like a 6 000 metre (19 685 feet) peak, just in case.

We set off in high spirits, keen to tackle the head-wall. We heard on the radio that Mike Hodges and Dave Hahn were slowly making their way up and were roughly a day behind us. It was comforting to know that there were others behind us who were following the same route. Above us, the headwall stretched about 400 metres (1 312 feet) upwards to the neck between Mount Vinson and Mount Shinn, Vinson's neighbour. The headwall lay back at about 35 to 40 degrees so it wasn't that steep, but it was still the most technical part of the trip. We made our way up it in a series of slow zigzags, stopping frequently to rest and drink. Way below us on the other side of an intervening ridge, one of the pyramidal peaks was slowly coming into view. This one had been hidden the whole time but, now that it was clear, we were amazed at how symmetrical it was. We turned and continued walking. Camp Three was close.

The slope fell back and eased off at the top of the head-wall. We seemed to be in a broad valley that separated the upper slopes of two of Antarctica's biggest peaks. To the left of us, Mount Shinn rose steeply to the summit. It seemed so close. To the right, the slope rose gently in a series of small knolls and then disap-peared. We couldn't see Vinson or anything of the summit and would have to wait until morning to see what it was going to be like. We quickly set up camp and then climbed inside our tents. By now we were well acquainted with what would happen when the sun dropped behind Shinn. I looked across at Lawrence and was impressed by how strong he looked. Lawrence had been a professional cricketer before turning to business.

I imagined that his hours of discipline on the field had prepared him well for the rigours of tent life in Antarctica.

'How are you feeling?'

'Good so far.'

'No headaches or anything?'

'No, nothing. I'm just worried about whether my gear will be warm enough.'

'How are your hands and feet doing?'

'So far so good. What do you think the weather is going to do?' This had been the one thing that Lawrence had been concerned about.

'It's hard to tell. The skies look good but there is still a slight breeze about. Who knows what it's like up there.'

We started the routine of boiling water and eating something. Cooking had become harder and harder as we got higher up the mountain, mostly because it was just becoming colder and colder.

Soon we were trying to sleep. The night before summit day is always a difficult time for sleeping, no matter how tired you are. You are always slightly nervous about what the weather will be like and how you will be feeling on the day. Most times you just toss and turn, finding it impossible to fall into a deep sleep. This time, however, I felt calm. I lay back, content to drift in and out of a trance-like sleep for a while. I wondered why it felt different. Then it occurred to me that all my other pre-summit nights had been spent in darkness, but here it was still light outside. I realized there was something ominous about the dark – some-thing unknown that just compounded the mysteries of the day to come. That feeling wasn't present here. The dangers were the same but there wasn't an over-whelming feeling of the unknown. When sleep came this time, it was deep.

Our summit day started late in the morning. On any other mountain this would have spelt disaster, but up here it was vital as the sun had just reached the tents. Preparing for summit day in the confines of a tent is always an ordeal. Layer upon layer of clothing has to be carefully put on and at the same time you have to make sure you are boiling water for your bottles. When all of this is done, you finally climb outside and strap on your crampons while you rope up.

It was freezing outside. A light breeze blew from the other side of the valley. Roping up at −20°C (−4°F) is not a pleasant experience, especially when the sun is shining down on you without any hindrance – it just doesn't feel quite right. Lawrence and I roped up together and were ready about 20 minutes before the two Seans. We wanted to start but Wisedale insisted that we wait so that he could film us. My feet were already starting to get cold and this was just the beginning. When we finally got going, I knew it was going to be a struggle.

From Camp Three, the route climbed a short knoll that had been hiding the higher slopes of Vinson from view. Once we were above the knoll, a broad plateau opened out that seemed to stretch for miles and there were many small peaks spread about. As we climbed higher, the shelter of the valley was lost and we soon realized that the breeze had developed into a wind. We climbed on. The terrain was easy and the skies were clear, but the wind concerned us. Before leaving camp we had decided to press on despite the breeze. But, in the backs of our minds, the warning from Dave Hahn was ringing like a bell. He had said that we shouldn't even think about going for it if the wind was blowing, and should rather wait it out. We had discussed the issue but agreed that the weather had been so bad

on this trip that we would take our chances if the sky was clear.

Four hours later I was losing the battle to keep my feet warm. The temperature was well below −40°C and the wind was howling. It was the coldest I had ever experienced. I pulled up in the snow.

'Guys, I need to warm my feet.'

'How bad are they?'

Sean Disney pulled up next to me.

'They're still there but I can feel my toes going.'

While we stood around I desperately tried to wriggle them about so they could warm up. This worked for a while but it wouldn't last. I looked at the others.

'How are you all feeling?'

'Good, just flipping cold.' Sean was waving his arms about.

'Lawrence, how are you doing?'

'I'm okay. I'm just worried about the weather.'

'Guys, we need to try to move a bit faster so I can generate some heat.'

We set off again a little faster. A while later our pace had slowed once more. It was difficult to maintain any kind of pace in the howling wind and the cold. This was all we could manage. Once again I stopped.

'I have to rub my toes, otherwise they're gone.'

I sat down in the snow with my back to the wind. Wisedale approached with the camera. I could not believe he was still filming in this cold.

'Alex, just tell me what's happening there.'

'My damn toes are too cold. We're not moving fast enough to generate any heat and, unless I can warm them up, I'm going to get frostbite.'

The others crowded round me trying to give me some shelter. I quickly pulled my double boot off and then my socks. It was a grim task but I knew it had to be done. When my foot was bare I rubbed it vigorously, trying to bring back to it the warmth it had lost. It worked, but just barely. Then I did the other foot. The problem was that snow was being blown around by the wind and it was impossible to be completely sheltered. I was fighting a losing battle. I turned and looked up along our route.

'Anyone sure which one is Vinson?' The plateau we were on headed upward towards some peaks dotting the skyline but they were all indistinct. At this stage it was still impossible to be sure which one of them was Vinson. They weren't really peaks as such, because we had now spent the entire day on Vinson, but they were more like high points poking out of a long ridge. One of these high points was the very top of Vinson, but which one? We couldn't be sure but hoped it would become clearer as we got closer. Again I resolved to move faster and we set off. But deep down I knew we couldn't keep up the pace.

When I stopped again, it was for the last time.

'Guys, I can't go on.'

'Why? What's wrong?' Disney was peering at me through his ice-encrusted goggles.

'It's my feet. They're too cold and I can't seem to warm them.'

'Are they that bad?' he asked.

'Bad enough to get frostbite. I can feel them going and they haven't got long.'

'Well, what do you want to do?'

It was a good question. Deep down I wanted to continue. That same feeling as before was welling up inside me.

I wanted to get there with the others, bag the peak and be the first South Africans to do so. It seemed crazy to turn around now that I was so close.

There were four, maybe five hours to go, and the terrain was relatively easy. But I also knew that, if I carried on, I would have to pay a price. I stood in the snow with the wind blowing around me. Damn the wind, I thought. Once again it's going to be my bloody downfall. I turned to Lawrence.

'How're you feeling?'

'Okay.'

'Your hands and feet?'

'They're still fine.'

'Are you happy to go on without me?'

Up until that point we had been tied together for the entire trip and I knew what it was like to sever that bond and tie up with someone else. Once you had got used to the rope, being tied to someone else just wasn't the same.

'*Ja*. Look, if it doesn't get any worse I should be all right.'

'Alex, why don't you keep on for a while? Maybe the wind will die down.' Sean Disney was keen for me to stay with them.

I knew that it might, but I also knew that my toes were past the point of no return. If I didn't do something now, I would certainly get frostbite. They had just started to lose sensation. From here on they would go numb and then it would be too late.

'I can't. I have to head back down.'

'Are you sure?'

Sean was concerned about the route down but I was happy to do it alone. The route was safe and we hadn't been near any crevasses. But I was torn. I looked up towards the ridge and then looked at the others, who were huddled together.

'Good luck, guys. Just take it easy up there.' I turned and headed down alone. After 50 metres (164 feet), I stopped and looked back. The others were pushing ahead, heads bent into the wind. They were no more than 100 metres (328 feet) away but it felt like there were miles between us, and for a moment I thought about heading back up and joining them. Then I remembered that I'd made a decision and needed to stick with it. I continued, increasing my pace as I went. The warmth slowly returned to my feet and, by the time I got back to the tent, my toes were stinging with that familiar re-warming sensation. I crawled into the tent, pulled off my boots and surveyed my feet. They were fine. There was no permanent damage but the tips of my toes would stay numb for the next few months.

I lay back and drifted in and out of sleep for the rest of the day. Hours later the others returned, exhausted. They had succeeded but had been battered by the wind and cold. Lawrence collapsed in the tent, looking completely exhausted. Part of me was sad that I had missed out on this important first South African ascent, but I was happy for the others,

Standing on the summit of Mount Vinson on a rare warm day. To my right is the ski pole belonging to the legendary Chris Bonington.

especially Lawrence. It was an honour to be able to make a chance like this possible to someone who had only recently started climbing and I knew he would be chuffed with himself.

Over the next few days we made our way back to Patriot Hills and some decent food and red wine. We had hoped to fly straight out and get to Punta Arenas as soon as we could, but the weather was against us. In the end we were stuck at Patriot for another 14 days. After a while it became desperate. The season was winding down as summer came to an end and the weather was becoming increasingly unsettled. Within a week the good food and red wine had run out. All we wanted to do was head home, but we couldn't. Every day something else was wrong with the weather and soon we began to believe there were economic reasons for our delay. It was the same as before. Some of the team were convinced that we were waiting for passengers to fly in on the last flight of the season. At one point, one of the Russians decided to go on a hunger strike until the Hercules came in. It lasted for all of three days before the camp doctor convinced him to start eating again.

Just when our tolerance had reached its very end, a distant drone brought us racing out of our tents. Far in the distance we could just make out a shape in the sky. As it grew bigger, the drone grew louder. When we were sure it was the Hercules, we ran about in the snow shouting and waving our arms. We were on our way home.

But fate was to deal us one last card. The Hercules turned out to be a Chilean Air Force Hercules that was bringing supplies to a small military base nearby, and we weren't allowed anywhere near it. With broken hearts, we retreated back to our tents where we stayed in near silence for three more days. When that familiar drone was heard again sometime during the quiet morning of the fourth day, we hesitantly poked our noses out of the tent, fearful of being disappointed yet again. But this time it really was ours. We were finally on our way home. Vinson had taken four days to climb, but the expedition had lasted for 42 days.

Love moves in strange and sometimes mysterious ways.

Just when you think that part of your life has been pushed into a quiet drawer to be forgotten for who knows how long, it gets swept open and you are reminded of what it was like that very first time. That's how Brit [pronounced Bri:t] came into my life, although I had caught a glimpse of her several years before we finally met. On that occasion, I had just started going out with my girlfriend at the time, Daniella, and she had invited me to a corporate day at a country club. It was a clear summer afternoon and people were socializing outside. I didn't know anyone, so stood around making sure there was always something in the glass I was holding. At one point I turned and glanced over my shoulder. That's when I saw her. Brit was standing in a similar group and at the same moment had looked up and over her shoulder. We looked at each other for just a second, then she turned back to her group. But, for me, that glance was enough. I remember thinking: 'Wow, that woman is stunning.' She was tall and was wearing a white dress that dropped from her long black hair. Clearly I hadn't left the same impression because Brit doesn't even remember the incident. As I was already spoken for, I quickly put her out of my mind.

Four years later, and I was now established on the speaking circuit. Around about this time I was doing quite a bit of work for Accenture, formerly called Andersen Consulting. The company regularly hired new consultants and felt it was appropriate for the newcomers to be exposed to Adventure Dynamics' team-building expertise. On one particular day in 1997, a year before my first trip to Vinson, I delivered the Everest talk to one of their divisions, and Brit was sitting in the audience. After the talk I had lunch with a few people from the company and asked one of them about her. I was told to forget about it as she had a boyfriend. Besides, I wasn't that keen to get involved with someone who worked for one of my biggest clients.

Anyway, the years went by and the work with Accenture slowed down. One day a friend called me up and said that there was someone I needed to meet. Heidi did a lot of corporate work with Accenture and spent some time interviewing some of its people.

'Alex, there is someone you need to call.'

'Why?'

'You just *have* to meet her. I think the two of you will get on great.'

'Heidi, you know how I feel about strangers, especially clients. What's her name?'

'Brit.'

'Brit! That's a funny name.'

'She's Norwegian. Alex, she's lovely.'

'What does she look like?'

'She has long black hair and she's beautiful.'

Suddenly the glimpse of that woman I had seen years before came back to me in a flash. I quietly wondered if it was her.

'Heidi, I'm not going to phone her, but I don't mind if you give her my telephone number,' I whimped out. I was still adamant that I wasn't going to call a strange woman.

Two days later the phone rang and it was her. I was on the golf course so I must have seemed pretty distant. Anyway, we agreed to meet for breakfast at the weekend.

When Saturday morning arrived I was like a young, excited kid. I even went out and bought a new shirt. Heidi was joining us and, as we arrived at Hyde Park Centre in Johannesburg, I remember hoping beyond hope that it was the woman I had seen all those years ago. I can't say why but deep down I was pretty sure it was her. And, when I turned the corner and saw her once more, I knew this was it.

The two of us hit it off instantly and started going out soon afterwards. This was all shortly before my first trip to Antarctica. Brit was very supportive of what I did. In fact, it was the biggest reason we had met in the first place. She had told Heidi she wanted to meet people who were living their dreams and loved the outdoors. In a sense we had been match-made, but it definitely helped that she also believed in what I was doing.

By this stage Adventure Dynamics was going strong. We had developed a solid client base and were doing a lot of corporate work which included speaking on the circuit and doing team building. The corporate work complemented the expedition side of the business nicely. The work was completely different and also far more profitable, opening doors to many prospective clients.

Slowly, the idea of climbing the Seven Summits was forming into something more concrete. We had a very good idea of those we still needed to climb and how to go about reaching them. One mountain, though, had constantly posed a problem. It was the Seventh Summit.

'... the ice was here, the ice was there, the ice was all around. It cracked and growled, and roared and howled, like noises in a swound.'
The Rime of the Ancient Mariner
Samuel Taylor Coleridge

THE MOUNTAIN GUIDE:
Carstensz Pyramid

- ALSO KNOWN AS: Puncak Jaya, meaning Victory Peak.

- HEIGHT: 4 884 metres (16 023 feet).

- FIRST ASCENT: 1962 by H. Harrer, P. Temple, A. Huzenga, R. Kippax.

- LOCATION: The Sudirman Range in the Indonesian province of Irian Jaya, West New Guinea.

- POINT OF INTEREST: Named after the Dutch navigator Jan Carstensz, whose reports of tropical ice after his voyage of 1623 were widely disbelieved.

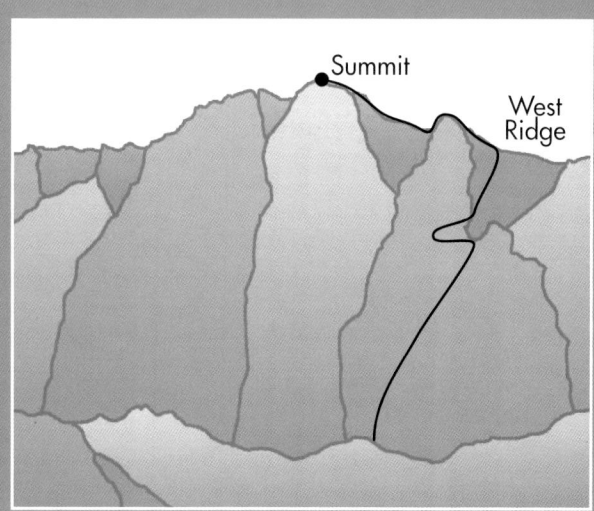

Carstensz Pyramid is composed of a pure but rough limestone.

CHAPTER EIGHT
Stone Age

Ever since I first read Dick Bass's *Seven Summits*, the story has inspired and intrigued me. In 1984, Dick became the first guy to climb the Seven – pretty recent when you consider that Everest was first climbed in 1953.

While Dick was finishing the Seven, a man called Pat Morrow was also trying to climb

them. Pat narrowly missed out on bagging Vinson before Dick, and so Dick beat him to it. Not to be outdone, Pat contrived a theory that the Seventh Summit was not a mountain in Australia, as Dick had climbed, but rather Carstensz Pyramid in Indonesia. Pat went on to climb Carstensz and claimed to be the first to have climbed the Seven Summits. However, the records correctly show that Dick was the first to climb the Seven, with Pat coming second. But, ever since then, a debate has raged through the mountaineering world about which is in fact the Seventh Summit.

The argument is based on whether or not the seventh continent is the country of Australia alone, or whether the surrounding islands of Australasia are included. Added to this, Kosciuszko, Australia's highest peak, is in fact a small hill under 3 000 metres (9 842 feet) high, which can easily be ascended in a 4x4. But, if the surrounding islands are included, then the highest mountain must be Carstensz Pyramid, which towers just under 5 000 metres (16 404 feet) and is technically demanding. I have never subscribed to the Carstensz theory, believing that it was far too contrived and was conceived out of ill feeling. But there is no denying that Carstensz is the more fascinating peak of the two. Interestingly enough, the statistical records show that you have climbed the Seven Summits if you have climbed either of the two. It seems the debate will never end and both now qualify for the Seven.

From a business perspective, Kosciuszko has no appeal, even though I believe it to be the Seventh Summit. Your grandmother could guide you up it. Carstensz, on the other hand, is difficult to reach. The mountain requires sound logistical planning and, once you're there, it also proves difficult to climb. In short, it was right up Adventure Dynamics' alley.

For the previous few years we had been sussing out the possibility of offering it to prospective clients as another first South African ascent. The only problem was that Carstensz was off-limits big time. Carstensz is situated on the island of New Guinea but lies in the western half of the island, in the Indonesian province of Irian Jaya. It is one of the more politically and ethnically unstable parts of Indonesia and experiences constant unrest. For this reason we had been turned down for three consecutive years. Our Indonesian agents said it just wasn't possible.

Then, early in 2000, Adventure Dynamics received an e-mail from the agents saying the province had opened up again but they couldn't tell us how long this situation would last. We knew this was our chance and quickly set about trying to put a trip together. By the end of March we had created a small team happy to cover the enormous cost of getting out there. This trip wasn't going to be quite as expensive as Antarctica had been, but it was still going to cost a small fortune. Sean Disney and I would guide the trip and our clients were: Mike Hodges, whom we had met on Vinson; Roy Fouché, also from the Vinson trip; Mike Aldous and Louis Carstens – no connection but a nice ring to his name. Louis couldn't say no when he heard what the mountain was called.

The team set off for Jakarta, Indonesia's capital, at the beginning of April 2000. We only spent a day meeting our agents before setting off again on a long sequence of flights that took us from one island to the next. From Jakarta, we flew to Sumatra, and on to the Japanese islands and Biak, before finally arriving in Jayapura on the island of New Guinea. We then flew to a town called Wamena, where we climbed aboard a small missions plane for our last flight. Wamena was already in the middle of nowhere and its small airstrip was guarded by some fierce looking pigs. As the group

squeezed into the plane, we commented on how fortuitous it was that Roy had pulled out, otherwise we would never all have fitted inside (unfortunately Roy had contracted a form of pneumonia at the last minute that had made it impossible for him to join us)! Once we were all on board, the pilot took off and quickly covered the last leg of our flying.

This was a spectacular part of the trip, with the hills of Irian Jaya opening up beneath us. The place was as unspoilt as one could imagine. Lush green hills stretched on forever in all directions. We bumped along in and out of clouds, craning our necks against the windows as we tried to make the most of the scenery. Finally, the pilot dipped the nose of the plane and we came low over a hill and landed on a tiny, muddy airstrip. We had landed in Ilaga and had officially gone back in time.

About 200 languages and almost 800 dialects are spoken on the island of New Guinea. Language divisions are closely related to tribal divisions – different tribes occupy specific valleys. It's not hard to imagine why there is so much unrest in Irian Jaya when it's virtually impossible for one tribe to understand another.

Apart from our clients, our team was made up of two Indonesian guides. They were from the main islands of Sumatra and Sulawesi and even they struggled to understand the locals. Ilaga was in the middle of the land inhabited by the Dani tribe, a people who at first glance appeared to have come straight out of the Stone Age. For the most part, the women were naked and the men had a penis gourd attached to their waists. We were told that the size of the penis gourd was proportional to both what it contained and the stature of the man in the tribe. We believed this theory up to the point when we saw an old man who had a gourd stretching right up to his chin!

The Dani had *National Geographic* written all over them. As we climbed out of our small plane, it was hard to tell who was more fascinated with whom. The crowd of onlookers quickly grew until the airstrip was swarming with Dani. We struggled to keep check of our gear as they moved in amongst us, poking their noses into everything. Once the plane had taken off and left us behind, we made our way into the village, followed closely by the throng of Dani. I turned to glance at the crowd and noticed one last Dani leaving the airfield. He was a cripple who had been left behind, slowly hobbling along. His fascination for us was no less intense as he struggled to keep up but he had soon been left far behind. Judging by the way he was struggling I was sure he had been helped to the field. But now he had been abandoned for something far more interesting.

Ilaga would be our base for a few days as we finalized permission and logistics. This wasn't so much permission to climb the mountain, but rather permission to cross the various tribal lands. Remember, this was a place where the last reported case of cannibalism was as recent as 1968. Stories were rife about the eating habits of the Dani and similar tribes.

Another element of the logistics involved sorting out the porters. One would have thought that a team of five could have got away with a small group of porters, but it wasn't meant to be. By the time the last porter had signed on, there were almost 50, and it didn't end there. That was just the number of men who would be carrying food and gear. When the men leave the valley for a lengthy period, as they were now doing, they take their wives and children along. So, all told, our porter group was about 100 strong, and every last one of them was smelly.

Before leaving South Africa, we had been meticulous in our planning and in following the gear list given to us by our agents. One thing stood out: take the biggest umbrella you can find. At first I laughed at this but a few

e-mails later it was pointed out that we would be travelling in one of the wettest places on the planet. Without a second thought I packed my golf umbrella – a great, big colour-burst of a thing. But it lasted all of five minutes. Before we had left the landing strip, it had already been pinched. I still hadn't realized quite how valuable these things were until it rained that afternoon. When the heavens opened, almost as sudden as the deluge of rain was the burst of colours as one umbrella after another was opened. But mine was nowhere to be seen. Our guides found me another but it just wasn't the same as my old one. I kept my eyes peeled for that familiar pattern but wasn't too sure what I would do if I did spot it.

The next day we set off early with our army of Dani. Women, children, old-timers; you name it, they were all there. We slowly climbed out of Ilaga and wound our lazy way up and over the surrounding hills. The landscape was green and fresh, and small streams flowed everywhere. At times our path would end in a swamp and we would have to backtrack. Other times it would intersect a river and we would wade across it. It was difficult to track whether we were going in any one direction as we darted about all over the place, trying to find the driest path onwards. But we were invigorated. The air was clean and heavy with expectation, as there was no way we could know what lay around the next bend.

'Mike, how are you doing, big guy?' Seeing as there were two Mikes, and they were both over six foot three (1.90 metres), we called them Big Mike One and Two, or BM One and BM Two. Big Mike One was Michael Hodges from California. He had tried to summit Mount Vinson the day after our team but had also run into bad wind. He had got even closer to the top than I had, before turning back. But he wasn't upset about it. He took the disappointment in his stride and just kept on going. When he heard we were coming to Carstensz, he was dead keen to join us.

'Alex, this is fantastic!'

The porters were carrying most of the heavy stuff so we were able to walk along and enjoy the scenery.

'How long should the walk take us?' he asked.

'If it doesn't rain too much, we're looking at about seven days.'

'No kidding!'

After we had been walking for four or five hours, we arrived in a clearing and noticed the porters had dumped their loads. We were still fresh and wanted to continue walking.

'Stephen, why are we stopping here?' I asked. Stephen was one of our Indonesian guides. He was short with a round face and was always smiling.

'Porter say next day is steep, so today enough. We camp here.'

We would soon discover that there was no arguing with the Dani. They did as they pleased, which most of the time was different from what we wanted to do. They also had an uncomfortable habit of staring. No matter what you were doing, you could be sure there would be a group of three or four of them quietly watching. They even went as far as following you to the toilet in the bush and standing some metres away, gazing intently.

On the previous night in the village we had slept on the floor of a hut. As we were lying about preparing for bed, we noticed that a group of them had quietly drifted into our room and were standing in a corner, staring at us. We joked about it, saying they were sizing us up for their next meal. I was the last one to get into my sleeping bag and I politely informed them that I was about to put out the light and they should be moving along. They ignored me, which they always

did, so I put out the light, turned on my torch and crawled into my bag. With my torch still on, I looked up at them and told them one last time that I was about to turn it off. Silence. I switched it off and lay back. I could still sense their presence and after about a minute I heard some scuffling. Suddenly a torch went on and I was caught in its beam. One of the buggers had pulled one out and they were still standing in their quiet, unnerving way. I pulled myself out of my bag and physically escorted them out of the room. Despite the consistency of their staring, we could never quite get used to it.

The rains arrived on cue that afternoon, and the place was soaked. We camped in mountain tents which, for the most part, kept us dry. The porters erected a giant piece of plastic strung over two big logs. They lay under it in a haphazard pile, like a pride of lazy lions, and built a blazing fire in the middle of their throng to keep warm and dry.

In the morning, we set off through the wet bush. Within minutes the path had turned steeply upwards and it was evident we were about to ascend the plateau. For the next 100 or so metres, we climbed up steep banks by clinging to the roots of trees. Once up, we were in the jungle proper, surrounded on all sides by trees of incredible proportions. From here the trail became indistinct as it followed the path of least resistance. But it was fantastic hiking. On occasion we came across a giant tree that had fallen over, and the trunk became the path we followed through some of the thicker bush. Sometimes we would walk for 50 metres (164 feet) along a trunk, and always slightly upwards. Like a long train of termites, our army of porters wound their way through the jungle. How far it stretched was anyone's guess, but it was so thick that it was impossible to see more than 10 of us at any one time. Often a bird would break the silence with an exotic call.

Suddenly, out of the soaked depths of the jungle I heard a faint squeal.

'What the heck was that?' I asked.

'What?' responded Big Mike One.

'That noise, listen.'

There it came again, far off and different from any bird call we had ever heard.

'It sounds like a pig. Stephen, what's that noise?' As I asked him, the others huddled up together, staring into the surrounding bush.

'Jungle.' I was sure that the gist of our questions was sometimes lost on our guides. We shrugged it off and continued. But the faint, squeal came again, softer than ever.

By afternoon our day was brought to a halt by the front porters who had settled down in a convenient spot. We seemed to have come out of the thicker stuff because the trees weren't nearly as big and the clearings were wider than before. A myriad colours were splashed about on the ground as umbrellas lay open in preparation for the deluge. We quickly put up our tents and crawled inside them, keen to escape the flood. When the rain started, it fell with a monotonous patter and we were soon asleep.

Over the next week we trudged across

the high plateau of Irian Jaya. Our maps were marked with large blank areas labelled as 'territory uncharted', and we wondered just how many people had previously seen the valleys and ridges we were now crossing.

The jungle really only covered the fringes of the plateau up to about 3 000 metres (9 842 feet) in elevation. Once we had passed through it, the landscape became karstic as the rock was replaced with limestone. The trees vanished as we reached an altitude of about 3 700 metres (12 139 feet), and pockets of bushes now dotted the plateau in thick clumps. Everywhere, limestone outcrops stood in sharp isolation, and there were many dark holes and hidden caves. It seemed that God was still trying to decide what He wanted to do with this land. It was almost as if it had been kneaded and bent in one way, and then He had changed His mind and bent it another. This was a place rife with the potential of discovery.

On about the fourth day, the mystery of the squealing pig was revealed. We had decided that it must have been some of the younger porters imitating wild forest pigs, but found the truth far more disturbing. We had just arrived in a clearing chosen by the porters as our next camp, when we noticed a woman who had in her hands a tiny piglet that she was breast-feeding. Another woman had tied one of the animals to her leg with a piece of string. The tiny piglet was scratching around in the dirt. As we gaped and asked questions, we were told that some of the tribes in Irian Jaya practised a form of animal husbandry. The Dani were no different. It seemed that pigs and the like were treated with the same care as children. If the family headed to the hills for a spell, the animals were taken with them. However, this respect only lasts for as long as it takes for the piglets to get big enough to eat.

After three days of hiking, we had long since given up the attempt to keep our shoes dry. It was impossible. A little after noon every day, the grey clouds would thicken and the downpour would start. It was never the torrential drenching that one experiences in the African tropics, but it was strong enough to soak one through – and it was incessant. The weather was like this all year round, so the ground was a muddy swamp that was knee-deep at times. We trudged on like beetles crossing a vast land, thinking only of completing the next mile or climbing the hill ahead. At most, the sun poked its head out for an hour a day. But, in the cool of those damp afternoons, the agony of wet socks was soon forgotten in the thrill of where we were. The landscape played out like a scene in a mysterious play, never revealing too much too soon.

By the fifth day we were about as remote as we could possibly be. Our train of Dani was stretched out over the better part of two kilometres (1.24 miles) and I was somewhere in the middle. I had spent much of the previous two days pottering around near the back, investigating every nook and cranny I could find. Being a keen caver, I couldn't stop myself from peering over the edges of bottomless holes. The caves of Irian Jaya are seldom explored and the vertical relief means the region could contain some of the world's deepest caves. But few people get out there with ropes and head-torches and, as much as I would have loved to, there just wasn't any time to go spelunking. But I kept my eyes open and took many photos, making mental notes in case I returned some day with different objectives.

On this particular day we had hiked up a steep valley until we crested yet another plateau. Ahead of me I could see the line of porters make a sudden turn to the left and then skirt in an arc, before continuing. I was pretty sure it was a cave and judging from the way the group had moved around the depression, it must've been huge. I hastened my pace.

Big Mike Two had stopped at the turn and was staring down.

'Is it a cave?' I asked, barely able to contain my excitement.

'Oh *ja*, and how!'

I got to the turn and stared down. 'My word, that is unbelievable!'

The ground dropped away in a depression the width of two or three tennis courts. At the bottom, maybe 50 or 60 metres (164 to 197 feet) down, the depression ended abruptly in two dark holes. On the left, a river fell in a steep waterfall and then disappeared into one of the holes. It was incredible. I had never before seen so much water disappearing into the ground – normally the sign of a very big cave. And, if you think the two holes at the bottom of the depression were small, forget it. They were each the size of a squash court.

'Mike, do you know how high we are?'

'3 752 metres! Why?' He wasn't called Metric Mike for nothing.

'Well, you know what that means?'

'What?'

'You could be looking at the world's deepest cave.'

'Why do you say that?'

'Well, the deepest is Gouffre Mirolda in France, I think, which is about 1 800 metres deep. This thing starts at 3 700 metres and the limestone must be at least two kilometres thick. I wonder if anyone has been inside?'

'No.'

'No?'

'Stephen said no-one had ever been down to the drops.'

'You're kidding me? Well, I'm going to head down.'

'Just don't be long. Stephen reckons we need to all hike together here. He said something about another tribe that the Dani are fighting with, or something like that.'

'Really? Do me a favour: when I get down there, can you take a couple of pics of me?'

'Sure thing.'

I dumped my pack and started the descent. The depression was steep but it was lined with thick grass and the same small shrubs that we had been hiking through. It flattened out near the bottom, before disappearing into the inky blackness of the holes. I pictured falling inside and disappearing into some icy wormhole that took me into the heart of Irian Jaya.

I stepped forward gingerly, making sure that I didn't slip and fall on the wet rocks. The hole to the left that swallowed the river was impossible to get near. The rocks were steep and slippery and the place was soaked. I moved to the right hole, realizing that it was far bigger than it had seemed from above. I could just peer over the edge to see it open into an immense cavern. It dropped down about 30 metres (98 feet) and then I could see no more. But it appeared to be at least the size of a tennis court. I couldn't see the maelstrom but I could hear it. Somewhere below, the river was churning and grinding and eating away at the limestone, carving out the very heart of Irian Jaya.

Above, I could hear the others shouting for me to hurry up. I turned around and made my way back up the steep slope. I was breathless when I reached the top, having forgotten that we were almost at 4 000 metres (13 123 feet). For the next few hours, until the supposed danger from other tribes had passed, our group consolidated into a large mass. But the place was remote and lonely, and we didn't see any other tribes. When the rain came in the afternoon, the group drifted apart again until one long line of people slowly picked their way along, lost quietly in thought.

By the time we reached camp the land was covered in a grey twilight and the range of peaks we had glimpsed earlier were hidden somewhere in the gloom. During the day the porters had been pointing to the horizon and shouting 'Puncak Jaya', which is the local name for Carstensz. We couldn't see anything but a grey shape, but we knew we were close. That night was the wettest of all. We had been on the go for six days and it had been raining for most of that time. Now it poured down but, as we went about the chores of the evening, we forgot about things like our soaking wet socks. Instead we talked about what the first sighting would be like, and joked that there might not be one if it continued to rain.

When the morning sun broke the skyline and poured into our steep valley, it chased away the mist and left us gasping in wonder. It was spectacular. We were surrounded on three sides by steep peaks. It seemed that in the gloom of the previous day, we had found a path amongst the mountains without even realizing it and were now hemmed in. We were amazed that there in the distance stood a peak capped in snow. We'd certainly never expected to find permanent snow up here. Behind the peak, the sky was a deep blue and bits of cloud seemed to tug at the upper slopes. The Dani pointed in that direction, shouting in their usual excited banter. It wasn't Carstensz that we were staring at, but a neighbouring peak. Carstensz was hidden behind it. We set off that morning, wondering how we would find a suitable way up the ever-steepening valley.

We scrambled up a steep, rocky slope and then came upon a lake. It was deep and clear and stood at the foot of the pass that would take us up to a higher plateau. On the far side, another steep slope climbed madly upwards and, as we stared in disbelief, Stephen told us that it was a way only the craziest of porters would take. Our route followed the left bank and then climbed up the bed of a stream that bubbled a muddy froth. It was tough going but we had the help of trees and shrubs which we could cling to. Below us, the lake opened up and turned that deep, clear brown you see back home in the mountains of the Western Cape. As we climbed, the tufts of cloud that had been stubbornly lurking about vanished, and for the first time we felt the warmth of the sun pressing down on us. It was the best day yet.

At the top of the gully we seemed to have breached the pass, but it turned out to be an intermediate step to take us to a higher level. The path skirted around along the top and back end of the lake – and then it got complicated. There were a great many routes we could follow. Peaks jutted out here and there, and lakes filled the spaces between them. We followed the Dani, who walked on deliberately, picking a roundabout route towards the snow-capped peak.

At some point along the route around and through the lakes, I stopped. Only Mike Aldous and Louis were with me. The others were either somewhere behind or ahead of us. I looked down at my feet and realized that for the first time in seven days we were on dry ground, standing on a patch of hard, white sand. We could only speculate about how it had got there, but it was in such contrast to the land we had moved through, that we had to savour the moment. We crouched down and pressed our fingers into it. A light breeze had picked up, adding to the sense of isolation. Whether we were the first or the thousandth person to stand on that spot didn't matter right then. We felt like the first. That's when a part of me began to understand why it is I go to these places and climb these mountains.

For the rest of the day we climbed higher up into the mountains, heading towards the pass that would take us to Carstensz Base Camp. By afternoon, the weather had deteriorated and we were surrounded by thick cloud. It was time for the umbrellas. The rock was soon wet and slippery and we had to scramble with caution. The route was unbelievable because we were now really scaling the sides of a peak. At times, we used our hands and scrambled up small cliffs, not daring to look down. Then we walked along narrow paths hugging the cliff face with no end in sight. Below us the world seemed to sink into a grey, endless pit. Finally, when we could climb no higher, the trail ended in a narrow neck between two peaks. From here we would have to scramble down the other side.

We stopped in the neck for a rest and it was while we were staring out into the gloom that the clouds cleared for the briefest of moments. But it was enough to show us why we had come. There, on the far side of the valley, Carstensz seemed to grow out of the murky depths and soar impossibly high into the sky. It was a cold, grey and intimidating sight. We gasped. It was like staring into Mordor for the first time. We felt tiny. Just a blink later and Carstensz was gone, swallowed by the gloom. We sat down, feeling stunned. It looked desperate.

We carefully made our way down the steep gully, knocking rocks as we went. It wasn't the safest of places to be but we had no choice. We knew that a knocked rock could spell disaster because it could easily trigger a landslide in the gully, but there was no other way to Base Camp. An hour later we were down and walking into camp. We had arrived. Our pilgrimage was over. In a way it was an anti-climax. We had seen and

experienced so many different things over the previous week that it felt like a lifetime had passed. I don't think we or the Dani had got to know each other any better, but boy had we learnt heaps – the kind of stuff that no book could teach you. And to top it off, we still couldn't see Carstensz. It was hidden behind a ridge that rose right next to our camp.

The next day was a rest day which was welcomed by all. It's not that we were exhausted by the hiking of the previous week. In fact, it had been kind of easy. But there hadn't been any time for us to stop and think. Rest day was great. In the clear morning we dried out some of our stuff, which was a treat. The others lazed about but I decided to follow Stephen over the ridge to Carstensz and see what he was up to. Our two guides had brought along a section of fixed rope that they hoped to use on the first section of the route. As with many of the popular technical peaks, sections are often 'fixed' with rope. This makes it easier and safer to get up and down reasonably quickly. The problem is that sometimes the ropes lie for months, even years, getting frayed in the wind and sun. Using these ropes is foolish and dangerous, which is why Stephen was hoping to replace these sections.

By the time I arrived at the foot of the face, Stephen was already 100 metres (328 feet) up a gully, stretching out a section of rope. Grey clouds had started rising out of the valley and hiding the upper slopes, but I could still see enough to be impressed. The main face of Carstensz swept up 800 metres (2 624 feet) into the sky. It was pure limestone.

The route we would follow was the original line of ascent, which traced a gully from the foot of the face up to a point halfway up. Then it traversed a broad band before once again ascending a gully. I couldn't see above that but I had a pretty good idea of what the terrain was like. The upper gully topped out somewhere on the summit ridge about a kilometre away from the very top. This was the most technical section. The ridge climbed steadily along a section of pinnacles before finally topping out. The photos we had seen of this final section had horrified us. The ridge was like a knife edge, but I didn't think about it for too long. My eyes dropped from the clouds and scanned along the gully until I spotted Stephen. He was still up there, slowly working away. I left him and his partner to the afternoon clouds and made my way back to camp.

Sometime that evening I decided I wanted to marry Brit. You're probably thinking: yeah, typical of a guy to decide something like that a million miles from anywhere. Well, I had been thinking about it for a while and I knew that my proposal would have to be different. In my mind I had conjured up an elaborate plan to drag the satellite phone all the way to the top, and then phone her and propose. I told Sean about it because I knew he would wonder why the heck I wanted to carry the phone all the way up the mountain when we had hardly got the thing to work previously. There was nothing wrong with the phone, it was just the battery. Once it was dead, it was nearly impossible to try to charge it with our solar panel. When the one hour a day of direct sun did come on the odd occasion, we weren't always in a position to stop and charge the phone. At one point we even had the solar panel strapped to the back of a Dani in the hope of getting some charge time as we hiked on a particularly bright day. Sean agreed with the plan. He thought I was nuts but he was keen to play along.

We were up at one am the next day to check our last bits of technical gear and try to decide what to wear. The range had been very warm and we thought it wasn't likely to get below freezing, even on the summit at just

below 5 000 metres (16 404 feet). The problem was the rain that was sure to come. We set off at about two am and made a noise as we climbed up and over the ridge and along to the base of the gully. Soon we were sweating. At the foot of the gully, a rope hung limply over the edge. It had that new sheen to it which was always comforting. We stopped and began the process of gearing up. This involved putting on our harnesses and checking the straps, tying knots and checking each other, and then clipping on our jumars – the metal devices that would help us get up the fixed ropes. When we were all done, I gathered the group in a huddle and said a quick prayer for protection. One by one, in the small glow of our head-torches, we clipped ourselves onto the rope and disappeared around the corner. Around us, the night was black and still.

The going was slow for the first two hours, as we slowly worked out a rhythm that worked best for the group. The light from our torches was sufficient to light up only the next section of rope. We could see nothing higher up, or for that matter nothing of the growing void below us. I climbed at the front with Stephen, and Sean brought up the rear. The others laboured on between us, making sure there were never more than two on any section of rope at one time. Once we had the sequence going, it worked well and ensured everyone was always on the go. Technically, this first section of the gully was a doddle. It was a broad ledge that sloped upwards at about 50 degrees. It was steeper at some times than at others, and there were occasions when we could walk along it. This went on for about 400 metres (1 312 feet), which was a perfect way to get into some kind of rhythm and see out the dark hours of the dying night.

By daybreak we had reached the broad band halfway up the face of Carstensz. Across the valley, we could see a small glacier and some snow on a neighbouring peak. It was the same peak that had been tempting us from a distance, making us believe we were closer than we were. Base Camp was hidden behind that small ridge but we knew it was down there somewhere. At the very end of the valley, some three or four kilometres (1.86 to 2.48 miles) away, we could just make out the tailings of one of the largest opencast gold and copper mines in the world. We had read much about Freeport McMoran and how it was a wonder of engineering. Also, its location on the slopes of Carstensz made it somewhat controversial. Mountaineering history in this part of the world was rife with epic tales of climbers sneaking through the mine to avoid the seven-day march through the swamps. The problem was that the mine was off-limits to all climbers. We sat on a ledge staring at the dumps in the distance and wondering if we would have a good chance of getting through.

Before long Stephen was muttering about the rain and motioning for us to get going. We agreed that this wouldn't be a great place to get caught in the deluge that was sure to come. The broad band was a tricky place to be. It was flat to a degree, so ropes weren't really needed, but it had sections of loose rock that would start sliding when just the slightest weight was put on them. So we couldn't go bounding along. Instead we had to creep forward, making sure that we put our feet exactly where we wanted them to be. If a clump of shale started moving, we would very quickly end up sliding down the face of Carstensz. The team followed the band for about 100 metres (328 feet) before it joined the upper gully.

Once in the gully we felt safer, realizing that a slip here would not be as disastrous. We continued unroped for a while, scrambling from boulder to boulder as we headed upwards to the ridge. After an hour of moving from one rock to the next, we arrived at the foot of a vertical face. It stretched up for 50 metres (164 feet) before joining the summit ridge. It

was time to clip ourselves to the fixed rope again. I attached my jumar and peered up. Stephen was crouching next to a boulder somewhere at the top of the face. I started up, taking it slowly at first to ease myself into that familiar rhythm. I glanced around and noticed how beautiful the limestone was. It was as pure as it gets, and so coarse to the touch that it was necessary to climb with those thick gloves that handymen use. Without them, our hands would've been cut to shreds.

I heaved myself upwards on the rope, keeping my legs spread apart and balanced on the rock. A pull with my jumar, a lift of the leg, and a pull on the rock with my other hand. So it went, hand after hand, until I reached the end of the rope. I unclipped and sat back on the rock to wait for whoever was next. Stephen was already ahead on the next section.

While I was resting, I was suddenly struck by how quickly the clouds had come in. I stood up and looked over the edge of the ridge, hoping to catch a glimpse of the other side of Carstensz. But it was already thick with cloud. I glanced at my watch. Shit, it was 11 in the morning. Where had the time gone? I sat down again. We would now almost certainly be caught in the rain.

Louis arrived at the end of the rope and unclipped. 'Howzit going, Louis?'
'Alex, this is awesome! I'm just a little bit nervous of the ridge ahead.'
So was I. 'Look, all you've got to do is take it one step at a time and make sure you're comfortable where you are.'

Truth be told, in the back of my mind this next section freaked me out. We had seen very few photos of the summit ridge, but they all looked hectic. Narrow rock with gaping drops on either side and dodgy little rope sections reminded me of tightroping across the neighbour's yard as a kid. It was not a section of the climb where you could afford to slip up. If you did, you would nosedive straight down to Base Camp.

Louis moved slowly ahead of me and I clipped on soon after. From here the route followed the ridge slowly upwards in scrambling sections. Occasionally we had to balance around a giant boulder or creep along the edge of a narrow ledge. Sometimes there was a fixed rope to clip onto, but on other sections there was nothing.

After an hour of exhilarating but nervous climbing, we arrived at a gap in the ridge that seemed familiar. This was one of the places I had seen in a photo. The ridge suddenly ended in a mind-boggling drop. Two metres (6.56 feet) across the gap, a pinnacle stood suspended in space.

'How on earth can that thing stand like that?' was my first thought. 'Shit!' was my second.

Louis turned and looked at me wide-eyed. 'How the hell are we supposed to get across that?'

I moved closer to the edge to have a better look. A rope dangled across the gap and seemed to be tied to the top of the pinnacle.

You could clip it, but if you slipped you would almost certainly be hanging five metres (16 feet) below the gap, suspended above the biggest drop you could ever imagine. It was nauseating stuff.

'Louis, if you scramble down a bit you might be able to stretch over and just reach the other side.'
'Are you nuts? Have you looked down there?' Louis had a point.

'Let me go first and then I can give you a tight rope if you need. Just don't fall.'

I clipped the rope, knowing that this was more psychological protection than anything else. I wasn't convinced it would hold a gerbil, let alone my fat ass.

I carefully scrambled down a foot or so. With my back to the gap, I grasped a hold on the rock and slowly stretched my leg out. It fell just short. I shuffled around and then tried again. Still short. I realized I would have to let go with both hands if I was going to reach it. Holding onto the grip again, I stretched my leg out as far as I could and, just as I reached the end point, I let go with one of my hands. This carried my leg a touch further and, as I felt the momentum pulling me off balance, I let go with the other hand. Then, as slowly and with as much control as I could manage, I kind of fell over and twisted round until my foot just touched the far side. An instant later, my hand slammed into the rock and I was balanced again. But only just. I was now spread-eagled across the abyss. Quickly, I reached across with my other hand, grasped onto whatever I could, and then heaved. I was across.
'Whoooweee! Man, that was wild!' I was pumped with adrenaline but wasn't keen to do it again.
'Alex, you've got to be joking!'

Louis had quietly been observing me but I don't think he could have repeated exactly what I had done, even if he had memorized it perfectly. It was one of those moves that involved many ifs and buts.
'Don't worry. Clip onto the rope and I'll give you a heave as you step.'

Louis grabbed the rope, balanced himself, and then stepped forward. With a tight jerk of the rope he was across. We turned and carried on, not even thinking about the fact that we somehow had to get back across that abyss.

If we thought the technical stuff was over, we were wrong. Within a short while we arrived at the edge of yet another drop. Again there was a pinnacle standing in the gap, but this time the gap was about 10 metres (33 feet) wide. To get onto this pinnacle involved doing a diagonal abseil under tension. Once on the pinnacle, you kind of had to skirt around the side of it, and then clip onto another rope that was suspended from the top of the other side of the ridge. Once clipped onto this, you had to jumar vertically upwards while all the time hanging in space. It was time-consuming and dizzying stuff. To get all of us over that took more than an hour.

When we pushed on, the cloud had become so thick it was impossible to see more than 10 metres ahead. The ridge seemed to end in a series of slabs and broken faces with lots of crumbling rock. It was unclear what was the best route to take and we ended up splitting up and choosing a few options, listening to one another calling through the clouds. Then something to the side of me caught my gaze because it seemed way out of place. I did a double take and, on looking more closely, realized it was a metal plaque. For a moment I was confused. I couldn't figure out what the heck that plaque was doing in the middle of nowhere. Then I looked around and realized there was nowhere else I could climb. The plaque marked the summit and we were there, on the very top of Carstensz Pyramid. Louis was sitting to the side of me in tears and it wasn't long before I, too, was gripped by emotion. I can't tell you what it was but there was something different about this mountain. Yes, we had become the first South Africans to climb another of the Seven Summits, but it was more than that. For so long, something about this mountain had been haunting me.

For the previous week I had been filled with fear and doubt, and these two things combined are far more dangerous than any mountain. Alone, they have caused the downfall of countless people.

But the whole time I had been casting these feelings aside, hiding them behind thoughts of home and destiny and my soon-to-be fiancée. I kept on reminding myself that God had a destiny for me, and it didn't end here on Carstensz. I felt sheer relief and great joy to arrive, finally, on the top of that mountain.

Soon we were all sitting on top, hugging and taking the necessary pictures. I pulled out the sat. phone and prepared for the big moment. By the way, I didn't carry it up. I had decided that I had enough on my plate worrying about clients, so had asked Stephen to carry it for me. He happily agreed. It was about midday, local time, which meant it was close to the middle of the night back home. I wasn't too concerned about that. I knew that Brit would appreciate the effort and I was sure she would say yes. I turned it on and began dialling. It buzzed in my ear for ages and then went dead. I looked down at the display and realized the battery was struggling. Damn!

'Pull the battery out and stick it in your armpit, or your groin even. Anywhere where it's warm,' advised Mike Aldous.

'Great! Brit's going to can herself when she sees this.'

Mike Hodges was filming this odd scene on his small video camera. I pulled the battery out and shoved it into my armpit. As I looked around, I realized that, as far as places to be in the world went, this was an odd one. But it was the right place to be. After a while I wiped off the battery and slotted it back into the phone. Again I dialled and again it buzzed in my ear. Then it went dead. This time it wouldn't even go on again. I had really screwed up. I knew now that I should have put a bit more planning into this. 'It's not happening, guys. This thing's dead.'

Stephen looked at me indifferently. I don't think he knew what I was up to, even though I had tried to explain to him. All I could see around me was the group of us huddled on the small summit, surrounded by cloud. It could have been anywhere: Melville Koppies, a hill in the Magaliesberg or even an outcrop in the Drakensberg. Who could tell? The only thing that made it different was the journey we had undertaken to get there, and the feelings inside us as we sat for a while in silence. Then we began the dangerous process of getting down.

The rain began within an hour of us

leaving the summit. It was a light drizzle at first but, by the time we reached the last gully, water was gushing in tiny rivers down the face, and the gully itself had become a series of waterfalls and one big stream. We were soaked through by the time we reached the bottom of the face in the late afternoon. But the worst of it was behind us and we were justifiably elated. As we took the last few steps back into camp, the afternoon clouds had grown dark and the day was over. At last it was time to celebrate.

I woke the next morning with that 'summer holidays feeling' – free to do whatever I wanted without a care in the world. The pressure of having to get up the mountain, and possibly failing, was now gone. The fear of falling down some great big face had vanished. It was time to relax. The morning sky was clear and brought with it the promise of another adventure. But we still had to get back.

Slowly, one by one, we dragged ourselves out of our tents and walked over to the mess tent. Water was on the boil and the aroma of coffee and cocoa filled the small tent. Anything was on the menu! 'Whatever you wish!' Stephen said. We picked through the bits of food in our packets, looking for those favourite titbits that had somehow been missed. On everyone's minds was the question of how we would get home. Mike Aldous's knee had packed up and he was concerned about spending another week walking through the swamp. 'There's no way my knee's going to last through another seven days of that mud!'

'Look, it shouldn't take us that long on the way out. Stephen reckons five days, max.'

'Still, I don't think my knee's up to two days of that crap.'

'What do the rest of you think?' I was pretty sure they felt as I did: great adventure in, but no ways were we going to walk it on the way out.

'I wouldn't mind the walk out, as long as we took it easy.' For Louis, getting to the top of Carstensz, and being one of the first South Africans to do so, was probably his lifetime achievement in climbing. He was beyond ecstatic. I could understand how he wouldn't mind the adventure of returning through the swamps. 'And the rest of you?'

'The mine.' Sean was thinking of getting to Bali, where he could chill out and relax. The jungle and swamp held no more appeal for him.

'Do you think we will get through the mine?'

'We could ask them.'

Mike Hodges was being as practical as ever. He was the only American in the group and, considering it was partly an American mine, we decided he should call the General Manager on the satellite phone.

Mike took the phone outside and plugged in the charger. The sun was bright so we were pretty hopeful that he would have some juice within the hour. The rest of us milled around, eating and drying our kit. An hour later, Mike had spoken to the GM of Freeport McMoran.

'It's a no go.'

'Did you get through to the guy?'

'Yeah, he was pretty friendly. He's got no problem with Big Mike Two going through along with one helper, but the rest of us will have to go back the way we came.'

'That's crazy, even if we just want to sneak through and head on out the other side?'

'Yeah, they're pretty strict about that kinda stuff here.'

'So, what do you guys reckon?'

We talked about it for the next hour but it was pretty clear that, as a group, we definitely weren't keen on heading back through the swamp. Even Louis had been convinced. This didn't leave us with much choice and in the end we decided to chance it and sneak through the mine. Well, we weren't really going to try to sneak through, we were more likely going to show up and try and smooth talk our way inside. It was decided. We had an hour to pack up because next stop was Freeport.

Soon we were bustling down the valley along with our porters, heading for an obscure side entrance to one of the world's largest mines, and boy were we excited. We knew that, whatever happened, we were about to have our second adventure in Irian Jaya. Our faithful army of Dani porters followed loudly behind us. They would accompany us as far as the gate to Freeport and no further. The porters still had to make the journey all the way back to the small village of Ilaga. Their fate was certain, while ours had yet to be decided.

Two hours later, we scrambled down a steep path and arrived in a clearing. In fact, there was no gate, only a small corrugated iron shack and a pile of gravel. We had followed a gorge from Base Camp down to the mine, and were now at the point where the gorge ended and opened up into the expanse of Freeport.

Beyond the shack, giant piles of grey gravel lay in long lines. Trucks drove between these lines, moving still more gravel and creating more piles. The trucks were the biggest I had ever seen, the kind you could quite easily drive your car underneath, and there were plenty of them kicking up dust and adding to the mess of the place. We pulled up outside the shack and greeted the guard.

And so began the long and uncertain process of trying to convince a whole bunch of people that it was vital for us to pass through the mine, when all along we knew damn well we weren't allowed anywhere near the place. I can't begin to count how many times I have found myself in similar situations, making up the most ridiculous stories to try to sneak through some or other crazy place.

Sometimes they work and other times they don't, but something I have honed over the years is an ability to resign myself to whatever fate awaits me, especially when I'm pushing my luck. This time, we were seriously playing games.

The guard decided early on that this little 'surprise' was beyond his authority and so referred the problem higher up the chain of command, which meant getting on the phone. This was a good thing for us. The longer it took, the more chance we had of bamboozling them.

A while later a van pulled up and we were told that Mike needed to go to the mine hospital to have his knee checked out. He was allowed one companion and it was decided that I should tag along, being louder and all. Off we sped, wide eyed as we gazed at the monstrosity that was Freeport. It is supposed to be one of the world's largest opencast gold and copper mines, and we saw no evidence to the contrary. The place was enormous. All around us, giant mounds of tailings lay about like pyramids. In every corner there were huge contraptions that played a role in the processing of gold or copper. In one place we passed a cliff that had been stained bright blue from years of having copper minerals leaching down its side. The place was as ugly as it was impressive. I had never seen such a mechanical mess.

The van pulled up outside the hospital and we were escorted inside. Truth be told, it was more like a general practitioner's private rooms than a hospital.

'So, what's wrong with your knee?' The physician was Indonesian but his English was good.

'Well, I, uh, I think it's a bit of inflammation.' There wasn't much wrong with Mike's knee. Sure, it was sore, but we were using it as an excuse to avoid walking out across the swamps.

'Okay, just lie back for a minute.' The physician bent Mike's leg so that it was at a 90-degree angle.

'Does that hurt?'

'Uhm, mmm, a little bit.'

'How about that?'

'Um, no, that's okay. Ooh! Yes, that's sore.'

After five minutes of Mike's leg being pushed and pulled in various directions, he was given a heat pad, some salve and we were told we could go.

'Where to?'

'Don't worry, just follow this man.'

Sean takes in the first view of Carstensz Pyramid.

We left the room and were escorted back into the van. From there we were taken to the cable car that linked the top section of the mine with the lower sections. We asked what was happening to the others but they couldn't tell us. Soon, though, we forgot all about them as the wonders of the mine distracted us.

The top section of Freeport is at an altitude of 4 000 metres (13 123 feet), while the lower section is closer to 2 000 metres (6 562 feet). Connecting these sections is the longest single-span cable in the world. It hangs suspended above the cliffs more than 300 metres (984 feet) up, and the ride, which is both terrifying and exhilarating, takes a little more than five minutes. As we sped off down the steep incline, we noticed that we were above the clouds. They would open up every few seconds, revealing a mysterious world way below us, filled with steep slopes and bizarre machinery.

By the time night finally came, we had made it to the small town of Timika, home to the Sheraton. Timika is a town rotting away under the filth of decades, but cut into a quiet corner is the Sheraton Hotel, built by Freeport to service the mine's executives.

It had been a bizarre day filled with many surprises and uncertainties. The others had caught up with us after somehow making it through the mine. When we sat down for dinner later that evening, no-one could quite point their finger at a single definitive move that had brought success. It was more a case of everything subtly combining to get us through the mine. Had we quietly slipped past the guards, or blazingly cajoled our way in? We couldn't quite decide but we didn't care. We were free, and, as for Mike's knee, well, it was doing just fine.

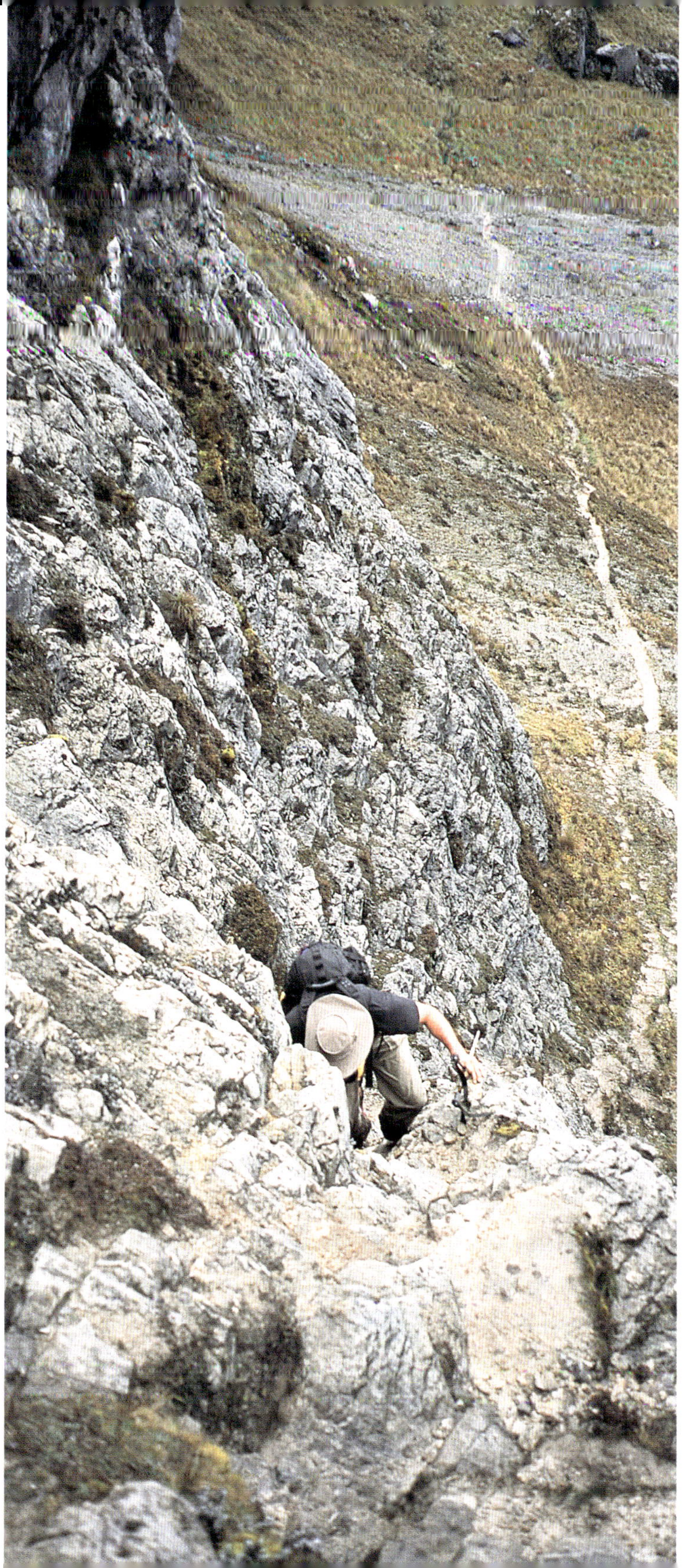

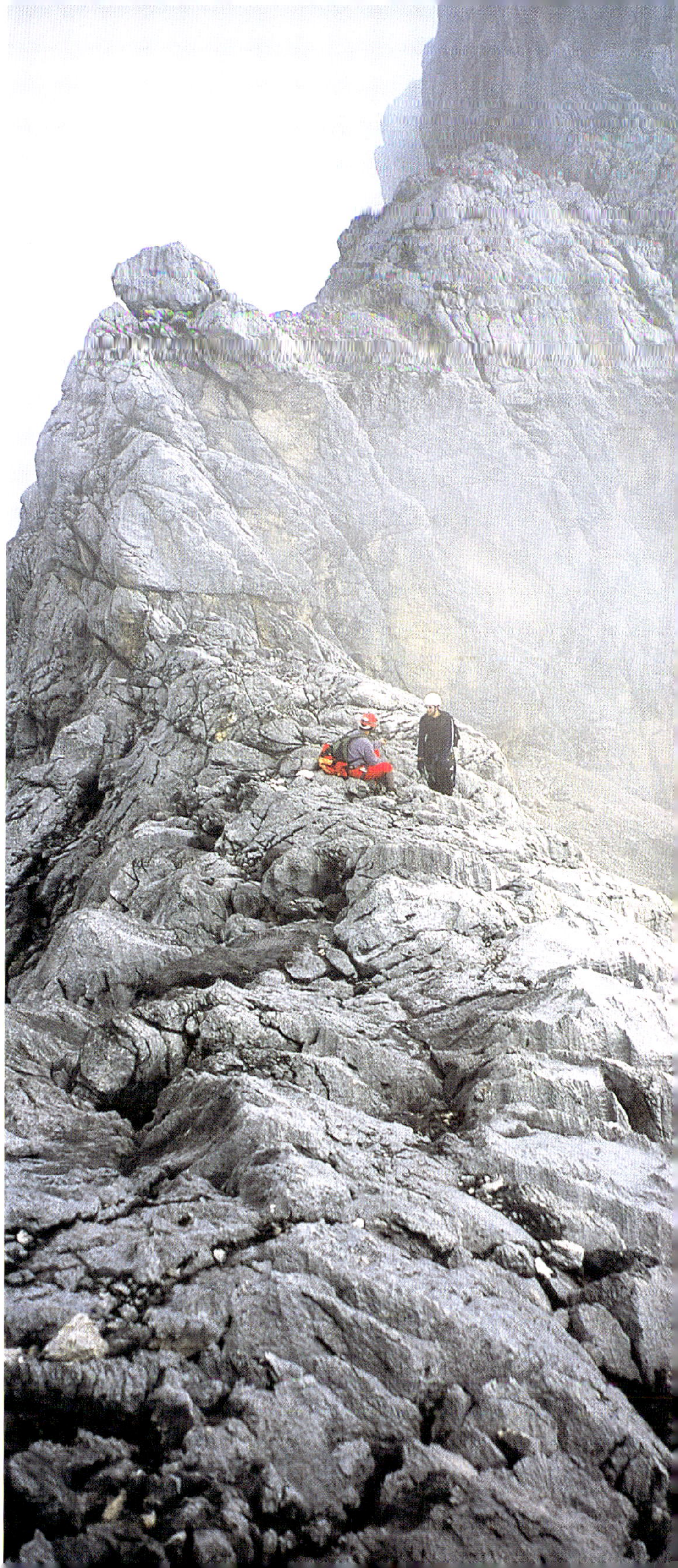

PAGE 146: *Mike Hodges climbing the fixed ropes in the gully.*

PAGE 147 LEFT: *Big Mike Two, Mike Aldous, on the way in.*

PAGE 147 RIGHT: *Behind me, the summit ridge disappears into the clouds*

OPPOSITE TOP: *Our first glimpse of the high peaks of Irian Jaya.*

OPPOSITE BOTTOM: *Stephen, our guide, leading the way up the broad gully.*

ABOVE: *The Dani children were intrigued by the spectacle our group presented.*

ABOVE: *Carstensz can only be reached by hiking for a week through Irian Jaya's swamps and rain-soaked jungle.*

RIGHT: *The Dani inspect two echidnas, or spiny anteaters, which are indigenous to Australia and New Guinea.*

OPPOSITE RIGHT: *Women, children and old-timers – our Dani porters brought their entire families with them on our trek.*

THE MOUNTAIN GUIDE:
Denali

- ALSO KNOWN AS: Mount McKinley. To the Athabascan Indians, 'Denali' means 'The High One'.

- HEIGHT: 6 194 metres (20 320 feet).

- FIRST ASCENT: 1913 by W. Harper, H. Karstens, R. Tatum, H. Stuck.

- LOCATION: Alaska, North America.

- POINT OF INTEREST: Denali National Park is located approximately 482 kilometres (300 miles) south of the Arctic Circle. During the summer solstice, the Park has nearly 21 hours of sunlight.

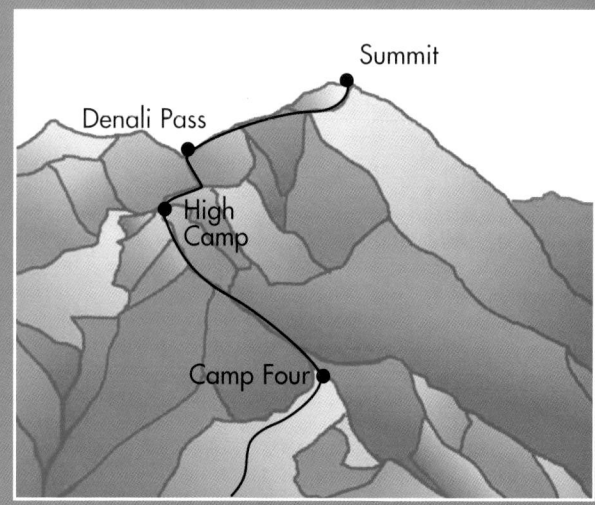

Summit

Denali Pass

High Camp

Camp Four

High winds blow off the summit of Denali.

The construction of protective snow walls is vital to survival on mountains like Denali.

CHAPTER NINE

The High One

The year 2000 marked the beginning of a few good climbing years. We made the first South African ascent of Carstensz Pyramid, and I got to go back to Mount Vinson to complete those last few hours. In sharp contrast to my previous Vinson trip, this time I reached the summit in a fleece top and temperatures of about −5°C (23°F) – balmy for Antarctica.

It was also a special trip for other reasons.

Our small team of four who reached the top on a beautiful clear day comprised Gilad Stern from South Africa, Jaime Vinals from Guatemala and Joby Ogwyn from the United States. Jaime went on to become the first Guatemalan to climb the Seven – such a big thing in Guatemala that the President met him at the airport upon his return. His book was also turned into a school setwork. But it was number six for Jaime on that day on Mount Vinson, and for Joby it was number seven. I stopped about 50 metres (164 feet) short on the ridge and watched Joby climb those last few steps. At that very moment, at the age of 26, he became the youngest person ever to climb the Seven Summits. He was also the youngest American to have climbed Everest. I remember watching him kneel down and grab hold of the summit ski pole. I wondered what he was thinking and feeling, and when my turn would come. Deep down I knew I would have to be patient.

I had also made four ascents of Kilimanjaro in the previous few years. I guess you could say it had become 'old hat', but the truth is that I loved it. It was always a good break to spend a week in Tanzania climbing a mountain I had got to know so well. Kilimanjaro was one of Adventure Dynamics' most popular products and it seemed growing numbers of people were becoming interested in climbing mountains. Kilimanjaro was a good start for beginners, and, soon after climbing it, a few people wanted to go on to climb Elbrus. The Seven Summits had a ring to it that appealed to the more ambitious of our clients, and, while it was true that it was unlikely they would go on to climb them all, it gave them a good reason to travel the world and climb some of the greatest peaks.

This meant, of course, that I got another opportunity to go back to Russia and climb Elbrus – the right summit this time!

By the end of 2001 I had climbed five of the Seven Summits and had also eventually plucked up the courage to ask Brit to marry me. I guess I hadn't proposed straight after the Carstensz trip because I'd whimped out after the satellite phone had let me down. But I eventually popped the question the night before leaving for Antarctica. There'd been no time for glamorous and romantic options, so I'd resorted to buying a small toy lion and tying the ring around its neck. When I later told her about the failed Carstensz proposal, she thought I was crazy but she had a good laugh.

I wanted to get married high up on a mountain in the Drakensberg but Brit pointed out that some of our guests were well into their 70s, and having them traipse up a mountain to watch us tie the knot would almost certainly result in one or two heart attacks. In the end we settled for the side of a hill at a place called Montusi in the Drakensberg. We even organized a 4x4 to cart up the more elderly of our guests.

Towards the end of that year, out of the blue, Everest came into our lives again. Part of me had forgotten about the cold slopes leading to that sacred summit. I was content to drift along trying to climb as many of the Seven as I could, not too worried how we would find the money to go to Everest. Over the years we had become fairly good at writing up sponsorship proposals, and we had been slowly refining the art. We also had a few well-connected clients who had become good friends. The deal was simple: find us the money to go to Everest, and you get to be part of the team.

Part of the team moving up to the 3 352-metre camp (11 000 feet).

The long slog up to Windy Corner.

Abseiling down the headwall.

Errol Gottlich was one such individual. A successful paediatrician with his own practice, Errol had begun climbing mountains far later than the rest of us. But he enjoyed it and saw it as an escape from the hectic demands of looking after other people's kids. Errol had climbed Kilimanjaro and one or two similar mountains. He wanted to go to Everest and was sure he could get us the money. Errol also happened to know the Marketing Director of Discovery Health, Neville Koopewitz. None of us knew that Errol had informally mentioned the idea to Neville, who thought it had merit but said he wanted to meet us before taking it further.

Several days later I got an excited call from Sean Disney:

'Dude, howzit going?'

'What's up?'

'You won't believe it but Errol has found us a sponsor.'

'You've got to be kidding me! Who?'

'Discovery Health!'

Climbing up Motorcycle Hill.

'That's awesome. How much are they putting up?'

'Two million!'

'Are you serious?'

'Yup, they want to meet with us.'

I couldn't believe it. In the past, most sponsors had given us token amounts and, to be fair, hadn't expected much in return.

A few days later, most of the team had met with Neville and it was a done deal. Discovery Health would agree to underwrite the expedition for two million rand. Considering that our proposed budget was more than that, they also agreed to find a co-sponsor to cover the rest. It was official: we were going back to Everest. The hardest part had been accomplished, just like that. Now we had to formalize our team.

At the time the team consisted of me as leader, Sean Disney and, as before, Sean Wisedale as our camera-man. As Errol had found us a sponsor, he was invited to join the team. That left place for three more. Truth be told, there weren't too many people on our short list. The criteria were simple: be experienced, and get on well with the team – in other words we had to know the person. David Ker, who had been working with Sean at Adventure Dynamics, filled the fifth place. David had been up a few of the easier mountains of the Seven more times than I could count. We also decided to invite Lawrence Seeff who had quickly become more than just a competent client, he had become a friend as well. Lawrence wasn't as experienced as the rest of us, but he had a good attitude and the right character.

As the weeks went by, we racked our brains for a seventh person. This was the total number of people our permit would allow and, while we didn't have to fill all seven places, we felt that it would strengthen the team if we had that many involved. Robin Walshaw's name came up on the short list, which included two or three other people. He had done well on Everest in 1996 and had even helped Adventure Dynamics guide some of

David Ker and Robin Walshaw on the summit of Denali.

Sean Disney celebrates after a successful summit bid.

I spent most of the Denali trip roped up with Robin.

the smaller trips. Robin was desperate to go. He knew this was a unique opportunity and dearly wanted to be part of the team. After much debate, however, the final decision was made by Discovery: we needed to be representative of South Africa and this meant finding a woman, preferably black. Only one person fitted those criteria: Deshun Deysel.

I had know Deshun ever since her first trip to Everest. She had been a member of Ian Woodall's expedition but had never really been allowed the opportunity to climb high on the mountain. She still wanted to go back to Everest and we had kept in touch ever since. In the interim, she had busied herself with smaller projects like Kilimanjaro and Mount Kenya. Deshun had reminded me time and again of how much she would love to be part of our team if the opportunity ever came along. Well, it did, and when I called her up and told her she had a sponsored trip to Everest if she wanted it, she was ecstatic. Deshun was definitely in.

This was all happening towards the end of 2001. In our minds, we imagined returning to Everest in the pre-monsoon season, which was only five months away. But it wasn't to be. Discovery felt that an investment of this magnitude required serious planning on the marketing side if they were to turn it into a successful campaign. This would mean delaying the expedition by a year and going in March 2003. While the urge to go as soon as possible was overwhelming, having more than a year to plan the trip was a good thing, as it allowed us to sit down and put together a plan for preparing the team.

First on the agenda was deciding where we should go for a training expedition. There were a number of options but we agreed that, wherever it was, it should have similar conditions to Everest. Going to another 8 000-metre (26 247-foot) peak was out. It wasn't

necessary and would be too costly. We also didn't want to go back to Kilimanjaro as most of the team members were very familiar with it.

That was when Denali was mentioned. It was not only one of the Seven Summits, being the highest in North America, but also had very similar conditions to those we would encounter on Everest. While nowhere near as high, Denali is certainly as cold and windy. It seemed like a good choice and because the Everest idea had been sold to Discovery on the back of the Seven Summits concept, it also made perfect sense.

By now I had climbed five of the Seven, just in case you've lost count, and Sean Disney had done six. He had climbed Denali the previous year and had invited me to join him but unfortunately other commitments had prevented me from making the trip. If we succeeded on Denali, then both Sean and I would have completed six of the Seven, giving Discovery a better shot at sponsoring the first South Africans to climb the Seven Summits successfully.

Discovery Health weren't just any sponsor. In truth, they were the perfect sponsor. I know as I write this that poor Suzanne Stevens and Neville Koopewitz are soon going to have their desks inundated with proposals, if they haven't already. But that's a good thing. I am sure some of the ideas will be harebrained, but somewhere in that pile there will be a great idea or dream that will inspire someone and possibly change their lives. (Sorry, guys, I take full responsibility!)

Right from the start Discovery understood that this wasn't just any trip. This thing was big and it involved more than just giving us money. It was about identifying the dream, the characters, the risks, and all the accompanying ups and downs. This was also an expensive endeavour. Everyone knew that the permit for Everest would cost a fair amount, but there was a lot more to it than that: there was also the equipment we would need, medical expenses and the cost of the entire Denali trip – and that was just for the preparation. In all of this, Discovery Health was superb, becoming more than just a sponsor and more like our own family.

When April 2002 came, it was time

to head off to Alaska and our 'training' expedition. While we knew that the objective of this trip was for us to bond as a team and test our gear, no-one was deluded by the serious nature of the Denali expedition. It was a big mountain. It lay four degrees south of the Arctic Circle and towered above 6 000 metres (19 685 feet) in height. Some said its proximity to the North Pole made it the world's coldest mountain. People regularly died on Denali, so we wanted to make sure that things went smoothly. Remember that this was a precursor to the big one.

We were in high spirits when we set off for the United States and Alaska, home to Mount McKinley, or, as the local Athabascan Indians call it, Denali. Our team had also grown somewhat. We had invited Michael Aldous along to be our technical guy at Base Camp. Mike had climbed five of the Seven and he was a technological whiz. After the successful Carstensz trip, Big Mike Two was the logical choice for this important role.

Then there was good old Robin, frustrating us once again with his stubbornness. When told that he couldn't join us on Everest, he'd been distraught and took it as any Englishman would, cursing and fuming. He bugged us by sending e-mail after e-mail to justify why he should have been included in the Everest team. Robin had moved to Canada with his wife, Natalie, a year previously, so he

was 'close-by' as he put it. The team didn't mind when I suggested he join our expedition. Robin was a good guy, he got along with most people and it would be fun to have him with us on Denali. Lawrence was the only one who stayed at home, as his job as our Base Camp Manager on Everest meant he didn't need to join us on Denali.

If you had to take a map of the earth and try to find all the points that are furthest away from South Africa, Alaska would be one of them. Getting there involved a number of lengthy flights: first to Amsterdam, then on to Minneapolis, followed by Seattle. Seattle was still a few hours away from Alaska but it had been chosen as the town where we would do all our equipment shopping – a small expedition in itself. Down suits and jackets had been specifically made to our sizes. Gore-Tex suits and sleeping bags had to be bought, and they had to be the best in the world. There was no scrimping on this trip. When the mayhem of four days in Seattle finally calmed down and we were officially equipped, we decided to head to a small peak in the Cascade Mountains to familiarize ourselves with our truckload of equipment. We didn't want to arrive on Denali to find that any of our gear didn't fit. It was great to finally get onto a mountain after all the frantic rushing of the previous few weeks. But we were restless. This was fun but none of us could wait to get to Denali.

Finally, after yet another long flight, we arrived in Anchorage and the wilderness of Alaska. We had barely stepped off the plane before it became pretty clear where we were. Greeting us in the arrivals lounge was a three-metre (10-foot) giant of a polar bear standing in a glass display cabinet. A short way down, a grizzly bear crouched menacingly behind another glass pane. Alaska was already promising to be everything we had ever heard of the place, and we weren't yet out of the airport.

Anchorage is a windswept place that has a cool air of mystery about it.

Streets run steeply down to the ocean and the sun hangs low in the sky, giving the town a false appearance of warmth. All around there seems to be the potential for a great adventure or a desperate epic. We strolled around, amazed at the relative quiet of such a large town.

In the morning, we began the next leg that would take us closer to Denali. The team piled into the biggest 'mini' van we had ever seen and set off for Talkeetna, a four-hour drive away. As we left the outskirts of Anchorage, the scenery became noticeably wilder. Spring had only just found its way into North America and most of the lakes were still frozen in the last grip of winter. The forests were a mottled mixture of greens and browns, with log cabins scattered about at regular intervals. Ten minutes before arriving in Talkeetna, we crested a small hill and were surprised by the staggering vista that sprawled across the horizon. The van pulled off the road and we all climbed out. The massive bulk of Denali stood supreme, stretching across the cold sky. We stood and stared, amazed at how much of the horizon it filled.

It wasn't long before we became aware of a loud buzzing around us. Mosquitoes were going crazy and biting the heck out of us. These weren't the piddly little bugs we get at home; they were huge things from the swamps of the outback. They seemed to appear out of nowhere and before long we were covered in them. We ran back to the van, thrashing our arms through the air. The mozzies hovered around outside, trying to find a way into the van while we laughed our heads off. We headed off on the last stretch into Talkeetna.

Talkeetna! It's a small, dirty and boring town. In a way it's a frontier town – not between borders but rather between people who are either coming to Denali or leaving it. That's the only reason the town exists. People drive into Talkeetna and then fly to Denali.

As bleak as the town is, there is almost a quaintness about it that makes you want to see what's around the next corner. Most times you will be disappointed, but that won't stop you from being inquisitive. The locals walk around with foot-long hunting knives strapped to their legs and call their dogs by funny names, like Sky and Commander. It's also a town where you won't go hungry. Walk into any bar or restaurant and pick whatever you want from the menu. Chances are it will include the tastiest hash browns you've ever had, and you won't be able to finish your meal.

Talkeetna is also the place where all the formalities are sorted out: planes are chartered, luggage is weighed, fuel is purchased, snowshoes are rented and exotic beers are consumed in large amounts. Climbing teams are also required to attend a briefing at the National Parks Board office, where the rules and regulations of Denali are made clear. This includes the operation of the small canisters that are used to ferry human waste. They're small, grey plastic buckets that you somehow have to position beneath your buttocks before doing the necessary deed. We had a good laugh although I'm sure each of us was quietly wondering just how well the buckets would work.

After a couple of days in Talkeetna, we were packed and ready to fly. The airstrip was buzzing with small aircraft ferrying climbers to destinations all over the

Looking down along the summit ridge of Denali.

Alaskan range. It was easy to see who was returning and who was setting out. People who had just finished a climb had that weathered, sunburnt look about them, while new arrivals like us still looked fresh and clean.

Our group packed into two small planes and before long we were airborne and droning along towards the mountains. Mountain flights like these are always short but spectacular. The wilderness seemed flat and an endless network of small streams twisted and turned in a dizzying maze. In the distance we could clearly see Denali, flanked by Foraker and Hunter, two giants of the Alaskan range.

Forty-five minutes later we were in amongst them, blinded by the bright glare from the snow. It was hard to imagine how the pilots could see anything. After making a couple of steep turns, the plane flew through a tiny gap between two peaks and dropped suddenly. My stomach lurched like I was on a rollercoaster ride and for the briefest of seconds I believed we were going down – all the way. Then sanity prevailed and I realized we were banking towards the area where Base Camp

was situated. Out of the window I could see a line of tents forming tiny specks in the snow. Immediately next to them was a stretch of snow with a slightly greyer tinge. This was the runway, if you could call it that. It still seemed miles below us but within seconds the pilot had the plane lining up for final approach. As we came in for touchdown, Base Camp seemed to rush up to meet us. The plane landed in a flurry of snow and went skidding up a slight incline. The pilot didn't waste any time in bundling us out and packing the next guys inside. In fact, the plane wasn't even switched off. It just spun around, reloaded and then took off in a mad buzz. High up in the sky we could see the next plane coming in to land.

We stood watching as our plane slowly disappeared into the Alaskan sky. Then someone shouted for us to get off the 'apron' because the next aircraft was heading towards us. We felt disorientated for a few moments, then quickly gathered our wits about us and started dragging our gear off to the side of the 'landing strip'. Base Camp was located in an intimidating setting. Behind us, the North Face of Mount Hunter rose steeply into the sky. It was a mixture of rock and hard ice that was strewn with desperate routes. Across the valley, Mount Foraker stood in sharp contrast. There wasn't a stain of rock anywhere on its slopes, it was just ice and snow. We knew that Foraker was considerably lower than Denali, which made it hard to imagine how high Denali would appear. We couldn't see our destination as it was obscured by a small peak directly behind Base Camp.

emergency supplies from our gear and buried them in a marked spot just to the side of camp. If for some reason we were on the mountain for longer than we had planned, we could always return to base and dig them up. If they weren't needed we would dig them up on our way out and take them with us.

From Base Camp, the route drops down Heartbreak Hill into a valley. We were told we would figure out why it was called that on our way out but for now we had other troubles to worry about. It is often said that you

Robin and Deshun climbing towards Windy Corner.

In a way, climbing in the Alaskan range is similar to climbing in Antarctica. Daylight lasts for almost 24 hours, which means you don't have to worry about being caught out at night and you can climb whenever you want to. Most people fly in to Base Camp and spend a day sorting out things before they set off. But our group was in high spirits and our gear was pretty much organized, so we decided to carry on, rather than camp at 2 000 metres (6 561 feet). Before leaving, we pulled our

'camp' your way up Denali. This is testament to the bad weather that is a notorious part of climbing the mountain: most teams end up being bogged down at a camp for days, even weeks, before they can continue. You move up the mountain carrying a pack and towing a sled. As with Mount Vinson in Antarctica, you end up with most of the heavy gear sliding along behind you. This works fine when you are moving along a flat section, or even up marginally inclined slopes, but it definitely doesn't work when you are heading downhill. Then the sled has a mind of its own and seems hell bent on beating you down. What normally happens is that it starts sliding behind you as it gathers speed, and then whacks into the backs of your legs and knocks you over. It's an incredibly frustrating process. Add to this problem the fact that you haven't quite worked out the right distance for all the slings that connect you to the sled, and you have a period of glacier-crossing that includes some of the most profane language you are ever likely to hear.

For this section I was tied to a rope with Deshun and Robin. Robin has the patience of an umpire and a head like a football. It's the biggest of anyone's I know and it's round. One of Robin's great problems in life is trying to find a hat that fits, but he can endure the most irksome of teasing and quietly takes it in his stride. But there are times when enough is enough – even for Robin. That's when his head will start to shake from side to side and his skin will change from pink to a dangerous crimson. In the right light, those who know him really well might just see a flash of red. I was leading, with Robin bringing up the rear and Deshun between the two of us. Robin was constantly being tugged and pulled as we slid down Heartbreak Hill.

'For crying out loud, Alex, cut that out!'

'What's it now?' I pulled up in the snow.

'Stop pounding on ahead like that, you keep pulling me off balance.'

'What are you talking about?'

'I agree with Robin, just slow down. I won't be able to keep up like this.' Deshun had stopped roughly in the middle of us.

'Okay, what would you like me to do?'

'Just go slower!'

'Fine!'

We carried on down the hill and I made an effort to slow down. But it was frustrating stuff for all of us. The tricky thing about moving across glaciers is that everyone has their own pace. It's as difficult to speed up to the pace of someone who is faster than you are as it is to calm it down a bit for someone who is slower. By the time we got to the bottom of the hill we had achieved some form of rhythm, a compromise between the different paces. The rest were somewhere ahead of us, moving along in two groups.

It was now noon and the glacier was blazing. We stopped regularly in the heat, needing to rest and drink often. The glacier had widened around us, revealing peaks that had been hidden till now, Denali included. It towered above the smaller peaks, shining in the sky with a mixture of white and a shade of granite pink. But it was still a long way off. For the next 10 days we would follow a semi-circular route as we wound our way up the glacier, steadily getting closer to the peak. For now, though, we just had to get to the next camp.

The route was pretty flat for the rest of the day. Ahead of us was a rise marked 'Ski Hill'. This was the point where we would have to decide whether we would set up camp at the base of the hill, or somewhere above it. I knew the decision wouldn't have to be debated. This was our first day on the mountain and I was sure that everyone would be tired. I was right. As we neared Ski Hill I could see that the others had stopped in a suitable place and were already setting up camp.

One of the biggest problems on Denali is making sure that your camp is strong enough to withstand the atrocious weather. You have to consider not only the ferocity of the conditions, but also the lengthy duration of some storms. For this reason, a couple of snow shovels are mandatory equipment, even if you do manage to find a vacant site. The first thing you do when you arrive in camp, assuming there aren't any vacant sites, is to start building some walls. Some of the higher camps will be home for a number of nights, so small fortresses are required there. Down here, though, we were only going to spend one night before continuing. Of course this meant there was a great temptation to build a small wall, or even do without one.

What you certainly don't want to do is build nothing and then get hammered in some awesome Arctic whirlwind that keeps you pinned down and hanging on for days. But you also don't want to waste energy building a small version of the Great Wall of China, only to pack up and go first thing in the morning. Somewhere between is a compromise, and this is where experience kicks in, finding the right balance between what is necessary and what you can get away with doing.

That night we put in about an hour of effort and then settled in for our first night on Denali. Most of our tents were ensconced between snow walls varying between half a metre and one metre (1.64 to 3.28 feet) in length. It was a clear and calm night, although, in its strange Arctic way, it was devoid of darkness. The temperature outside was about −15°C (5°F), but the hues of pink and red in the sky could easily have fooled you into believing it was a lot warmer. I was in a tent with Robin snugly wrapped in my new −50°C (−58°F) sleeping bag. Between the both of us and our billion goose feathers, there wasn't much room left to do anything but sleep.

In the morning the sky was clear so we hustled about packing up camp and setting off while it was still cool. One of the most important rules on Denali is: when the weather is good, move! This is because there's a good risk of getting stuck at any one camp for longer than you'd like if the weather turns.

We were in high spirits as we slowly made our way to Ski Hill. The day before it had seemed like a small rise in the glacier. It was only as we began making our way up that we realized it was actually much higher than we'd imagined. It was foreshortened, which meant that it was initially quite steep, but then tapered off gradually. This tapering off was hidden from view, so you could never quite see where the top was. Often you would think you were there and speed up a touch, only to realize that it was still a way off. Then you would really have to slow down because you were completely out of breath.

This was a short day in both time and distance. The previous night we had camped at roughly the same height as Base Camp. Today we would camp at 3 352 metres (11 000 feet), meaning a gain of 600 metres (1 968 feet), and we would travel for around five kilometres (three miles). At noon we caught up with the others already setting up camp. This section of the route had a number of possible campsites, depending how far you wanted to go that day. Some were better than others. I didn't like where this camp was situated, as I felt it was too close to an ice cliff that towered above.
'How are you guys feeling?'
'Fine, why?' Deshun and Robin had caught up to me and were both sitting on their packs. We were still roped together.
'Well, I don't like the look of that chunk of ice up there.' I pointed to the slope above.
'Do you think that could reach us?' Deshun asked.
'I'm not sure, but why take the chance?'
'Well, I'm too tired to carry on, so I think I will just spend the night here. Besides, David has already put

his tent up.' Deshun was sharing a tent with David. 'Robin, what do you think?'

'I'm fine. If you want to carry on for a bit then let's go.'

We unclipped Deshun from the rope, shortened the section between the two of us, and then continued. The others weren't about to take down their tents and were quite happy where they were, so we agreed to see them in the morning somewhere along the route.

We made our way along the snow for another hour before reaching a flat spot on the glacier that was well away from the ice face off to our side. From here the glacier turned sharply to the right and headed up closer to the main camp. We hadn't gained much in terms of altitude, so the risk of altitude-related problems was small, but we still had to be wary. Another similarity between Denali and Mount Vinson is their proximity to the poles. Being so close to the North Pole meant Denali had a relatively lower atmospheric pressure than other 6 000-metre (19 685-foot) peaks around the world. We were treating Denali like a 7 000-metre (22 965-foot) peak, and that meant taking it slowly.

Again the night was calm and brought with it a clear day. There were still no streaks in the sky to give evidence that things might get hectic. As we packed up camp, the others slowly passed us as they headed up to the 3 352-metre camp. The two Seans were on one rope, Mike and Errol were tied together a short distance behind them, and bringing up the rear were David and Deshun. They stopped briefly to chat and then set off again. We would see them later. On these flattish sections the only hazards were crevasses. Each person made sure they had the necessary equipment to help rescue their partner if they should be unfortunate enough to fall into one. This equipment included a pulley and a couple of jumars. You also had to ensure that you were always tied to your partner by a rope.

This would be our last easy day on the mountain. From here on up things would get technical and exhausting, so we took it slowly and enjoyed the trek. By now we had pretty much found the right combination of slings and lengths for our sleds, which made it an entirely different experience from that first day. The sleds slid silently along behind us as we settled into a steady rhythm. The smaller peaks were closing in again, hiding Denali from view. Gone was that wide sweeping glacier we had been following for the previous few days. It was now squashed in between peaks and was slowly getting steeper. The last section up to camp was a steep slope that required every effort to prevent the sled from slipping back down. It was a punishing job that involved taking two steps forward and having your sled pull you one step back. When the slope flattened out, camp was barely 100 metres (328 feet) away.

Camp was situated at the base of Motorcycle Hill. This snow hill, which was fairly steep, as we would soon discover, was named after a hill that they race motorbikes up somewhere else in the States, and the original was supposedly even steeper than the one we would have to climb. Motorcycle Hill led to a ridge that swept up towards the West Buttress of Denali, our chosen route on the mountain. We would only follow the West Buttress for a short section higher up, but that would still be days away. For now we could only stare upwards at the pink granite in wonder.

The camp at 3 352 metres (11 000 feet) is a very important one because it's here that teams have to decide whether they will continue up to 4 000 metres

It is a strange experience to climb in the middle of the night and see the sky filled with hues of early evening.

(13 123 feet) with sleds, or make a couple of load carries and then do without. Either way, most teams will spend a couple of nights here to acclimatize. But you also don't want to spend too long because you could be trapped for days. Halfway between the two camps is a section called Windy Corner. I don't need to tell you how it got its name, only that, whatever impression the name gives of the place, trust me it is worse than you can possibly imagine. Windy Corner is a natural trouble spot on the mountain where the wind can be blowing so strongly that it's impossible to move either up or down. Even when the weather at both 3 352 and 4 267 metres (11 000 and 13 999 feet) is fine, Windy Corner can make climbing impossible.

Teams at the lower height have to decide how long they want to hang around before moving up. Being stuck at 4 267 metres is a good thing because you have time to acclimatize and might have access to the upper slopes of the mountain. Being stuck indefinitely at 3 352 metres, however, can only be frustrating. It was still early in the season but already a number of teams had settled in at the lower camp to assess the weather.

Up until this point everyone in the team had been doing great. No-one had any altitude problems and they were all feeling strong. What I hadn't realized was that Errol had been quietly suffering but he'd been stoically plodding on regardless. Errol's feet had the most hectic blisters that had first formed when we'd gone testing our gear near Seattle. The three days of pulling sleds across the snow had made them much worse and he now felt excruciating pain with every step he took. I winced when Errol showed me his feet in the morning. They really did look bad. Being a doctor, Errol didn't need to hear it from me. Where at first there had been blisters, there were now big

suppurating holes. It also turned out that there was far more to Errol's pain than just his blisters. He called me over to talk.

'Alex, I've been thinking. I'm not sure I can carry on.'
'Are your feet that bad!'
'It's more than that. I've been thinking about something for a while now.'
'What's that?'
'Well, remember the talk we had a while ago?'

Errol had mentioned that this whole Everest adventure was taking a huge toll on his relationship with his family.
'*Ja*, I do.'
'Well, I have thought long and hard about this and I don't think I can do it.'
'Are you talking about climbing Denali?'
'I mean this whole process. Denali and Everest next year.'
'What are you saying? Do you want to pull out?' I could sense that Errol had been having an emotional battle about this for a while.
'In the beginning the idea was great but, as this process has developed, I've begun to understand just what is required. And it's too much. I'm not where you guys are at. You know I've got two kids and a wife and it's just not fair.'

There was the faintest hint of a tear in Errol's eye. I could empathize with him. He was further down the road of family commitment than any of us. Brit and I had been married for almost a year and I knew how much of a toll it took on her.
'So, what do you want to do?'
'Well, I still want to be part of the process but I can't climb.'
'Look, I don't think anyone will object to that. What about Denali?'

'No. I need to get home. Sure my feet will be fine in a day or two, but I need to go. And I'm sorry if I'm causing you any hassles.'

'Errol, don't worry about it. If you have to go we'll all understand.'

I knew some of the guys would think Errol was just bailing. But I also knew what time on a mountain can do. It crystallizes things in your life and shows you just where you are. It also lets you know what's really important in life. Errol had reached the point where enough was enough. The lure of Everest and the Seven Summits wasn't as strong in him as it was in me. We all sat around watching Errol pack and then leave. He was tied onto a rope with two strangers who were heading off the mountain. By day's end he would be back in Talkeetna and soon thereafter on his way home. Errol would still be an important part of the process, but he would no longer be climbing Everest.

After Errol had left, we decided to hold a council of war of sorts. There were things on people's minds that needed expressing and this was as good a time as any. The first thing that had to be decided was whether or not we were going to spend an extra night resting at 3 352 metres (11 000 feet). We also had to consider whether we wanted to take a rest day. It was quickly decided that the extra night would be a good idea, but, as for a rest day, that wasn't as simple. Deshun had been moving more slowly than the rest of the group and she was keen for a break. David was paired up with Deshun, but he wasn't so sure. He was on a tighter schedule than the rest of us, as he had to get back to South Africa by the end of the month to guide a trip up Kilimanjaro. The rest of us were feeling strong so we decided to carry a load up to around 4 000 metres (13 123 feet) and then return to camp.

After a night's rest, we started the upward slog. David and Deshun stayed behind for a rest day while the rest of us pushed on. First we had to climb up Motorcycle Hill, which lay a short way out of camp. This wasn't too bad because, for the first time on the trip, we were moving without our sleds. Instead we had a portion of our load in our backpacks. We were only making a carry today so, if we didn't get all the way to 4 000 metres, then we would stash the load somewhere along the way. At the top of the hill we joined a thin ridge that turned to the right and headed up towards Windy Corner. The sky was clear and it was a warm day.

We were now on the first really tricky section of the route so we were still roped together. The ridge snaked along at a gentle angle, then steepened across an awkwardly angled slope. At the top of this slope it eased off again into a fairly broad glacier. We stopped along the way, checking on the weather and taking regular breaks. Up ahead we could see where the glacier ended and Windy Corner started. We reached the end of the glacier an hour later. Instead of ice and snow there was an area the size of a football field that was covered in rocks. This seemed to be the point at which the West Buttress started in earnest. To our left we could see it rising steeply upwards. Thankfully, our route didn't go anywhere near this prominent point. Instead, it skirted the base of the buttress, through Windy Corner, and then on to the high valley of the 4 267-metre (13 999-foot) camp.

As we neared Windy Corner we could understand why this was the scene of many an epic disaster. The trail now hugged the steep side of the West Buttress. To our right the slope dropped off a dizzying precipice to an isolated valley way below. A slip here would almost certainly be fatal. We were lucky. There was only a breeze blowing but it still demanded careful climbing. When we had turned Windy Corner, the trail opened up again and we could rest in safety. The camp was still an hour or so away, and we were all pretty tired, so decided to stash the gear off to the side and call it a day. It didn't make much sense to push ourselves too hard when we were probably going to come all the way up here again the next day.

We quickly dug a hole about a metre deep by a metre long (3.28 feet by 3.28 feet) in which we put the gear, which had been wrapped up in plastic bags. We then filled the hole with snow and compacted it. Finally, we took a couple of snow wands made of bamboo and prodded them into the snow about 30 centimetres (one foot) deep. The cache was now marked as ours. We turned and headed back down to 3 352 metres (11 000 feet) with our empty packs. It had been a successful day.

About an hour after 'sunset', just as we were settling into our bags, a frightening rumble sent us scampering out of our tents with our hearts in our mouths. On the other side of camp, a gigantic chunk of ice had peeled off the face high above us and was hurtling down the mountain. For all of a second we felt the overwhelming fear of impending doom, and then we realized the ice was going to miss our camp. We watched in awe as it plunged down the slope, gathering momentum. It seemed to be the size of a bus and was heading directly for a similar-sized chunk. At the instant of collision, the second piece disintegrated into a million pieces of ice.

Robin Walshaw approaching the summit of Denali.

When the clouds settle in, Denali quickly becomes a frightening place.

We stood about dumbstruck, watching the last pieces slowly grind to a halt on the glacier below. Then we noticed we were all in our undies and it was −15°C (5°F). We dived back into the tents and zipped ourselves in our sleeping bags, still pumped with adrenaline. The rest of the night was quiet.

In the morning the first thin streaks of white cloud appeared. They were high up and still far away but their presence was ominous. Again we discussed our options. David and Deshun would make a carry but they would spend a further night at the lower camp. The rest of us would move to 4 267 metres (13 999 feet). We decided to take our sleds along and leave them at the next camp while we moved higher up the mountain, but we had hardly gone 50 metres (164 feet) up

Motorcycle Hill when we were regretting the decision. The slope was only at about a 40-degree angle, but it was steep enough to make the task of hauling the sleds a backbending mission.

The next section was fairly easy, and, when we reached the flat glacier, it was a piece of cake. But in the backs of our minds we wondered what it would be like to tackle the icy slope of Windy Corner with our sleds. All too soon we were there, and this time there was more than a breeze blowing. As we slowly made our way along the narrow ledge, gravity tugged at the sleds, threatening to pull them down the slope, and us with them. With the sled rope in one hand and a ski pole in the other, we carefully dragged our way along the ledge. Halfway along my sled began an insidious slide sideways, and I only knew about it when its full weight suddenly stretched the rope and almost knocked me off my feet. I held on like a mad man, clenching my teeth and desperately trying to keep my balance. If I let go, I knew it would hurtle down at high speed with me screaming behind it. Robin would no doubt follow just as spectacularly. I held on. The sled stopped its sickening slide and sanity returned. We quickly crossed the last section and collapsed in a pile, breathing hard.

We only rested for long enough to dig out our buried rations. When they were securely tied to the sleds, we set off for the last hour up to camp. The breeze had now become a strong wind and the temperature had dropped. The cold and wind made the going difficult, even though the terrain had eased off. But it was too windy to stop and talk, so we just plodded on upwards, knowing that we would arrive sooner rather than later.

For a while the trail followed a zigzag path up the glacier before cresting a rise, and suddenly, there the camp was. It took us by surprise but we were glad we had made it although in the back of my mind I was worrying about David and Deshun. The thin streaks in the sky had been slowly getting closer and I knew that, if the weather did turn bad, they could be snowed in for ages and effectively cut off from the rest of the team. In a previous ascent, Sean Disney had once been stuck at 3 352 metres (11 000 feet) for 11 days before abandoning his climb. The last thing we wanted was to be separated for any lengthy period. But, then again, Deshun had also needed the rest. These are the compromises one has to make on big mountains. Nothing is guaranteed and anything can happen. All we could hope for was that the bad weather would stay away for

just a few more days. Then it could snow, or do whatever it wanted to, but not before we were reunited.

This camp would be the one where we would spend the most time, so we made pretty sure that our tents were well secured. Except the two Seans, that is. They bailed into a small hollow, pitched their tent and collapsed inside it. That night it snowed about two feet (61 centimetres) and by morning the Seans were buried alive. They whinged and moaned and cried for us to help to dig them out, but we laughed, pointing out that they still hadn't learnt their lesson from Vinson, and that they probably never would. When they were finally out of their 'prison', they muttered something about saving energy. But we did see them make an effort to put up a modicum of a wall after that.

After our first night, we settled in for a

hard-earned day of rest. This included checking in at the National Parks tent where we were given the turd bins and briefed on how they worked. They were small, cylindrical plastic buckets with screw-on lids and rubber padding on the rims. To top it off, a set of small straps made sure the containers could be wrapped up and 'bomb proofed', or made indestructible, if necessary. Up until this point on the mountain, going for a dump had been similar to the experience in Antarctica – you did it in a plastic bag. The only difference was that on Denali there were certain crevasses that were designated as dump holes. When a bag was frozen and full, you could dump it into the crevasses and condemn it to the frozen pit. But that all changed now. From here on up you had to dump in the buckets and they had to be brought back down to the National Parks tent, where they would be taken care of.

We wandered around camp for the rest of the day, checking out some of the other teams and watching the sky closely. The streaks were certainly closer to us but seemed to be holding out. We hoped that David and Deshun would be well on their way and by the time we were settling back into our tents, we could just see them coming over the rise.

It was at this height that we first started feeling the effects of the high altitude. We now had to start paying careful attention to what we were eating and how much we were drinking. Food consisted mostly of freeze-dried rations that were packaged in foil far brighter than their contents, although we had packed a few extra things for the odd surprise. Two of the packs had supposedly been developed for NASA astronauts. Both were types of ice cream, although one had pictures of dinosaurs on it. Robin and I couldn't quite follow the instructions and we ended up with a flaky, brothy type of choc-mint flavoured mess that we doubted any astronauts would eat, regardless of how long they had spent in outer space. We gave it up as a lost cause and tossed the other packet.

But there was still fun to be had with some of the food. One evening Robin and I had finished dinner but were nibbling on a few snacks before settling in for the night. He turned to me with an odd expression on his face.

'This stuff tastes old,' he said.

I looked up from my bag. 'What's that?'

'This biltong. Where's it from, your last expedition?'

Robin had a packet of small meat pieces in his hand. I smiled but it took everything I had in me not to burst out laughing. I remembered the day clearly. Pick 'n Pay had given us a cheque for R10 000 to spend on whatever food and treats we wanted. It was quite a thrill, rushing down the aisles with five trolleys and pulling boxes of sweets and chocolates off the shelves.

At some point in the frenzy Sean Disney came up with the idea of buying some cat treats that looked very much like biltong.

'What the heck for?' I asked.

'To sneak into Robin's pack, seeing as the bugger has been in Canada all this time while we've been missioning.'

We all laughed and the cat food did get into Robin's pack. As I watched him slowly chew through a piece I could no longer contain myself and burst out laughing.

Robin looked at me suspiciously. 'What's the matter?' he asked. 'Oh no, don't say.' Robin knew, without me saying anything, that he had been the victim of some prank. But he took it in his good-natured way and swore to do something disgusting to Sean Disney's toothbrush.

In the morning we geared ourselves up for a tiring day. Deshun would rest but the others in the group would make a carry higher up the mountain. This meant first climbing the fixed ropes of the headwall, and then the ridge that followed on from the West Buttress. The night had brought with it a covering of cloud and it seemed pretty bleak. But there was no wind, so we agreed to set off and take it one section at a time. As long as the wind kept at bay, there wasn't too much problem with climbing higher. If things started getting hectic, we would just dump our loads wherever we were and head back down.

The headwall was the first really technical section on Denali. It was a 400-metre (1 312-foot) face of hard ice that angled up at about 50 degrees. It almost always had ropes fixed to it, which would make the climbing far easier and safer. Normally there was a rope for going up and one for descending. In recent years the main American guiding companies had taken on the responsibility of ensuring that the ropes were put in place and then maintained. This not only meant an easier journey for their clients, but it also made the mountain much safer, which of course kept the clients happy. But this part of the mountain could also be the scene of many a drama. It is not uncommon to see someone stuck on the headwall, clueless as to how all their equipment works.

We set off early in the day with the objective of getting as high as we could while weather permitted. If we could make it all the way to the camp at 5 200 metres (17 060 feet), great. By this stage on the trip we had established which two or three members of the group were roped together, and we pretty much stuck to it. Once again Robin and I set off together, slowly making our way over a flattish section that headed up to the base of the headwall. I kept my eyes peeled to the sky, watching for any sign of deteriorating weather. I also used the time to think about a lot of things.

It's common to allow your mind to drift as you make your way along monotonous parts of mountains. Thinking helps to pass the time and turns what would otherwise be a long and boring slog into a relatively quick section. Robin was following at a safe distance, keeping to my set of tracks. I thought about how far the two of us had come in the previous decade. So much had changed. On that first trip to Russia, getting to the top had meant everything – at any cost – and I had been blind to all around me. Now I was more circumspect and observant. I watched the sky like a hawk, trying to spot any telltale sign that would hint at changing weather, or even an impending storm.

I have also gained the habit of keeping a constant watch over my body, knowing it like no-one else;

judging when to push, and when to back off. But I guess the biggest change has been learning to understand the consequences of certain actions, and when a risk is acceptable and when it is not. There is a saying in the mountains:

> There are many bold mountaineers, but there are no old bold mountaineers.

I guess it was starting to become more important to me to be old than bold.

We arrived at the base of the fixed ropes and stopped for a rest. Robin was looking strong and the weather seemed to be holding. In fact, we had just about climbed out of the cloud and the sky above us was a clear blue. Above us stretched a long line of climbers all slowly making their way up the fixed ropes. Some were moving faster than others but, all in all, it was a slow affair. When our turn finally came to clip on, I suggested to Robin that we climb off to the side with our ice axes and avoid the queue.

'You mean off to the right there?'

'Yes, about 10 metres right of where the rope is.'

'Dude, that looks a bit steep.'

'I don't think it looks that bad.'

'Are you sure about this?'

I wasn't, but, by the time we had finished bantering, the crowds seemed to have disappeared. We gave up the suggestion as a bad idea and each began the difficult task of climbing using a jumar – a clip that grips the rope when weight is applied, and runs freely along the rope when the weight is removed.

In essence the fixed rope was one long rope, but it was secured to the ice with snow stakes or ice screws every 30 or 40 metres (98 or 131 feet). We would jumar along a section and then rest at these points. These were also the times when you had to be super careful. In addition to the jumars, we each climbed with a sling and karabiner. As we got to a 'rest point' we would clip the sling to the rope above the point while still connected with the jumar. Only once we had done this would we unclip the jumar and then attach it back to the rope above the point. Lastly, we would unclip the sling and continue jumaring. Most accidents on fixed ropes happen when people take chances with their slings and don't clip when they should.

The headwall took about an hour and a half of jumaring before we topped out on the ridge. It was not a big place but it was often used as an intermediate camp for those who couldn't quite make it to the high camp. I looked around me, wondering how on earth anyone could safely pitch a tent in this place. All around us the ice sloped away steeply, and it was a hard wind-blown ice that had been compacted over aeons. Wands were strewn haphazardly about, some marking stashes, others lying on the ridge as testament to some or other hectic storm. In places the snow was stained yellow with urine and vomit. It was an awful place. We agreed that under no circumstances would we try to pitch a tent anywhere near the place.

We continued climbing. Our job today was not to pitch our tents, but only to get as high as we could manage and then stash some gear. We were following the old climbing adage of climbing high and sleeping low, and were banking on the weather holding, but were always prepared to dump everything in a heart-beat and make a hasty retreat. The group was also climbing unroped, mainly because the ridge had become so thin in places that it was knife-edged. If

one of us should slip, it would be impossible for the other person to hold the fall and both would go plummeting. With each person climbing unroped, we could concentrate on the climbing and not be worried about what the other person was doing. Short pieces of fixed rope made the more technical sections of the ridge safe. I felt ours was a safe strategy, but, in the final analysis, it was just a strategy. Other people might climb that same section differently. In these types of situations you have to decide for yourself and then deal with whatever happens.

In places the ridge was probably one of the more spectacular parts of Denali. To the right, it fell away steeply to the flat valley way below. To the left it was even more hectic. Way below a mess of jumbled ice fell forever into some forgotten valley. There was a slight wind about as we topped out at the end of the ridge and reached the flattish area of high camp. Situated at a height of about 5 200 metres (17 060 feet), it was a bleak place. Robin and I walked around looking for a suitable site that wouldn't require too much work. There were two or three other tents dug into the snow but the place was quiet, very different from the hustle and bustle of the lower camp. Soon we found an abandoned site that already had one solid wall in place. We knew with a bit of effort we could build it up into a suitable camp. In the corner of the site we dug a small hole, buried the gear, and then turned and hurried back to the ridge. We were keen to get back down to camp as soon as we could.

As we carefully made our way back along the ridge I started thinking about Deshun. I knew that she was inexperienced on this type of terrain and I also knew the risks of climbing unroped. Back in 1995 I had taken part in an exchange programme with some

New Zealand climbers, and we had spent a week climbing in the Mount Cook Valley on New Zealand's South Island. We had just climbed a technical peak and were descending late in the day. The snow was soft and the ridge we were on was similar to the one I was on now. Three of the climbers in our group were on a rope a short way behind me. Without any warning one of them slipped and started sliding down the ridge. Within seconds the other two were pulled off balance and were also sliding down. It was only a rock about 30 metres (98 feet) below the ridge that saved them from falling thousands of feet. With or without a rope, ridge climbing was dangerous stuff. There was no room for error. I wondered whether it was a little too much for Deshun at this stage. One of our objectives was to prepare her for Everest and we had to be careful how we went about this.

That night some of the guys mentioned similar concerns. They were right. I knew the terrain from here on up would be difficult. On Everest there would be far more fixed ropes, making the technical sections that much safer. There was also the fact that there was still a year to go on our road of preparation. I knew I had to have a talk with Deshun, but I also knew what it would mean. I would be robbing her of a potential summit. In the morning I walked over to Deshun's tent.
'Howzit going?'
'Fine thanks, and you?'
'Good. A little concerned about all this good weather we are having. We need to chat.'
'Oh yes? What's up?'
I knew Deshun wasn't going to like what I had to say but I didn't beat about the bush.

Robin makes his way to the summit through steep snow.

'Break my fall today, I lack the strength it takes to be invincible from this earthly toll. So many falls to break, please show me what it takes to be immovable when my spirit shakes.' — Plankeye

'I don't think you're experienced enough for the terrain higher up.'

'Okay. So what does that mean?'

'Look, I know it's still your decision, but I don't want you to go any further.'

Tears welled up in Deshun's eyes. I knew how much this meant to her but I had to think of the bigger picture. Then she did a surprising thing. In essence, she agreed with me. She told me how dearly she wanted to get to the top, but she had faith in my decisions and, if I felt she wasn't experienced enough, she would go along with what I wanted. I was impressed. This was what being a team was about: trusting your leader even if it meant sacrificing your personal goals. I made sure Deshun realized there were still many smaller peaks she would climb before Everest. This was just the first step in a long journey.

In the morning we decided to push on up to high camp and get ready for a summit bid. As hard as it was to believe, this was only our ninth day on the mountain and it seemed inconceivable that we would be summiting on our tenth day. After all, this was Denali – a mountain that normally took three weeks to climb, not 10 days. We talked about whether we were climbing too fast, but everyone felt good, and the weather was fine. In a way, we didn't really have any other choice. While those two things were in our favour, we had to keep pushing. We said goodbye to Deshun and started off towards the fixed ropes and, ultimately, high camp.

By the time we arrived it was late in the afternoon and we were tired. We all agreed we would need a rest day before trying for the summit. Robin and I settled into our tent for another night together. As much

as you know a person, and as well as you get on together, there are times when being cooped up in a small tent starts to test your patience. What started as the usual banter between us quickly turned into a heated argument. Robin flatly refused to carry the turd barrel. His reasoning was that he hadn't been for a crap in four days.

'Four days!' I said. 'That's ridiculous.'

'Alex, you've been using that thing every day since we got it. That means all five kilos of rot are yours. You carry it.' Robin was serious about this.

'That's crazy. You can't expect me to be the only one to carry this thing just because I'm the only guy going to the toilet.'

'Look, I'm not carrying it and that's that!'

'Fine. Just don't come to me when you need to park a turd.'

We carried on back and forth like this for a while before becoming too tired to argue. Eventually we fell asleep. I was the one who would carry the barrel.

Such is life in the confines of a tent on a high, cold mountain. Small, insignificant things that you would normally joke about turn into subjects of huge debate. But in the morning it was all forgotten and we could get back down to the business of climbing. After a while, Robin and I were both tired but we were keen to carry on while the good weather lasted. We asked the others how they felt and most of them felt they needed a rest. We agreed to wait an hour and then check again how we all felt.

An hour later and everyone felt much better. The sky was still clear and a slight breeze blew. We decided to go for it and, seeing that Robin and I had been keen for a while, we were ready before the others. The two of us set off at a slow pace, knowing that the rest of the group would soon be following.

From high camp we crossed a fairly flat section of snow before reaching Denali Pass. This was a notoriously dangerous section of the mountain where the bulk of Denali's accidents occurred, especially on the way down. Denali Pass wasn't that steep, being at only about a 35- to 40-degree angle, but the route slanted awkwardly, making climbing tricky. It wasn't hard to imagine coming down from the summit feeling totally exhausted and slipping somewhere along the pass. But I was climbing at a steady rhythm and felt strong, with Robin a short way behind me.

For the most part we climbed without being clipped together, and we occasionally clipped onto the odd section of fixed rope. The temperature was about −10°C (14°F) but with all my gear on and the hard work involved in climbing, I was soon pretty warm. But this lasted only until we got to the top of Denali Pass. Then, for the first time on the mountain, I started worrying about the temperature. A wind was blowing at about 30 or 40 kilometres (18 to 25 miles) an hour. Normally this wouldn't have been too bad, but, this high on Denali, it meant extremely low temperatures. It was now down to about −30°C (−22°F). The wind had been blowing all along, but we hadn't really felt it in the camp in the valley, where we'd been protected by Denali Pass.

Within half an hour I was losing heat fast and knew that I would soon be faced with choices similar to those I'd had on Mount Vinson. I stopped for a rest on a slight rise. The route above me followed a broad ridge. I knew that above that there was a large flat area know as the Football Field. If I could get there then I would be pretty close to the summit. I also felt

incredibly strong. Robin came up behind me and I told him what I was feeling: mainly that I needed to increase the pace so that I could generate some heat. Robin felt good but said he couldn't go any faster, so we agreed that I would stop at regular intervals to check on where he was. I put on my pack again and stormed up the slope. This was a battle I wasn't going to lose.

Half an hour later I had warmed up but my heart rate was sky high. I had my heart rate monitor on and it was telling me that my respiratory system was working overtime. I slowed down a bit. Ahead of me I could see the ridge flattening out a short way before the Football Field. I knew I was getting close. By the time I reached the edge of the field, the wind had picked up and I could feel my core temperature dropping. I stopped in the shelter of a large boulder and pulled out my down jacket. Even though I had on my Gore-Tex suit and a whole bunch of thermals, I was getting cold again. Trying to figure out the right combination of clothing to wear is always one of the big challenges faced on big mountains.

I stood up from the shelter of the boulder and stared across the Football Field. From where I was standing, it dropped slightly into a depression and stretched on for about 100 metres (328 feet). On the far side, a face of ice reared steeply upwards to a spectacular ridge. And there, to the left of the ridge, along a series of steep undulations, was the top of Denali, the highest point in North America. I could see it clearly. As my eyes gazed along the ridge, I caught sight of a group of climbers slowly zigzagging up the face. They were nearing the end of their goal. Suddenly I felt an overwhelming sense of excitement and a surge of adrenaline. I knew I was going to make it.

I get asked the question, 'Why do you do it?' so many times. Sometimes it's easy to explain; other times it's impossible. Sometimes I really want to give the person some idea of what it's all about, and, yet, there are occasions when I don't want to tell them because it's too difficult to explain and I feel like taking the easy way out.

There's an intuitiveness involved in climbing to the top of a mountain. That's it: the very top. Nowhere else to climb but down. Most of the time climbers set off not knowing whether or not we will get to the top, for whatever reason. We usually only realize we have made it when we are finally there. But this time was different. I knew I was going to get there sometime in the following hour and I was already savouring the moment.

I felt strong when I reached the Football Field and minutes later I crossed it and began the tiring ascent of the ice face. Halfway, I caught up with the climbers I had seen earlier. It was a group of Koreans who had been climbing Denali at a rate similar to our group. They were moving slowly but with determination and were also climbing the Seven Summits. For some of them this would be the last in their quest.

Without too much difficulty I made my way past them and continued up the face, stopping for a rest when I reached the ridge. In front of and below me, the South Face of Denali dropped in a dizzying scream into a valley miles below. Some distance off, Mount Hunter reared its steep and intimidating northern face into the sky but it was lower than us, much lower. I turned and carried on along the ridge.

This was now without question the most dangerous part of the route. It was a classic knife-edge ridge, in places no wider than the width of a pair of feet. The wind was still blowing up here, and on the exposed ridge, it threatened to topple me off at the slightest lapse in concentration. At one point the ridge was so narrow that I had a foot on both the north and south sides at the same time. Still further along, the path left the ridge and skirted round a face on the north side. The face was short but steep and it meant being pressed up against the snow with my ice axe. Then it was back on the ridge, climbing ever higher. A few more short, steep sections later and I topped out on the summit ridge proper. It was about 30 metres (98 feet) long, with a gradual rise to the highest point. I stopped and looked back. Robin was a short way behind. I decided to wait for him just below the ridge. This was a moment I had waited 10 years for, and I wanted to share it with someone.

Robin arrived and, without saying anything to him, I stood up and together we walked the last few steps to the very highest point on the continent of North America.

It was fantastic. A cold, white world dropped forever all around us and seemed to disappear into eternity. High above us the sun was bright, but its heat couldn't penetrate the cold Arctic sky to reach us. Warmth came from within. It came from the realization that we had dared to walk along the path that, until this point, had only been something we could imagine.

LEFT: *A procession of climbers arrive at the 3 352-metre (11 000-foot) camp.*

TOP: *Looking back from the summit of Denali.*

ABOVE: *A rare opportunity to rest.*

Everest, South Face

- **ALSO KNOWN AS:** Sagarmatha (Goddess of the Sky) in Nepal.

- **HEIGHT:** 8 850 metres (29 035 feet).

- **FIRST ASCENT:** 29 May 1953 by Sir Edmund Hillary and Sherpa Tenzing Norgay.

- **POINT OF INTEREST:** George Mallory may have been the first to summit Everest in the 1920s, but he disappeared on the way down. His body was recovered in 1999 but the camera which might contain photos proving whether or not he made the summit has never been found.

The classic view of Everest taken from Kala Patar.

Summit
Camp Four
Camp Three
Camp Two
Camp One
Base Camp

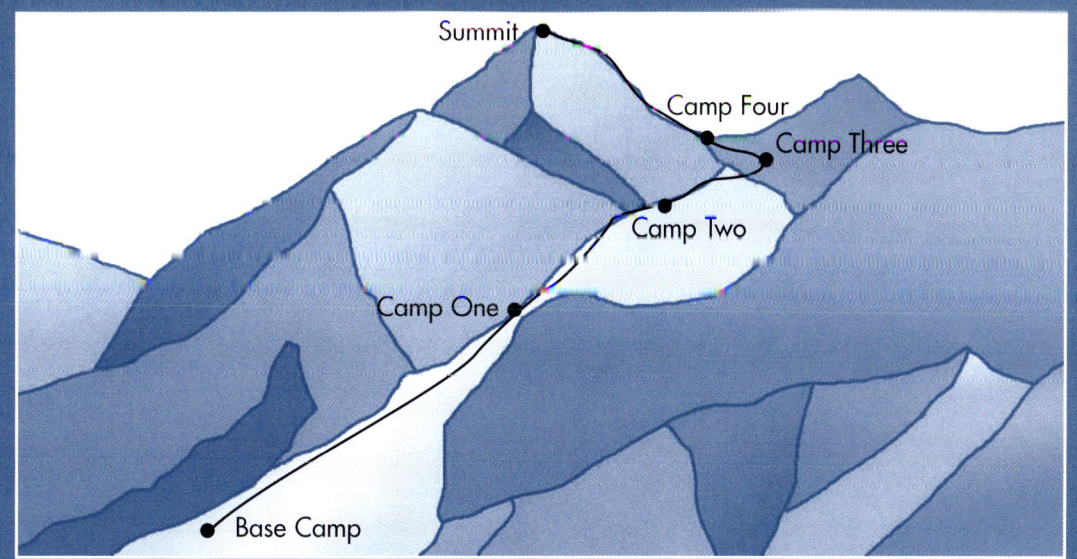

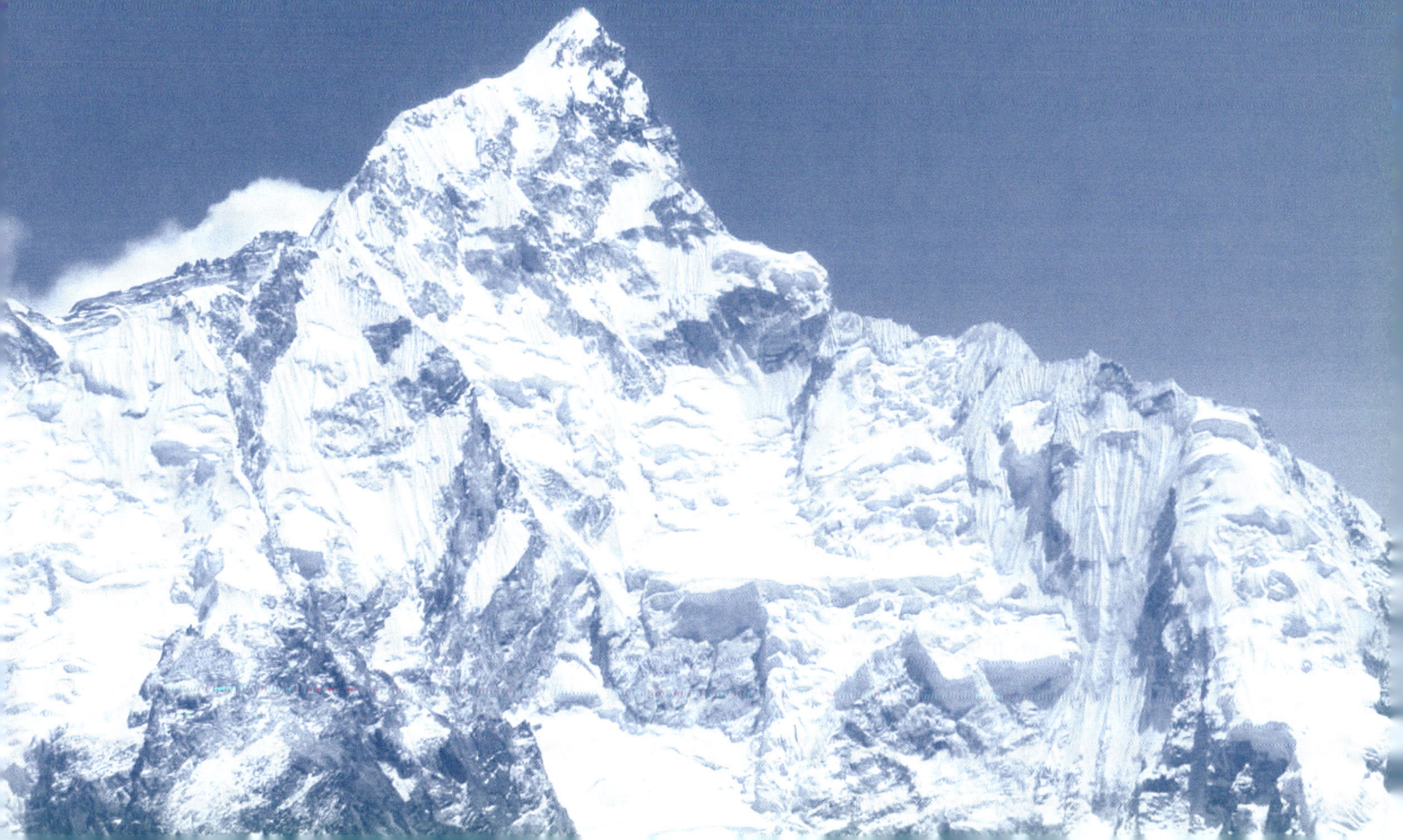

The jet stream winds are a permanent feature of Everest.

CHAPTER TEN

Over the Limit

The team returned home feeling jubilant. Everyone except Deshun had got up Denali, and that was not her fault. But she understood why and there was still a year for her to gain as much experience as she could. We had all bonded well and it had been the perfect preparation for Everest. True, we had summited in an unbelievable 10 days, which meant we hadn't even had a sniff of the bad weather Denali can throw at you, but we had still been there. We had also tested all our gear and were happy. Now it was just a case of keeping fit.

Before long, though, the issue of the seventh member of the team came up. With Errol off the climbing team, there was an empty place, and this was compounded when Lawrence unfortunately had to pull out. He'd been diagnosed as a type two insulin-dependent diabetic shortly after the Antarctica trip. His doctor was sure that his experience on Vinson had triggered his condition. It wasn't too much of a concern for Lawrence: ironically, it meant he had to adopt a healthier lifestyle and he was soon in better shape than he had ever been before. But it also meant he had to monitor his sugar levels carefully and administer insulin when he needed to. This was fine in the comfort of his own home, but on a mountain it would pose a problem, as he had previously discovered.

Soon after we had secured Discovery as a sponsor, Lawrence had gone with Sean Disney to climb Aconcagua. A week into the trip Lawrence had started having problems with his sugar levels and, by the time they left Base Camp for the higher camps on the mountain, his levels were dangerously out of control. With the cold temperatures and changing pressures, it was difficult to keep track of what was happening with his body.

Lawrence turned around and called it a day. He returned home without reaching the summit and was understandably upset. But he also came back with the realization and acceptance that climbing Everest in his state was an unacceptable risk. We were all dismayed that he had pulled out but he was still keen to be involved with the expedition. When we made him the offer of being Base Camp manager, he quickly accepted.

But what about another climber? Again the expedition members sat around the table and discussed the issue. When Robin's name came up, there was now far more in his favour than there'd been before the Denali trip. By now the team had all met and climbed with him and all agreed that he fitted in well. We were also keen to put this issue to bed so we could get on with the final stages of planning. It was decided. Robin Julian Walshaw was officially part of the Discovery Everest Expedition.

Unfortunately I didn't get to see his face when he got my e-mail inviting him along. He said he would have to think about it and talk it over with Natalie, but I knew he was chuffed.

As Robin lived in Canada, we would only see him again in Kathmandu at the start of the Everest trip. He felt bad that he was so far away and wanted to know how he could help. When the team remembered that he worked for Microsoft, the list of MS products that were suddenly 'needed' grew and grew.

As for the rest of us, we had all got back from Denali in pretty good shape, but the trick was to try to maintain that level of fitness. Discovery proposed that we hook up with the Sports Science Institute in Newlands, Cape Town. The SSI is run by Professor Tim Noakes and Morné du Plessis, and is a professional outfit that coaches and trains some of the country's top athletes.

Tim also has a personal interest in high mountain physiology and his knowledge about the human sports physique is unequalled.

We were all keen. In fact our initial assessment had taken place shortly before the Denali trip, so that the guys at the institute could get a benchmark of where we were physiologically and put something together for us.

As the months went by, the team members slowly increased their fitness levels and supplied the institute with weekly updates on how they were doing. Body IQ, the fitness and health assessment programme operating in conjunction with the Sports Science Institute, had kindly sponsored a step test kit that kept track of how quickly our hearts were able to recover after any exercise. Every Monday morning we would do the step test and e-mail the results to the institute. They would then compare them to their fitness models and give us feedback. This was represented in a percentage score showing whether we were either overtraining, or spending too much time watching television. It was a fascinating process as we slowly learnt more and more about our bodies. And, to top it off, I decided to take it one step further.

Part of me still wondered whether or not I was capable of climbing Everest without oxygen. I also had a better understanding of the risks involved and the unique physiology required to achieve such a feat.

I asked Tim if there was any way they could test my physiological make-up prior to me setting off for

Everest. He told me there were certain things that could be checked. The tests he had in mind would be able to tell if climbing without oxygen was a possibility for me, or if it was definitely out of the question. It wasn't quite the same as saying 'yes, you can do it' but it was one more thing that would add to my safety. Tim mentioned something about a hyperbaric chamber and oxygen and I said, 'Sure, I'm in.' I didn't quite know what I was letting myself in for.

One day in November 2002 I arrived at the Sports Science Institute and met Tim and some of his colleagues. From there we drove the short distance to Claremont Hospital which housed one of the few hyperbaric chambers in the country. The chamber was shaped like a capsule and was about six metres (20 feet) long. It was housed in a room with a whole lot of fancy equipment. Tim introduced me to the test team, which included Stephan du Toit, the biokineticist assigned to me, the anaesthetist, Dr Anthony Allwood, and Dr Paula Robson, who would administer a cognitive test. There were also a few technical people monitoring the equipment outside the chamber, and, lastly, a cameraman to record everything.

I looked around in amazement while I waited for all the necessary equipment to be set up. Then Anthony, the anaesthetist, called me into a side room and said we had to begin the tests. Basically, what they were going to do was put me into the chamber with a bunch of people and then slowly change the atmosphere to represent different altitudes. Ultimately, if possible, they would try to get to Everest's altitude. I would be breathing the air inside the chamber while the others who were with me would wear masks allowing them to breathe 'normal' air. The idea was that, as we reached each new height, I would do a step test and a cognitive test. What I hadn't realized was that they would also be

Tim Noakes (left) watches the readings as we near the simulated height of Everest's summit.

The mask on my face measures the gases coming from my lungs.

taking blood samples at the various altitudes. In order to do this, they had to stick a lot of needles into my body.

> Now I am really quite a squeamish kind of guy. Give me a vertical cliff face any day, but, when it comes to digging around in my flesh with needles, no way.

The test required samples of both my arterial blood and venous blood. To get blood from my veins, Anthony decided he needed to insert a catheter into my inner jugular. I was asked to lie down on a bed while he administered an anaesthetic to my neck, and, while it slowly adopted the numbness of a wooden plank, he proceeded to explain all the ins and outs of the procedure to me.

Soon the big boy was brought out: a needle about seven to ten centimetres (three or four inches) long. This was stuck into my neck in an effort to locate my jugular. Anthony poked and prodded for about five minutes with no luck. He made some comment about my neck having well-defined muscles, or something. Yeah, right, I thought, just shut up and let me think about that golf course. That's what I wanted to say, anyway, but I didn't. The harder I tried to think about some place nice, the more he told me what a difficult time he was having locating my jugular. Soon I could feel his prodding and asked if I should be feeling pain. When he gave me another anaesthetic, I guessed the answer was no. My feet were raised to drain blood into my neck so that the veins were really pumped.

Once more the needle was thrust into my neck and the prodding began, this time deeper than before. Just when I thought I was about to pass out, not from the pain but from the realization of what he was doing, he found it. With a gut-wrenching squelch the needle punctured my jugular and a stomach-turning popping sound shuddered through my head. It was awful, but it was in. How I didn't faint I will never know, but the worst was over. A small tap was attached to the venous insert that was deep inside my neck. The same process was then applied to the brachial artery on my wrist, but this was far less traumatic. Actually, compared to the neck job, it was a walk in the park. A small tap was attached to that one too. Now they were able to withdraw blood from my veins and arteries whenever they wanted to.

The next part of the test was to get everything set up in the chamber. In we trooped. Some of the team remained outside to monitor the equipment, but accompanying me were Stephan, Paula, Anthony and the cameraman. Once we were all inside, the door was sealed with a loud clang. It took half an hour for everyone to get rigged up with the masks that would allow them to breathe normal air, while I had to breathe the thinning air of the chamber. In fact, they weren't really masks; they were more like transparent plastic bags. I was put at one end next to Anthony, where I was connected to various pipes. At my feet was the 'box' on which I'd be doing the step test. On the other side of the chamber was a small centrifugal machine that stood idly by, waiting to separate the plasma from my blood samples. Next to that was a container of liquid nitrogen which would be used to flash freeze certain of my blood samples. At the last minute a mask was strapped to my face. It would be measuring the gases coming out of my lungs. Finally, we were ready.

A suction noise indicated that the process had begun. Slowly a machine extracted the oxygen in the

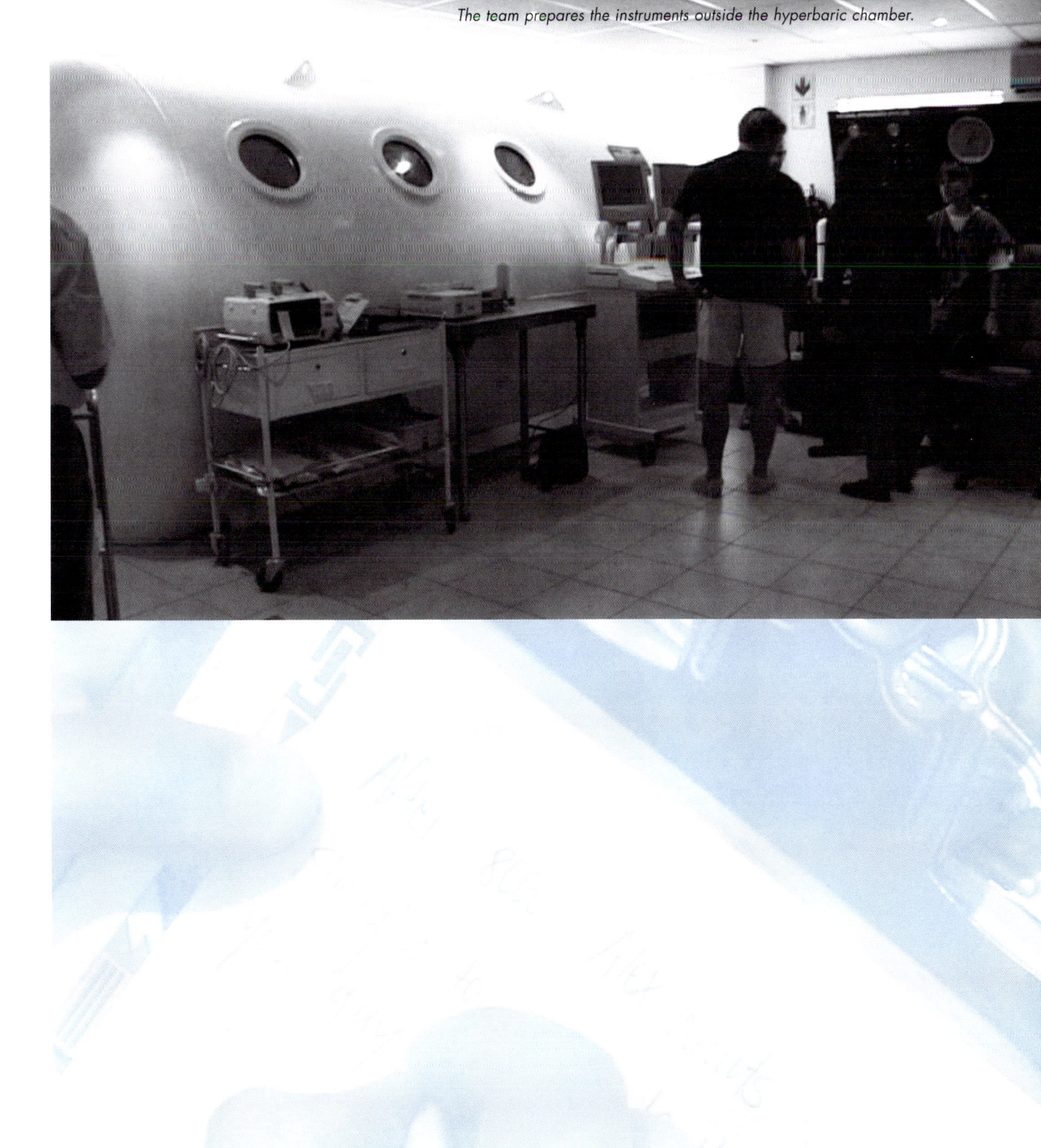

The team prepares the instruments outside the hyperbaric chamber.

chamber and replaced it with nitrogen – basically mixing the gases. The team started me out at the equivalent of sea level, or what was called 'normal' air. The idea was to change the gases in the chamber so that it contained the same amount of oxygen that you would find at 2 000 metres (6 561 feet), 3 000 metres (9 842 feet), 4 000 metres (13 123 feet) and so on, all the way up to 8 850 metres (29 035 feet), the height of Everest's summit. As this happened, my body would slowly become hypoxic, or short of oxygen. Now this was the key thing: how my body reacted to becoming hypoxic would ultimately determine whether I was capable of climbing Everest without oxygen.

I was nervous. When I heard that first suction sound, a slight change in pressure made my ears pop. I knew that the pressure in the chamber was going to stay pretty much the same, but it was still unnerving to hear that noise and then feel it. To add to my concerns, the mask on my face felt almost claustrophobic. Suddenly my throat felt dry and soon it became scratchy. I can only imagine it was being irritated by the moisture from the mask. I coughed.

'Are you all right?' asked Stephan.

'I think so. I think it's just the mask.'

'Two thousand metres,' a voice boomed over a PA system connected to the chamber. It was Tim. We had 'arrived' at our first altitude.

Truth be told, I had already done the sequence of tests at sea level. This was really the benchmark to which all values would be compared. But now the fun would start. Anthony tweaked at the small taps on my neck and wrist and soon had six vials filled with my blood.

'Are you ready?' Stephan asked. He was about to start the step test.

'Yup, let's do it.'

Stephan pushed a knob on a CD player and a metronomic tune played out. I spent a minute stepping up and stepping down in time with the beat. Stephan's hand

if the step test goes good, go to 950M!!

Alex harris

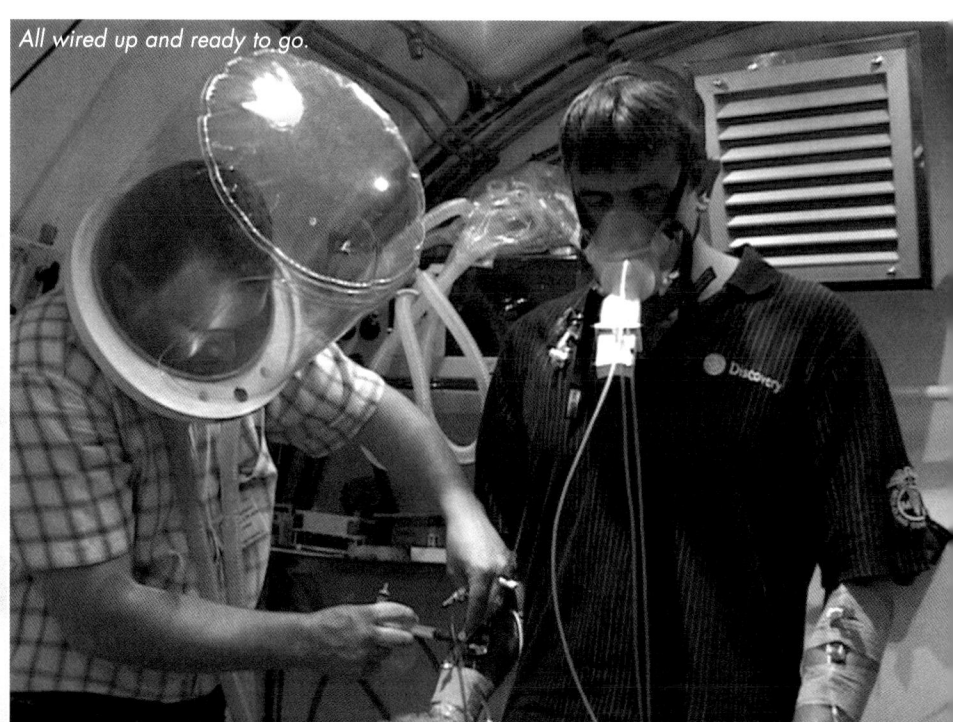

All wired up and ready to go.

indicated when we were five seconds from the end, then four, then three. At the end of the minute I had to step down and stand still for three minutes. At this point blood samples were tapped from the pipes connected to me. Then I sat down on a chair and stared at a laptop screen. It was time for the cognitive test.

The test involved three different screens. The first had the words 'red', 'blue', 'yellow' and 'green' scattered randomly across it. The second screen displayed small rectangles, in these colours, arranged from left to right. The third screen showed those same words but this time the words and colours didn't necessarily correspond, in other words 'blue' could be written in the colour blue, or in red, green or yellow.

From the first screen I just had to read the words from left to right, until I had read the whole screen. From the next screen I had to call out the colours of the rectangles from left to right and on the final screen I had to read out the colour of the word and not what the word was. Tricky! Of course this was all timed and, as you can imagine, the 'higher' I went and the more hypoxic my brain became, the longer I took to do the test.

When all of this had been completed at the height of 2 000 metres (6 561 feet), we moved up to 3 000 metres (9 842 feet) and repeated the process. It was far more time-consuming than I had imagined. Also, the process of changing the air from one height to another took between five and ten minutes. By now my throat had improved and I felt much better. Then we moved to 4 000 metres (13 123 feet) and on to 5 000 metres (16 404 feet), which was when things changed slightly. We now stopped at 5 500 metres (18 044 feet) and every 500 metres thereafter.

When the test protocol had initially been proposed, it had been based on the assumption that I would have acclimatized by the time it was conducted, as I'd hoped to accompany Sean Disney and Lawrence Sooff to Aconcagua and climb to almost 7 000 metres (22 965 feet). This would have given me a far better chance of reaching Everest's altitude in the chamber. Well, for timing reasons I didn't get to go to Aconcagua and this posed a problem. Tim Noakes gave it some thought and in the end the test team decided to stick with the test protocol but change the duration of the step test from three minutes to one minute. It wasn't crucial how long I exercised for, just as long as they could measure some cardiac output. However, not being acclimatized meant that I probably wouldn't get anywhere near Everest's 'summit' in the chamber. Tim estimated that I would get to somewhere between 6 000 and 7 000 metres.

By the time I got to 6 000 metres (19 685 feet) I was still feeling strong and it was impossible for me to tell if there was a marked decrease in my cognitive abilities. The next levels: 6 500, 7 000, and 7 500 metres (21 325, 22 965 and 24 606 feet), all went by very fast and still I felt good, although everything seemed to be slowing down. I don't know whether this was just my perception or whether it was in fact taking longer to mix the gases the higher we went. By the time I reached 8 000 metres (26 246 feet) I had been in the chamber for two hours and still felt fine. Now I was certain I would get to 8 850 metres (29 035 feet), the next and final stop.

Before the test I had spent a while chatting to Tim about what I could expect and why he thought it would be unlikely that I'd get beyond a certain height.
'You'll reach a point where you feel exhausted and you just can't go on.'
'And what happens then?' I asked.
'Well, you will be out of breath and it will just be too tiring to continue.'

'And if I do carry on, what will happen next?' I was trying to understand the worst-case scenario.

'Well, I guess eventually you will pass out.'

'And is that a bad thing?'

'Well, no, if you had to pass out we would put you on oxygen and you'd quickly come round. But don't worry; you'll probably stop long before that.'

The last thing Tim said to me was, 'Don't pass out!'

Slowly the minutes ticked by as we neared that magical height. Then Tim's voice came over the PA. 'We're there, the top of Everest.'

It had taken almost two and a half hours but I had reached the simulated altitude of Everest's summit. Blood was taken and I sat down to do the cognitive test.

> The first two screens were easy but, by the time I got to the last screen, I knew things were slowing down. Sometimes it took seconds to say a word I knew but couldn't vocalize. It was as if my brain had become lazy.

At the end, I asked Stephan how high the protocol went. He said this was it, 8 850 metres (29 035 feet).

'Can we take it higher?' I wanted to know.

'Why? This is the top.'

'I know, but I feel really good. If I still feel good after the step test, let's take it to 9 500 metres (31 168 feet).'

Stephan thought I was nuts. In fact, he wrote down my request on paper and got me to sign it. Then it was time for the step test. The first 30 seconds went by fine, but then my legs started feeling sluggish. Stephan's hand went up to signal the end. Five seconds, four seconds, three seconds. It was over. I stepped back off the box and that's the last thing I remember.

I was having a strange dream and as it came to an end my eyes opened and I could see Anthony staring at me through the mask pressed up against my face. I wondered who the heck he was and what he was doing. Slowly I put together the confusing pieces of the puzzle and realized I had in fact passed out. Tim was going to be angry.

Tim told me afterwards that the monitor checking my arterial pressure had given him a warning sign that it was dangerously low. He knew the instant I stepped back off the box that it would drop below that critical level and I would pass out. Unbeknownst to me, he had signalled Anthony to be ready for me. But he was smiling. The test had been an unbelievable success. In effect, we had managed to do physical exercise at Everest's summit altitude without oxygen or acclimatization. To Tim's knowledge, the test with this protocol had never been done before. Stephan still has that signed request somewhere in his office at the SSI.

That night I missed my flight back to Johannesburg and spent a further day in Cape Town. For whatever reason I had an unbelievably huge appetite that would last for a couple of days. I also had a neck-ache that would last for about a week.

So what did it all mean? Well, on paper it seemed I had the physiology to get up Everest without oxygen. Whether or not I could achieve this in reality was an entirely different matter. So much would depend on the day and the conditions. I decided to leave that decision until well into the expedition.

As I pass out, Anthony straps me onto oxygen.

CHAPTER ELEVEN

Sagarmatha

It is an intensely exciting day when you realize that your horizon has changed. Yes, the sun still rises in the same place as before, and the landscape is still pretty much as you remember it. But something is definitely different. Something is making you get out of bed earlier and putting an extra zing in your step, and your smile feels a lot broader than it used to. At first, you aren't quite sure what it is. But, eventually, it starts to sink in. Slowly, at first. And then, finally, it dawns on you. You are going to Everest.

Now your days seem to pass more quickly than before, but you get more done. You see more people, and more things start to happen. For the first time in a long time you feel you are on the right road. And when you ask yourself 'why now?', you remember all the years of training and the long hours of preparation that have brought you to this point. But, deep down, you also know there's much more to it than that. You know that, just for a moment, in a quiet space in your life, you believed. And that made all the difference.

As 2003 began, the team finalized plans for the big trip. The climbing team had been selected and only the support staff needed to be sorted out. Lawrence was our Base Camp manager and Michael Aldous would be our technical guy. Errol would be expedition doctor but he would only spend the last few weeks with us. We realized that we needed a medical specialist with us for the entire time and Sean Disney suggested that we ask his brother Mark to join us. Mark was a qualified paramedic who also did a bit of climbing. Mark was keen, even if it meant spending 60 days hanging around Base Camp.

Lastly, we needed a journalist to fulfil our commitments to Discovery and the media. Our first choice was David O'Sullivan from Radio 702. David had shown an interest in my career and that of Sean Disney over the years and he was passionate about the history of climbing. However, at the last minute David's leave was cancelled and unfortunately he had to pull out. We didn't know too many journalists so, on Discovery's recommendation, Patricia Glynn was invited along. Our team was finally complete. We were ready.

All too soon departure day arrived. Brit and I had gone down to Cape Town for a week of rest and to get away from the mayhem of the media in those last few weeks. I also did the Argus Cycle Tour as the last part of my training. The next day I boarded a plane to Johannesburg and met up with the team at Johannesburg International that night for the long process of checking in. Farewells before big trips are always frenzied and emotional. The team members are excited, people are taking photographs, bags are being moved everywhere. On the one hand you are trying to make sure nothing goes missing and, on the other, you still want to try to spend time with your loved ones. After all, they are the ones who are really going to have a tough time. While we're off trying to climb the mountain, they're just trying to keep busy, hoping that all will go well and counting the days to our return.

Finally, after three hours of chaos, I kissed Brit goodbye one last time and ran through customs. Just then she shouted at me and told me my cellphone was ringing. I told her to ignore it but she answered and told me it was Adrian Gore, the Chief Executive Officer of Discovery Health. I turned around and took the call. Adrian wished me good luck and asked me to pass on his regards to the team. It was a great gesture from him. Once again I said

goodbye to Brit and disappeared through customs for the last time.

Twenty-four hours later we were in

Kathmandu. The big wheel of Everest was starting to turn again. Kathmandu was busier than normal. With the Golden Jubilee of Everest's first summiting by Edmund Hillary and Tenzing Norgay approaching, a great number of teams were hoping to commemorate that historic anniversary. For us it didn't matter when we got up the mountain – as long as we got there. We were there to complete the Seven Summits. We were a little concerned at just how many teams seemed to be around. It wasn't clear exactly how many there were, but we knew it would become more evident as we got higher up the mountain.

Three days later we were ready to move. Sean Disney had flown in a week before to lay the groundwork, and that had greatly simplified things. All that was left for us to do was to make sure we were at the compulsory ministry briefing about our permit and the number of Sherpas who would be joining us, and then it was time to go. From Kathmandu we boarded a small plane and flew to the town of Lukla. This was where we would start the long trek to Base Camp. Once we'd landed, we only hung around in the town long enough to clear our stuff and have some lunch. We were enchanted by Lukla, a quaint town built onto the side of a steep hill, but the novelty soon wore off as we discovered the whole valley was dotted with similar settlements.

From Lukla we dropped slightly into the valley and then followed the trail along the side, climbing ever higher. It was a beautiful place. The sides were steep and green and a river roared and tumbled way below the path. All around us small villages dotted the hillside, adding splashes of colour to the green hues that dominated the landscape. I took it easy as I walked, enjoying the rich air and vibrant colours. We stopped often at the small teahouses along the route, feeling there wasn't a care in the world. I knew that would all begin later when the madness of the mountain began. Now we felt carefree and relaxed as we made our way along the 70-odd kilometres (43 miles) to Base Camp.

This was the route of the classic Base Camp trek and the same way that Tenzing Norgay and Edmund Hillary had trekked to make their historic first ascent. In tackling the mountain from the more conventional south side this time, we were following in the footsteps of famous mountaineers, sleeping where they had slept and gazing at the same vistas that they had seen. Those first couple of days were magical.

> With each turning of a corner or cresting of a rise, a new peak would rear its head higher than the last. We felt tiny in a landscape of giants.

On that first day, just as the late afternoon cloud poured down into the valley, we arrived at Pheriche, our stop for the night. It was cool that evening and our bodies were getting used to the process of acclimatizing. We were at about 2 700 metres (8 858 feet) and over the following week we would slowly hike up to 5 300 metres (17 388 feet).

Over the next few days the valleys became steeper and steeper and the surrounding snow-capped peaks more dramatic. It was still too early in the season to see the area's famous rhododendrons in bloom but the place was fresh with the hint of spring. By the time we arrived in the town of Namche Bazaar, we had reached 3 500 metres (11 482 feet). We were close to the end of the tree line and the landscape was becoming increasingly brown. The nights were now cold.

The following day we decided to have a rest day of sorts and spend another night at Namche. We set off late in the morning to do a short hike up the hill, where we were promised a view of some of the higher peaks. I set off about an hour after the others, as I first had to report to the Sagarmatha police post and register the group. By the time I got going, it was late in the morning but it had warmed up. I zigzagged my way up a steep slope that started behind Namche Bazaar. Halfway up I turned and looked back down the slope. Namche was a multi-coloured sprawl across the small, steep valley below.

At the top I crossed a small meadow that led to a rise. As I crested the rise the unmistakable shape of Ama Dablam stood across the valley. I had read much about this peak and had seen so many photos of its unusual shape. It was said by many to be the most beautiful peak in the world. I stopped under a tree and gazed up at it sharp shape. It was just short of 7 000 metres (22 965 feet) high and I realized that our Advance Base Camp would be about as high as Ama Dablam's summit. The others had gone on a short way but I decided to head back down. I was feeling good and was happy with a short morning hike.

The following day we set off for Tyangboche monastery. Most of these days up to Base Camp were short and involved four or five hours of easy hiking at the most. By the time we arrived at Tyangboche, it was snowing. We were shown into a small, dingy room that stank of yak dung fires. The dining area was no different. It was also gloomy with a foul smell. After an hour one of our guides told us we had to go to the monastery for a ceremony. It wasn't clear if it was just for our team or whether it was a daily ceremony. We put on warm jackets and walked along the snow to the monastery. Inside it was dark and desperately cold. We all took off our shoes and lined up along the side on a mat. For the next hour and a bit we sat in silence while a group of Tibetan monks chanted out loud. By the end of the session my feet were numb and all I wanted was a warm fire, even if it was fuelled with yak dung.

From Tyangboche it took four more days to reach Base Camp. Most of the group members were feeling good, although one or two people had experienced a bout of the runs. This was normal though in the first few days, as our bodies quickly adapted to the changing diet. What was of more concern was possibly picking up a chest infection or the 'Khumbu cough'. This was a problem that seemed to plague most teams walking to Everest's Base Camp. As a result everyone was obsessed with making sure they stayed healthy. Some of the team wore surgical masks just to keep their throats moist. I tried it a couple of times but found it uncomfortable. Others just made sure they were constantly boosting their immune systems with a variety of nutritional products. I used a bunch of different products from a South African company called Sportron. I had been using them for over a year and was very happy with the results. When it came to using such products, climbing Everest was a bit like running a marathon – you didn't change what you'd been using the night before the event.

The final day to Base Camp was

the first time we got to see this side of Everest. We had just caught a tiny glimpse of the very top of it a few days before, but it was cloudy and indistinct and could have been any old peak. About an hour after leaving a small village called Gorak Shep, I crested a rise and saw the unmistakable shape of the summit ridge of Everest. I stopped for a few minutes and stared. After so many years, and going to so many places, and dreaming about this for so long, I had finally arrived. I was now really on the last leg of the Seven Summits journey. I looked around at some of the surrounding peaks that made up the world's most famous mountain vista. There was a light breeze in the air and some clouds were scattered about. But for the most part the sky was clear. I felt good. I pulled my hat tighter and then turned for the last stretch into Base Camp.

By the time I arrived most of the team were already in and had chosen their tents. Our Sherpas and camp staff had arrived a few days before us and had set up most of the stuff. All that remained for me to do was to pick one of the tents that was left and get settled in. This was going to be home for the next month or two, depending on how lucky we got with the weather.

There were two things that I had wrongly perceived. One, Base Camp, or the moraine that it was located on, was far greater in size than I had ever imagined. The second thing was that the Khumbu Icefall looked far smaller than I had thought it would. The icefall was one of the more famous parts of the south side of Everest. It was a section of the glacier that tumbled down between Everest's west shoulder and Nuptse. It measured 600 metres (1 968 feet) vertically and was somewhat more than that in actual distance covered. It also separated Base Camp from Camp One. No matter how you looked at it, if you wanted to follow in the footsteps of Edmund Hillary and Tenzing Norgay, you had to climb through the icefall, and not just once, but many times. From Base Camp it looked small, but I would soon discover that it was anything but that.

We used those first few days at Base Camp to settle in. It was an intimidating place. After all, this was

Everest Base Camp on the south side. This was where people became famous and dreams came true. Big teams strutted their stuff around camp with high-flying clients who'd paid them a fortune. It was also a place where people died. Not two days after arriving at Base Camp, a member of the technical crew of a large French expedition had died in his sleep. It wasn't clear what the cause was, but it was sobering news. The statistics had already started.

We took it easy, making sure stuff was set up where we needed it. We were also introduced to our team of nine Sherpas. In charge of the Sherpas was our *Sirdar*, or lead guide, Naga. He was tall for a Sherpa and I guessed he was in his late twenties. He had a charisma that earned the respect of his team and had an easy-going manner that was focused around one goal: pleasing us. Apart from the nine Sherpas, we had a cooking team of five. Three, headed by Kalu, would stay at Base Camp, and two would eventually cook for us up at Camp Two, also called Advance Base Camp.

As Mike and Sean Wisedale set about making sure the communications tent was up and running, some of us decided to hike up to Kala Patar, a small peak about two hours from Base Camp. It was a windy and cold day as we trudged back out of camp and then up the steep hill to its summit. I walked with Lawrence and Robin. Lawrence was going to be confined to Base Camp for the next two months while he looked after our logistics, so he was keen to get in any exercise he could. When we got to the top of Kala Patar, we were stunned by one of the most spectacular and famous views in mountaineering. This is where all those classic wide-angle shots of Everest are taken. We could see most of the Southwest Face stretching around to the South Col and then on to the summit of Lhotse. Across from us

Nuptse looked horrendous in sharp profile. The wind howled and tugged at us, making it difficult to stay at the top for long. I stared up at the distant summit of Everest. From the top I followed the route down past the Hillary Step and on to the South Summit. In just six weeks I could be standing up there, I thought. Just six weeks and this 13-year journey could be over. It was an amazing thought.

I guess in a way this was why I did it. To get to places like this. To stand and look at a view so awesome and feel the privilege of knowing I was going further, maybe all the way. So much of what lay ahead in the next few weeks was uncertain. So much depended on factors we couldn't control, like the wind and the conditions of the snow. But that didn't matter. I was starting to understand why it was that I had dedicated 13 years of my life to this dream. In those first few years it was all about standing on the top of a mountain, and being the first to do so. But I had discovered that it was far more than that. It was about the things that I could see and understand, like the spectacular vistas I would come across, or the unbelievable relief of arriving home after a long trip. But it was also about the things that weren't so clear. Those thoughts that come to you in the dark of the night or a quiet moment alone, when just for a while you know you're doing the right thing at the right time in your life. And that's just it. It's your life. When I figured that out, I realized I could do anything I wanted to do. And, right now, this was what I wanted to do with my life.

Ten minutes later we were out of there. We had taken our pictures and gazed in awe at our proposed route. Now it was time to go. We bustled back down the path and then trudged over the tiring moraine back to Base Camp. We were beat. It had been a short day but we hadn't taken much food or water with us. We had also gone up to 5 500 metres (18 044 feet) and now we were paying the price. We knew we would be doing nothing but resting for a few days. Life at Base Camp continued as normal.

> Over the next few days we came to understand a little more about our Sherpas. They were far more superstitious and religious than we had realized. For one, they would not go anywhere near the mountain until they'd had their puja ceremony.

The puja takes place on a predetermined day in the month. Each team has its own puja, and, on the set day, a Tibetan monk arrives and begins the proceedings. We had to sit around for a week until our monk arrived, which was incredibly frustrating. But this was how it worked and the Sherpas wouldn't budge until the puja was over, so we just had to be patient.

A huge stone altar was built and offerings of food were spread about. Our technical gear like ice axes and crampons were laid down on one side. Once everything had been set out, the monk began the ceremony, which involved much praying and chanting. We all sat around watching with interest. Once the ceremony was over, the Sherpas began to drink and party. For most of them, this was the only time they would drink on the mountain.

Finally, on the morning of 6 April, we got the go-ahead to make our first trip through the icefall. This would be a tough day for all of us because we were climbing above Base Camp for the first time. We would only go as far as Camp One and then return the same day.

At four o'clock the next morning we awoke, nervous but excited. We were finally going to climb on Everest. We spent about half an hour in the mess tent filling water bottles and trying to eat but no-one really had an appetite and we were all still feeling groggy. The night was cold but still and the faintest hint of light had begun to filter into the sky. As the group set off for the icefall, Naga and some of the Sherpas picked a route across the moraine in the darkness. Our camp was about 15 minutes from the icefall and it was an exercise in itself just to find our way through some of the other camps. This would be the only time that the Sherpas would wait for us, so I made an effort to try and memorize the route.

A short while later we had left the moraine behind. The first section of the icefall was fairly flat and easy-going. We stopped after a few minutes to put on our crampons. It was quiet except for the crunching of the Sherpas making their way across the ice. They said goodbye and headed off. From here on out we were on our own but all we really had to do was follow the fixed rope which led through the icefall and up to Camp One. The rope had been put in place by a team of Sherpas called the icefall doctors. They would be responsible for maintaining the ropes for the duration of the season. As long as you kept to the ropes, you were almost guaranteed of finding your way up to Camp One. All you had to hope was that a chunk of ice didn't collapse while you were moving through.

After five minutes of crossing the flat stuff, we reached a small rise and the start of the fixed ropes. We clipped on and began what would be a long day of slowly making our way upward. The team spread out as we each climbed at our own pace. After about an hour I reached the first ladder of many. This was a unique part of climbing Everest. On no other mountain would you cross numerous aluminium ladders such as these on the way to the top. It was the icefall and the way it tumbled that required ladders to cross crevasses and climb steeper sections. The ladders on the south side were an integral part of climbing Everest and there was no way to avoid them. Some people hated them. In fact Jaime, my Guatemalan friend, had unsuccessfully tried to climb Everest twice from the south side, before eventually getting to the top via the north side. On one occasion he fell while crossing a south-side ladder and twisted an ankle. He always hated the ladders after that experience.

The first ladder was about 30 centimetres (12 inches) wide and about two metres (6.56 feet) long – short compared to what would be found higher up, but long enough to make things interesting. I clipped onto the two safety ropes that also doubled as handrails. Holding as tight as I could to the ropes, I took my first step. Before the day was up I would figure out that there were two types of rungs. The one had a space of about 30 centimetres (12 inches) between rungs, and the other had a smaller space of about 24 centimetres (9.5 inches) between rungs. Both types required distinctly different techniques – well, certainly with my sized boots anyway. The longer type was just right for me to hook the front points of my crampons over the rung. This meant I had a definite point at which to aim. The smaller type required more care as I had to balance my boot over the two rungs and make sure I wasn't too far forward or too far back.

It took a while for me to work this out, so for the first attempt I just made sure I was well balanced as I carefully took one step after another. I remembered being told not to look down but I couldn't help myself. I took just a glance down and found myself peering into a deep blue crack. That was enough for me. I took two more steps and was across. It was over. I breathed deeply and had a short rest. I had crossed my first ladder. I'd been under the impression that the first would be the worst but it turned out that I'd been hopelessly mistaken. I had no doubt that, as the expedition progressed, I would become much more adept at crossing the ladders, but occasionally the icefall would move and alter the angle and tension of the ladders. The worst were the ones that sloped slightly downhill and were also tilted to one side. These were desperate, as you couldn't just 'walk' across them. They required a trapeze act of sorts, where you made sure your centre of gravity was on the up side of the tilt. You also had to lean back at the correct angle, all the time making sure you were stepping in the right rungs.

But Sean Disney had other plans. He was so big and heavy that the only way he could cross the tilted ladders was to get on his butt and slide across them.

For just a second he imagined himself being catapulted off and disappearing into some endless hole never to be seen by any of us again. A second later he was flat on his butt and this was the position he would remain in whenever he crossed one of the nasty ones.

I laughed when he told me that the first ladder had started shaking like a boat in a feeding frenzy of sharks when he was just halfway across.

The hours went by and the top of the icefall still seemed ages away. In a sense there was no 'top' because the icefall flattened out gradually, which meant you never quite knew when you were going to get there. By the time I was nearing the top, the sun had been up for several hours and the icefall was starting to warm up.

I had just climbed a seven-metre (23-foot) vertical ladder and topped out on a small ledge. In front of me stretched a crevasse about 10 metres (32 feet) across that was bridged by two long ladders fastened side by side. In fact, each 'ladder' consisted of about four sections of smaller ladders tied together. This was the biggest gap in the icefall and one of the trickier ladders to cross, as it both sloped downwards and tilted sideways. To get to the top of the ladder I had to swing around from where I was standing on the ledge. As I held onto the rope and swung my body round, I heard a noise behind me. I turned and just managed to see one of my water bottles flying down the crevasse. It had been stashed in my bottle holder on the side of my pack and all the movement had obviously loosened it. I cursed as I watched it disappear. I knew that I still had several hours left before I got back down to Base Camp.

About an hour later I finally arrived at Camp One on the fringe of the Western Cwm [pronounced ku:m]. I had reached 6 100 metres (20 013 feet) but felt bushed and too tired to look around and enjoy the spectacular view. I collapsed in a tent that had been pitched by our Sherpas and finished what little water I had left. I knew that at some point in the next few hours I would become dehydrated and then things would really get nasty. I lay back for about half an hour trying to rest as much as I could before setting off. When I got back to the top of the icefall, I had a pounding headache. Just

then I encountered some of the others. They were taking it slowly but were confident they would reach Camp One. We said goodbye and I continued my descent. The next three hours back down to Base Camp were a tiring thrash and I was spent by the time I arrived. That was my worst day on Everest.

The next two days at Base Camp were all about resting and recovering from the ordeal of that first climb up to Camp One. We also started getting a sense of just how many teams would be arriving in the following weeks. The mountain was still quiet, with only a few teams on its slopes, and we got to know two of them very well. One was the joint Indian-Nepalese army expedition and the other a smaller Irish team. The three teams had arrived at roughly the same time and we got to know each other early in the expedition. We would work especially closely with the Indian-Nepalese team as we formulated a strategy for summiting.

Apart from the fixed ropes in the icefall that are maintained by the icefall doctors, the rest of the mountain is fixed by one of the climbing teams. What normally happens is that a few of the bigger teams collaborate and share the logistics. From the beginning, the Indian-Nepalese team took it upon themselves to co-ordinate the effort. They then scoured Base Camp to see who was in a position to help. Our team readily agreed, although logistically our setup was far smaller than theirs. We still offered them one of our Sherpas on an ongoing basis, some rope, and also a couple of oxygen cylinders when the Sherpas would be fixing ropes on summit day. The Indians appreciated our gesture and from then on we got along really well. We would often have lunch with them in their grand mess tent and be treated to an Indian buffet. On occasion we would also be invited across to watch a DVD on their big television screen. Such were the benefits of being in touch with the 'big guys'.

Early on the morning of 9 April, our group once again set off for Camp One. This time we were going to spend some time up there and hopefully reach Camp Two. The icefall was quiet and a long string of lights higher up indicated the Indians had set off early. Most of their team were highly trained soldiers who fought high up in the Kashmir Mountains, so they were accustomed to the altitude. They were also incredibly fit and would often overtake us on the icefall.

I felt much better on this morning in the quiet light of early dawn. Behind Base Camp stood Pumori, a 7 000-metre (22 965-foot) mountain. The first hues of pink were just touching its upper slopes, telling us the day would be a good one. As the morning progressed and the sun filled the icefall, I was just topping out and still feeling good. A short while later I reached Camp One. It had taken five hours and fifteen minutes. I had knocked 45 minutes off my previous time.

Camp One lies at the start of the Western Cwm. It's a valley of sorts that stretches around the western shoulder of Everest and culminates in the Lhotse Face. At night and in the early hours of the morning the place is bitterly cold, but in the afternoon it becomes an inferno as the surrounding peaks reflect the sun's intense rays. Lying in the tent without a breath of wind about was draining stuff. If you opened the flap all the way, the intense brightness from outside almost blinded you. If you closed it, you baked. Mostly, we left the flaps partly open and prayed for a breeze.

The next day was a rest day and I was awoken by Tenzing and Gombu, our two high-altitude cooks. They were hustling about taking tea to the team. I just wanted to sleep but they insisted I take some and wouldn't stop

rattling my tent. Finally I capitulated and got up. I knew they were right to pester us with hot drinks because it was one of the best ways to prevent altitude sickness. For the most part the team just lay back and snoozed. It had been our first night above 6 000 metres (19 685 feet) and the rest had been well earned.

In the morning we put only the essentials into our packs and set off. The goal was to reach Camp Two, bury some stuff and then return to Camp One. This was where strategies on the mountain started differing between the teams. Some only spent a night at Camp One and then returned to Base Camp. Our plan would be different. I recognized the immense effort required in climbing through the icefall. It was also a pretty dangerous place and so we wanted to minimize our time there. This meant staying up at Camp One for a couple more days and then combining the trip up to Camp Two. But this plan also had its risks. By staying higher for longer, we had to be sure we were all feeling good and that none of us was showing any sign of altitude sickness. We kept an eye on one another and while the group felt confident, we pressed on.

The team left Camp One over the space of about an hour and we slowly made our way up the Western Cwm. It was an unbelievable place. To my left, the west shoulder of Everest blocked off Everest itself. To my right, the staggering steepness of Nuptse raced up to almost 8 000 metres (26 246 feet). It was only when we were about an hour out of camp, after climbing a short ice cliff, that the valley truly opened up. There, standing grandly in the distance, was the Southwest Face of Everest, the scene of the legendary British mountaineer Chris Bonington's mammoth expeditions of the 70s. Strangely close to Everest stood the Lhotse Face that would be an integral part of climbing the great mountain itself.

Within a couple of hours the Western Cwm had become like an oven. The route snaked closer and closer to the steep face of Nuptse. At one point the face curved inwards and reflected the sun's heat back into the cwm like a solar shield. I stopped for a moment and turned towards the face. Moving my hand to and fro across my own face, I was amazed to find that I could actually feel the difference in heat when I shaded my face. The temperature was now up to 40°C. I turned my back on the face and had a drink. It was too hot to hang around and, as much as I wanted to lie down and rest, I knew that lingering would only tire me sooner.

Apart from two small ice cliffs

of about six or seven metres, the route up to Camp Two was relatively flat. Camp Two was at 6 500 metres (21 325 feet), so the vertical gain was only 400 metres (1 312 feet). For the most part the route followed a slowly inclining valley. Towards the end it curved back to the Southwest Face of Everest. At its foot I could just make out the telltale small specks of colour that marked Camp Two. It seemed close but as I got to within a few hundred metres, I started feeling the altitude. Camp Two was actually spread out over a rocky slope of about 300 metres (984 feet), with one end at the bottom of a gully and the other end at the top. I came over a small rise hoping our tents were near the bottom but my gut told me they were at the top.

I was right. Those last 20 minutes up a seemingly innocuous slope were murderous. My head was pounding and my throat was dry, and it seemed as hot as I had ever experienced it in the mountains. Now I could go no further without resting every few steps. Finally I dragged myself up the last slope to what would become our Camp Two,

and eventually our Advance Base Camp, although there was nothing there but a couple of tarpaulins with some gear underneath them. A piece of rope marked the perimeter of our chosen site. I didn't waste any time pulling out the stuff that I had carried up and then burying it under the tarp. I turned around and set off quickly, knowing that the Western Cwm would be even warmer.

By the time I got back to Camp One I was beat, and it had been a short day. The sun had drained far more of my energy that I had bargained for. I made a promise to leave earlier the next time I was going to head through the cwm. That night the team settled in for a second night at Camp One. It was a night to look forward to as we all knew we would sleep better. But we had a problem deciding what we were going to do the following day. The two Seans were keen to head back up to Camp Two and stay a couple of nights. I favoured another night at One before moving up. It was easily resolved. We agreed that, since the two Seans were feeling good, they could head up the next day. The rest of us would spend a rest day at One and then meet them up at Two.

What a treat it was to wake up late in the morning and know that the only thing my body needed to do was rest. It was going to be a slow, easy day with no pressure to do anything other than drink lots of liquids and read. Brit had put a small book together for me that contained inspirational quotes and encouragement from my friends and family. I was meant to read one quote a day but I'm afraid I treat such things in the same way as I eat chocolate – all at once! It was inspiring to know that so many people believed in what I was doing and found hope in it. I would often pull the book out in camp and read what they thought and felt.

After four nights at Camp One it was time to move up to Two. The plan now would be to spend a couple of nights there and then head back down to Base Camp. All of this was part of the first phase of the expedition, in which we simply had to acclimatize. When we had spent enough time at One and Two, we would put ourselves in a position to spend a night at Camp Three.

We all knew that the night at Three would be one of the worst on the mountain, but we also knew that, with a night at Three in the bag, we would be ready for a summit bid.

As is usually the case with the process of acclimatizing, the first night at Camp Two was tough, with plenty of sleeplessness and headaches. By now a small mess tent had been put up that simulated some of the comforts of Base Camp. It made the task of getting out of our tents that much easier, because we knew that eating enough was a vital part of the process.

Camp Two was a relatively safe place that had grand views out across the Western Cwm. It was situated almost at the head of the cwm and the only way behind the camp was upwards. On our rest day we just hung about staring up at the route. Far above into the sky directly behind camp, I could just make out the summit. It was miles off and it topped the Southwest Face. Thankfully that wasn't the way we were going. It looked impossibly steep and desperate. Our route would head up the last short section of the cwm, and then straight up the Lhotse Face.

When our time was up at Two, we were all too keen to head back down to Base Camp. As bleak as it had been at the start of the trip, everything had become relative: compared to higher up the mountain, Base Camp was now luxury. This time round we would spend four days resting and recovering. Life at Base Camp was all about

routine and everyone quickly figured out what theirs was. This made it that much easier to deal with the rigours and boredom of Base Camp and it also helped me to keep a check on my body. At half past seven every morning I would wake up and lie in the tent waiting for the sun to arrive. In that time I would take my Sportron pills, read and pray. At eight o'clock it was up and to the toilet, followed by a washing session of sorts. Finally, at half past eight, it was time for breakfast.

The rest of the day would be spent reading in the mess tent, playing cricket on the ice, or visiting some of the other teams and trying to get a handle on what the weather was doing. Trying to predict the weather was one of the biggest challenges on Everest. Considering we were working closely with the Indians, we relied heavily on the reports they got from their military bases back in Delhi. Things were still looking good though. We were only halfway through April and we had already spent our allocated time up at Camp Two.

On the morning of 19 April we set off early, as had become routine. This was going to be our toughest day yet. From Base Camp we would bypass Camp One and climb all the way up to Camp Two. In fact, Camp One would no longer be used and we would now be moving straight through to Advance Base Camp. I felt strong as I climbed through the icefall, with Sean Disney close behind me. Near the top of the fall I arrived at the biggest ladder crossing, the wonky one that was also tilted. Just before starting, I had a drink, posed for the camera, and then began to move across the ladder. I hadn't taken two steps when one of my crampons got stuck at a joint. With my weight on the ladder, the joins between sections had buckled, allowing the two front points of my crampon to slip through. The joint then bounced up again, effectively trapping my crampon. No amount of shaking my foot could free it. There wasn't much I could do without falling off. Remember, I was just holding onto two ropes that provided an element of balance. Sherpas on the other side told me to take off my boot. Now how on earth was I meant to do that?

I was in a predicament but was also limited as to what I could do to get myself out of it. I remained calm. Slowly I took a step backwards and sat down on the ladder.

Sean then reached into my pack and pulled out my ice axe. With this in one hand, and my other hand clasped firmly around the rope, I wedged the tip of the ice axe into the joint and pried it open. It released my crampon with a jolt and I almost went hurtling into the void below. Now all I had to do was carefully stand up and cross the ladder.

'Well done, dude,' Sean shouted across at me when I reached the other side.

'Thanks. Are you going to walk across?'

'Forget that. My butt's warmed to these ladders.' Sean slowly slid across the ladder without any mishap.

I tried not to think about what might have happened but later on in the trip I was reminded of my incident when I arrived at this section again, only to find it had completely disappeared. I heard that two Sherpas had been on the ladders when they had collapsed and both had survived to tell the tale, only suffering broken bones. The entire chunk of ice that the ladders were tied to had fallen into a crevasse and what remained was a complex, tiring arrangement of vertical ladders. To get across them would involve climbing down a 10-metre (33-foot) ladder, then crossing two smaller ladders, and finally climbing back up the fourth ladder to the other side.

We were now well into the morning and my memory of the heat of the cwm urged me to press on. When I reached Camp Two I had been on the go for seven and a half hours, a good time for this section, but I was still beat. I dived into my tent and fell asleep. Over the next few hours the others would trickle in feeling similarly bushed. For Deshun, it was a particularly long day. She had been out in the heat for more than 10 hours and I could only imagine how she felt. But, regarding the altitude, she was fine, as were the rest of the team. We were all acclimatizing surprisingly well. Normally by this stage someone in the team would be showing signs of altitude problems. All around us people were succumbing to dehydration or similar symptoms and were being flown out by helicopter. We knew that if we could stay healthy up to the time of our summit bid, then we all had a good chance of making it.

This trip up to Camp Two had one objective: to spend a night at Camp Three. As we stood around in the morning we could see climbers slowly making their way up the Lhotse Face to Camp Three. It looked steep and grim.

As the day wore on we kept our eyes on the weather and the wind, which was increasing in strength. I was concerned about how much it had picked up in the last couple of days. It wasn't so much that the wind was strong enough to blow us off the mountain, but rather that it could keep us pinned down indefinitely at Camp Two.

After a couple of nights at Two the team was feeling much better and all were keen to head on to Camp Three. We decided to make a short trip to the base of the Lhotse Face. This was for two reasons. For one, we wanted to get some exercise while we hung around camp. Two, it would also give us a better view of the route ahead. We geared up and set off late in the morning, thinking we would be gone for three hours at the most. A light breeze was blowing when we left camp and I felt confident that we would reach our destination. But within minutes it became clear that the wind was in fact blowing much harder than it had seemed at first. Temperatures were below −30°C (−22°F) and the wind was relentless. Before an hour had elapsed the team turned around and gave it up as a bad idea.

When morning came we all felt reluctant to head out again but we also knew the importance of spending a night at Camp Three. If we could just get there and spend a night, the worst of it would be over. This was motivation enough, and the prospect of a rest lower down in the valley inspired us. The team set off feeling determined to reach Camp Three. As we approached the Lhotse Face we could see a line of climbers heading up somewhere above us. It was the Indian team. They were moving strongly and steadily as always and were only planning to make a carry to Three. But, by the time I got to the foot of the face, they were coming down. The weather was starting to turn.

At first it became cloudy with just the slightest of breezes. But, the higher I climbed, the thicker the cloud became until I could no longer see Robin, who was barely 20 metres (65.6 feet) above me. This was still okay. Fixed ropes led all the way to the next camp, so all we had to do was make sure we were clipped to them and we would be fine. The problem, as always, was the wind. If it increased in strength, the chances for an epic increased with it.

Halfway up the face, the wind started picking up. We had all left Camp Two at different times so some of the guys were ahead of me and some were behind. I was pretty sure that the guys ahead would be close to Camp Three and would decide to press on. I, on the other hand, was at the point where the decision wasn't that simple to make. I still had an hour to go. If I continued and things really got out of hand, I might end up in a serious predicament. I decided to give it a while longer. The wind slowly increased and, by the time I eventually reached Camp Three, I was a frozen, walking apparition. I dived into the tent without even taking off my crampons. A short while later Robin dived in next to me and collapsed. It had been a tough day. Deshun, who was lower down, turned around and headed back to Camp Two. In the circumstances she had made the right decision but it also concerned me that she would now be on a slightly different acclimatization programme from the rest of us. While it is impossible for the entire team to acclimatize at the same rate, reaching the various camps at the same time gives you a good idea of where people are experiencing problems.

As the day faded, the darkness began to herald the start of my worst night on the mountain. It was awful. We were now at 7 300 metres (23 950 feet) and were trying to sleep without oxygen. Now and again I strapped a small pulse oxymetre onto my finger to get an indication of my oxygen saturation. It's a simple device that measures how much oxygen is in your blood at any given time. At times it had dropped into the high 40s. In Johannesburg I would long have been dead with such a low saturation but up here, with the help of a partially acclimatized body, I was just hanging on. It was a long night. My head pounded and I tossed and turned, longing for the morning. When it came, it brought with it a sense of urgency. It was time to get down the mountain.

Outside the wind was still blowing at around 60 to 70 kilometres (37 to 44 miles) an hour. We had hoped to leave soon after sunrise but we quickly discovered this was impossible. It was just too cold. Trying to put

PAGE 209 TOP: Ancient huts dotted the valleys we passed through on our way to Base Camp.

PAGE 209 BOTTOM: Most treks to Everest start at Lukla.

LEFT: Suspension bridges occur regularly on the route to Namche Bazaar.

BELOW: Early morning light falls on Nuptse as we near the top of the icefall.

OPPOSITE TOP: Our Sherpas watch closely as the puja ceremony unfolds.

OPPOSITE BOTTOM: Looking down on Namche Bazaar.

ABOVE: *Lawrence, David and Robin enjoying the short rest lower down the valley.*

OPPOSITE TOP: *The climbing team and most of our Sherpas pose for the camera at Camp Two.*

OPPOSITE BOTTOM LEFT: *Sherpas from one of the other teams celebrating a record speed ascent by one of their members.*

OPPOSITE BOTTOM RIGHT: *Lawrence taking time out at Base Camp.*

PAGE 214: *A reflection of Base Camp, with the icefall behind it.*

PAGE 215: *Strong winds blowing off the South Summit.*

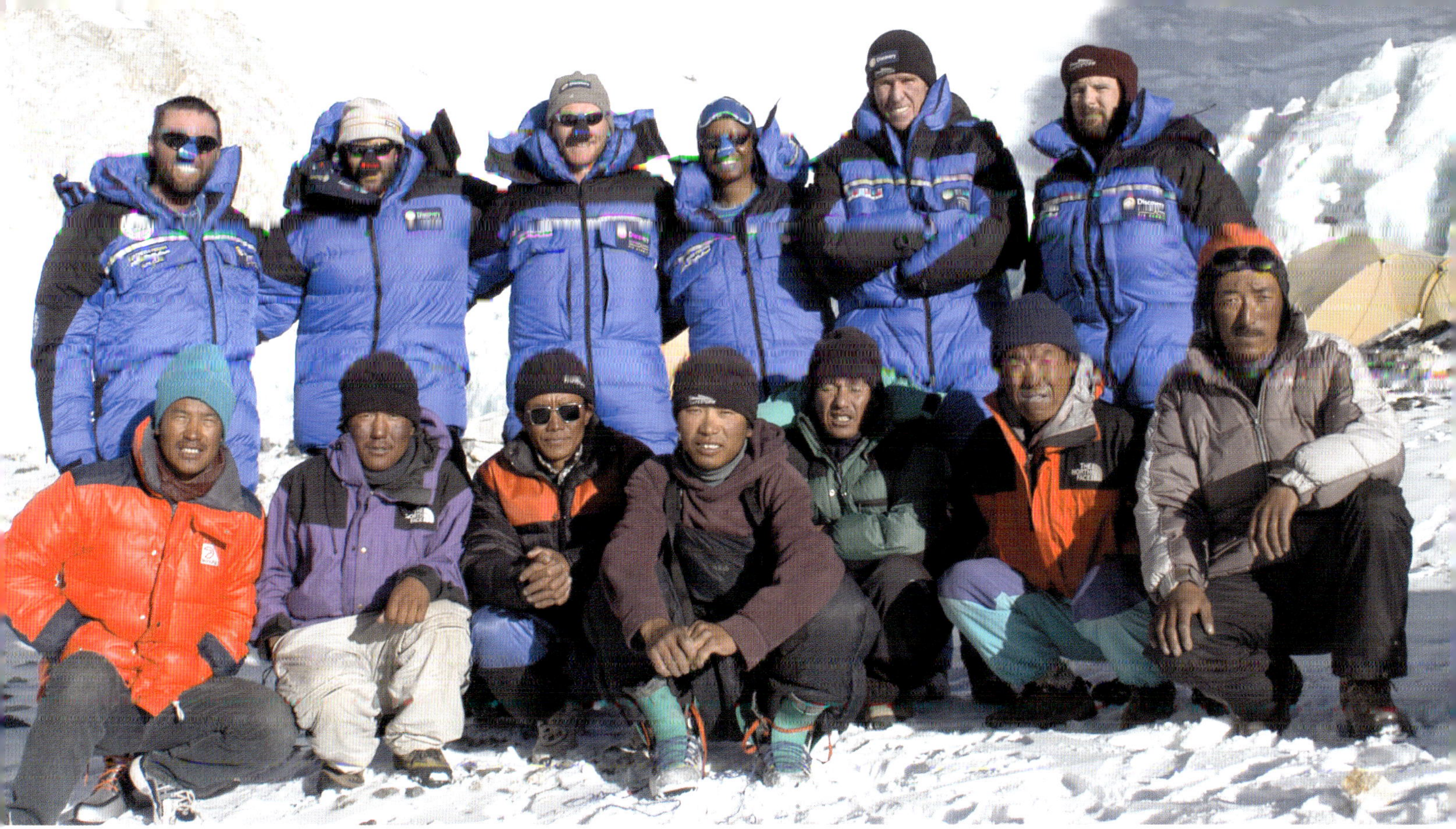

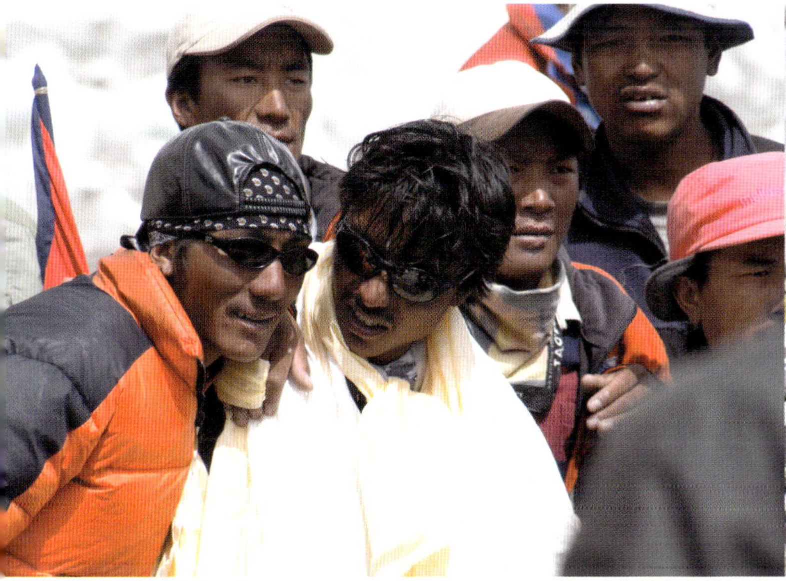

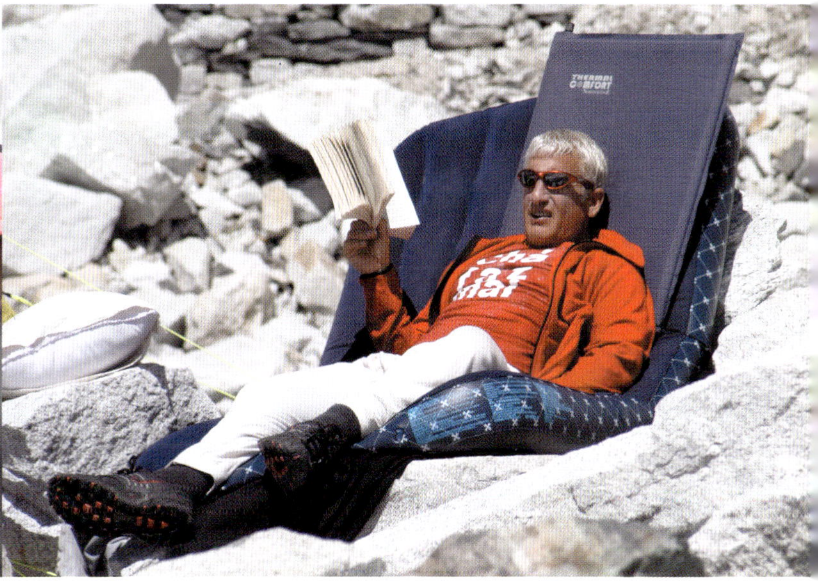

ABOVE: *As I reached the Yellow Band, I turned and realized for the first time how many people were trying to reach Everest's summit.*

OPPOSITE: *Strange plumes off Lhotse indicated high winds.*

PAGE 218: *Climbers moving up the Lhotse Face.*

PAGE 219: *Sean Disney disturbing the crows at Camp Two.*

crampons on with numbing fingers became a losing battle. We knew it was pointless and that we would just have to wait for the sun to hit the tents. When it finally did, temperatures improved enough for us to begin the process of retreat. And that is exactly what it was, a retreat. It was like being at the front during a war and constantly being hammered by enemy fire, trying to figure out how you could survive, and then realizing this could only be achieved by retreating. Get the hell out of there. That was the only thing on my mind.

Two hours later we stumbled into camp feeling humiliated. It had been a tough two days. David had fiddled with his crampons for slightly too long and had got a touch of frostnip. In the ensuing weeks the tips of his fingers would blister and then peel. But he'd been lucky – just a few more seconds and he would have got frostbite.

When we reached Camp Two we were effectively out of the wind and we stopped for a rest. But we didn't stay for long. The thought of warm air and green valleys filled our minds, reminding us that we had to reach Base Camp before we could have a 'holiday'. By the end of the day we were safely back in Base Camp with Deshun, who'd spent the night at Camp Two with some of our Sherpas and had had an early start.

Once the first phase of the expedition had been completed, we were both excited and relieved that we could finally head down the valley for some well-earned rest. It was 24 April and we had already spent our night at Camp Three. This gave us the edge on most of the other teams as they were still moving between Camps One and Two. Base Camp had filled up and it was incredible to see the long lines of prayer flags that stretched from tent to tent between the different teams. These were put up by the Sherpas as part of their supplication to the mountain gods.

Speculation was rife around camp as to the final number of teams on the mountain. The Indians had made a comprehensive log of everyone around and their number stood at 32 teams. That meant around 1 000 people at Base Camp. It was no longer a camp but had grown into a small village that even had a bar and an Internet café!

We had no intention of hanging around camp when the call of the lower valleys was tugging at our tired limbs. We had one rest day to recover from the ordeal of Camp Three, and then set off at high speed down the valley. Even though Deshun had missed out on her night at Camp Three, we still felt the rest would be beneficial

for her as well. In the back of my mind I hoped she would still have a chance to get there. A summit bid without a night at Camp Three would be a risky endeavour, even though it did happen quite frequently.

We were all in high spirits when we raced out of Base Camp and down the valley like madmen possessed. Even Lawrence joined us. He didn't have to considering that he wasn't going to climb above Base Camp, but the long periods of inactivity were beginning to take their toll and he was keen for any exercise, even if it meant hiking 40 kilometres (25 miles) down the mountain.

The support crew really had a tough time of it. Theirs was a completely selfless act while the climbers normally got all the glory. Mike was always busy fixing other teams' computers, so he didn't really have time to be bored. I guess Mark Disney had a similar experience. Even though our team was healthy, he was kept busy by tending to our Sherpas, as well as Sherpas from the other teams. Patricia definitely had the toughest time. When we were doing exciting things it was easy for her to write about us. But most of the time sitting around was boring for all of us, and yet she still had to make it sound interesting to all our followers back home.

The support team also made sure that we always had news from family and friends waiting for us when we arrived at Base Camp, as they knew how important it was for us to be in touch with our people back home.

Five hours later we arrived in

Dingboche, a small village situated in the valley just south of Lhotse. At the head of the valley the South Face of Lhotse reared up like an impregnable wall for a Fortress of the Gods. It was awesome. It was also one of the most difficult faces in the Himalayas and it was hard to believe that Camp Three was located just on the other side of it.

Dingboche was at about 4 400 metres (14 435 feet) but we would only spend a night there. The next day we sped on down to Deboche, even lower down the valley. Deboche was a small village at the very start of the tree line. Juniper trees were scattered about, along with small tufts of grass and bush. The village lay at 3 820 metres (12 532 feet) and was captivatingly described by Anatoli Boukreev in the 1998 book *The Climb*. Ever since then climbers have been more inclined to retreat further into the valley where they can properly recover. We stayed in the Ama Dablam Garden Lodge, the same place as Boukreev. He had written so much about it that it sounded like a destination you would find in a tourist

brochure at your local travel agent. And for us it was just that – a place where we could forget about the problems of the world and just chill out.

Deboche was cut into a broad ledge on the side of a mountain. On the one side a peak rose steeply upwards and on the other a brown, jagged slope dropped down to an aquamarine river. A wooded grove lay around the lodge and blocked out some of the light. In the mornings it was cool and in the evenings a glow would fall on Ama Dablam at the head of the valley, making it stand like a jagged peak on fire.

We spent three days at Deboche, eating as much as we could and even playing some cricket, until Sean Disney walloped the ball over the grove of junipers and down into the roaring river. We were despondent and the next day made a field trip out of searching for the ball. It was found and Disney was redeemed.

A day later I broke the bat. Again we walked back to the lodge and contemplated how we would fix it and what we would do if we couldn't. That's where Mark proved his worth. From his monstrous medical kit he pulled out a plaster of Paris set and went about 'repairing' the bat. All was saved. We had something to do again and rejoiced at our newfound luck. But one last twist in the plot would change things forever. The two Disneys collaborated in a villainous act and nailed the bat to a pillar in the lodge. There it stood, testimony to our youthful foolishness. The bat would have broken if any attempt had been made to remove it. There was no question now about what had to be done. It was time to head back and climb this thing.

It took two days to walk back to Base Camp and all the time we felt strong and invigorated. When we arrived, the place was mayhem. Teams were still trying to get to Camp Three and there were more people than

Crows were a constant scourge at Base Camp.

we could have imagined. It was 1 May – the 46th day of the expedition. We were ready for a summit bid. Our strategy had worked. There were only two or three other teams in a position to try to summit, which meant that the upper slopes of the mountain would be relatively quiet.

In the morning I went to the Indian camp and spoke to Major Shekhawat. The Major wasn't the leader of the expedition, but he was the logistics man and seemed to dictate their strategy on the mountain. He had a deep voice and chiselled good looks and rumours abounded that he had been a Bollywood actor before he joined the army. He had a warm smile and an easy-going nature and always welcomed us into his tent. He also kept daily tabs on the weather so he was a good man to know. As I walked in he was just putting down the satellite phone with Delhi.

'Alex, how are you, my friend?' His voice boomed through the tent.

'Good, and you?'

'You are well rested no doubt? How was the valley?'

'Green. It was just what the doctor ordered.' The Indian team had also been up to Camp Three but had decided to rest at Base Camp rather than head down the valley.

'So, what does the weather look like?'

'Not good, I am afraid. There is a big system over the northern part of India that is keeping high winds blowing over the mountain.'

'How long is it going to last for?'

'A week, eight days at least.'

'A week!'

I was disappointed, I knew that every day we spent at Base Camp would slowly deplete the advantage we had gained. But the weather was one thing we couldn't do anything about. I walked back to our camp and shared the bad news with everyone.

A sombre mood fell over camp. We had been keen and raring to go. Everyone was fit, acclimatized and well rested and now we had to sit around and play cards. Each day I walked over to the Indian camp and enquired about the weather. The answer was always the same. It was still bad. High winds were still blowing over the summit of Everest. By 5 May a potential window was opening up which was scheduled for around the 12th of the month. We slowly geared ourselves up for our summit bid. I was still praying and reading in the mornings, and was becoming increasingly convinced that things were going to work out perfectly. I remembered how clearly God had spoken to me on the north side in 1996, and how I had realized that His plan then was for me to be saved and had nothing to do with reaching the top of the mountain. This time was different. So many things had just seemed to fall into place.

On the morning of 8 May we set

off on our usual four am start. Even though it was still dark outside, the temperature was noticeably warmer than it had been on our first trip through the icefall. Most of the support team were up and about wishing us good luck for what lay ahead. It was a nice gesture – getting up at half past three in the morning was not something you wanted to do if you didn't have to. Our motivation level was high and we all moved through the icefall in record time. I took six hours to reach Camp Two, a little quicker than I had taken on my first trip to Camp One. I settled into my tent as the rest of the team arrived through the course of the afternoon. The Indians and the Irish were also on the move and there were several other teams that had managed to acclimatize while we were hanging around Base Camp. I wasn't too concerned. Yes, there were now more people trying for the top but we still had the advantage of being more acclimatized and fitter than most of them.

The next day was a rest day for us. Some teams pushed on straight to Camp Three without taking a break but we always felt the day to Camp Two was a long one that deserved a rest. In the morning I walked across to the Major to get the latest on the weather. It still looked good. After lunch I sat around the small mess tent with the team and finalized our summit plans. There was almost an air of disbelief that we were actually on an Everest summit bid and we joked about it. There would be enough time for getting serious higher up the mountain.

We would be shadowing the Indians and were still on track for a summit early on the morning of 12 May. We spent the rest of the day doing last-minute checks on our gear. Everything had to be perfect when we left Camp Two.

Late in the afternoon I walked across to the camp of a large American guided expedition. I knew an English client of theirs called Matthew Holt who now lives in South Africa. Matthew was also trying to climb the Seven and this was his second attempt on Everest. I had got to know him over the previous few years and we'd often been in contact on the mountain. The news in their camp was not good. As with the Indians, Matthew's team had a link to a weather bureau, but what they were saying wasn't at all promising. The predicted window was in fact deteriorating and the high winds would continue to blow. Matthew wasn't planning on a summit bid for another two weeks. That was their strategy: arrive late in the season and hopefully summit when it was a lot warmer. It was a good plan but it also had its risks. If the window came early, then they would miss out altogether. Right now they were hoping to spend their one night at Camp Three as part of their preparation, but they were happy to let us in on their weather reports.

I hadn't yet checked in with the Indians so I walked across feeling grim. When I told them the news, they said they were still waiting to hear the latest. The Major looked relaxed but I knew he wouldn't commit to anything until he heard from Delhi.

The next few hours were confusing as we heard conflicting reports about what the wind was doing higher up on the mountain. By nightfall it still wasn't clear what the forecast was, and, to complicate matters, there still weren't any fixed ropes higher than the South Col.

Climbing without fixed ropes on the higher slopes of the peak would be a calculated risk. Basically, it meant the Sherpas would have to fix the ropes in front of us as we climbed, or 'fix on the fly' as it is known. It's a process that doesn't leave a huge margin for error.

With heavy hearts the team met in the mess tent and discussed what to do next. As frustrating as it was, we decided to call off our summit bid for the time being and head back down to Base Camp.

By lunch time the next day we were all back in Base Camp feeling glum once again. The forecast now said that high winds would continue until 20 May. We couldn't believe our bad luck. If the winds were going to persist for only a few more days, then we could have hung around Camp Two before trying again. But, with more than a week of wind ahead, it meant we had no choice but to descend. Spending too long at Camp Two would negate all the benefits we had gained through rest and recovery. We sat around quietly and wondered how the next few weeks would pan out. It was a frustrating time but we had been here before and knew this was all part of the experience. We would just have to pass the time as best we could. For some it meant an opportunity to catch up with their diaries, while others preferred to read. For most of the time, though, we just hung around the mess tent hoping for better weather to arrive.

It was now clear that our strategy wasn't going to pay off. This was going to be a late season and there was nothing anyone could do about it. We had to bite the bullet and be patient. Another week went by as we slowly tried to regain our motivation. It was difficult. We had been on the mountain since 28 March and it was now halfway through May. We could have summited at any time in the previous two weeks if the weather had only played along. But that unpredictability was what climbing big mountains was all about, especially Everest. As we tried to figure out which reports to believe and which to reject, the struggle to stay positive continued. Finally there seemed to be hope on the horizon again – but it was going to be late. The word was out that a window was opening up around 21 May and this was confirmed by the Indians.

When we set off from Base Camp on 17 May it was our fifth trip through the icefall and I dearly hoped it would be the last. As unbelievable as it seemed, it had been almost a month since we had climbed up for our night at Camp Three. There was now a definite sense of *déjà vu* as we arrived at Camp Two. Everyone was pumping up on their protein shakes and making sure they were taking their assorted tablets. Each climber wanted to make sure he or she was as healthy as possible for a summit bid. After all, these would be the three hardest days of our lives.

It was now that I made the decision to use oxygen. I had been praying about this for a long time and had also spent hours weighing up the pros and cons. On the up side, I was feeling strong and healthy. In fact I was stronger than I had ever been on a mountain. I had no doubt that I would succeed with the assistance of oxygen, but part of me really wondered whether I could do it without. However, there was more to it than that. As the weeks went by it became obvious that there would be many people trying to summit Everest on the same day, maybe too many. Climbing Everest without oxygen deprives you of the very faculties you need to realize you are having a problem. It was a risk that, under the circumstances, I found unacceptable. Once I had made the decision to use oxygen, I felt much better. I knew it was the right thing to do.

On 19 May we set off for Camp Three. The morning was clear but it was bitterly cold as the team headed across the glacier towards the Lhotse Face. We set off early to avoid the crowds but there were already hordes of people heading up. It seemed that virtually every team had now acclimatized and all of them were backlogged for this first summit bid. And still the ropes above the South Col had yet to be fixed.

By the time we arrived at Camp Three, there was some good news. Our Sherpas informed us that a team had indeed fixed some ropes above the South Col, but only as far as The Balcony, a ledge on the Southeast Ridge at about 8 500 metres (27 887 feet) where most climbers would stop and change their cylinders. Ropes would still have to be fixed to the summit but the situation was better than it had been before. I hadn't been in the tent for half an hour before I had my oxygen cylinder strapped on and was breathing away. The change was remarkable. I suddenly felt completely lucid again and was ready for anything. I turned it off and waited for the evening.

That night we all slept soundly at Camp Three, even Deshun. In our previous summit attempt she had managed to get to Three and spend that vital night. It made everyone feel better as we were all once again on a similar plan. In the morning we set off at about nine o'clock for Camp Four. It was much later than I had hoped but we were still ahead of the crowds. There was almost a novel feeling about climbing with oxygen for the first time and there was no question that it improved performance.

From Camp Three, the route climbed diagonally up the Lhotse Face and crossed the Yellow Band. The band was only about 30 or 40 metres wide but it split the Lhotse Face from one side to the other and was a formidable landmark in an otherwise monochromatic land. I crossed the band feeling strong and then stopped for a rest. I turned around and was amazed at what I saw. Behind me, a long line of people curved around in an arc all the way down to Camp Three. There must have been at least 100 people. I had never seen so many people on a mountain at one time – and this wasn't just any mountain, this was Everest the day prior to a summit bid. After our first attempt had failed, we had often discussed what this amount of 'traffic' would mean for safety on the mountain. It worried us all but we were determined to do what we could to increase our chances of succeeding and remaining as safe as possible.

I spent the rest of the day feeling strong and positive. High up on Everest was an incredible place to be, both historically and geographically. From the Yellow Band the route split the Lhotse Face and then crossed the Geneva Spur. Once I was on top of the spur I knew I wouldn't have far to go. I gazed up at the summit pyramid and the final slopes to the top of the world. It was hard to believe that in a few hours I would be starting out on my summit day. It was even crazier to think that I could be standing on the very top of the world in just a few hours. Not days, but hours.

I crossed the last bit of the spur and made my way into Camp Four, all the time scanning the upper slopes. A series of gullies led from the col, the neck between Everest and Lhotse, up to The Balcony and the Southeast Ridge. From there, the ridge climbed up to the South Summit and eventually across to the main summit. I couldn't see beyond the South Summit but the trails of snow being blown off it were beginning to concern me. Surely the weather had to get better some time?

I arrived at the South Col and 8 000 metres (26 246 feet) – the death zone proper. For 14 years I had waited to climb above this magical height. But the truth was that only one height interested me now, and that was 8 850 metres (29 035 feet). The very top. I hadn't even bothered to fix my altimeter before I left. I knew the heights of most of the camps and, as for summit day, well, 8 300 and 8 400 metres (27 231 and 27 559 feet), or whatever, didn't interest me. There was only one height that I wanted to get to and I knew what it was: that small piece of snow that marks the highest point on our planet.

Why there? And why that height? Why is it that there are no mountains above 9 000 metres (29 527 feet), and why do experts believe Everest is exactly at the height to make it just possible for a very few people to climb it without oxygen? These were questions that I couldn't answer but I knew that God didn't do things by chance. He didn't make things by chance and He certainly didn't create people by chance. The funny thing is I was conceived out of wedlock and my father was a man I would only meet 20 years into my life. Some would say I was 'made' by accident and was illegitimate. Well, I can tell you there was nothing accidental about me coming into this world, and I knew the dreams and aspirations that lay so deeply in my heart weren't there by chance. I was starting to see God's hand in everything that was a part of my life. Oh, you can be sure there was some kind of plan. I just didn't know what it was all the time.

Robin arrived and we settled into our small tent at the highest campsite in the world. We were now hours away from our destiny. We changed our oxygen cylinders and went about doing the things that people do prior to setting off for the summit of Everest, like making sure the Sherpas were boiling water and checking that we had all the sponsors' flags, and enough food, and camera gear. I was even planning to take Bephu the teddy bear to the top of the world to raise funds for Cape Town's Red Cross Children's Hospital's trauma appeal. We had it all, including the passion and enthusiasm. As the hour dawned near, Robin and I smiled at each other. In minutes we would be setting off together, two lads from the neighbourhood who used to deliver papers together at five in the morning and cause trouble in the night. Two lads who knew nothing about mountains, but only bikes and books. Well, these two lads were about to make history.

A few minutes before nine I climbed

out of the tent and started my summit day. The rest of the team followed in their own time. The wind had stopped and the col was strangely calm. Above, the sky had darkened to a deep black but it was clear. Pinpricks of light were scattered about in a myriad stars. This was it. This was our moment. This was my moment. I couldn't believe it was so quiet. But then I realized it should be. After all, this was our day. Ahead of me I could see the lights of a small team of Sherpas. One of our Sherpas was amongst them and their job was to fix the ropes from The Balcony up to the summit. Behind them, about 12 climbers from the Indian team were making their way across the col. Then it was me. I got into a steady rhythm with my oxygen mask plastered to my face. Behind me Robin, Sean Wisedale and David were catching up.

Within an hour after leaving the tent I noticed that the wind had started to blow. My mind was so preoccupied with where I was and what I was doing that I hadn't noticed it and it had sneaked up on me. I guess it was somewhere around −25°C (−13°F) before the wind started, although through the down suit it didn't feel colder than −5°C (23°F). But the unexposed part of my face was starting to take strain. Icicles were forming around the bottom of my mask and I needed to break them off from time to time.

Once across the col we were on the fixed ropes of the gullies, and they were steeper than they had appeared from the Lhotse Face. The wind was getting stronger and I was starting to feel a little concerned. I stopped on a ledge and turned around. A long line of head-torches stretched all the way down back to camp. It was an impressive sight but it was also alarming. I knew there would be more than double the number of people on the summit ridge than there had been on that infamous day in 1996 when eight people had died on Everest. But then something really gave me a fright: I could no longer see a single star. They had vanished, as had the bulk of Lhotse that towered over the far side of the col. It had also started to snow.

I carried on with Sean Wisedale just in front of me and Robin just behind.

From nowhere I heard a whoosh and just had time to look up and see a rock the size of a loaf of bread whiz through Sean's legs and then through mine. In the same instant I heard a 'foomp' and felt something hit me. I looked down and saw a cloud of feathers billowing up.

The rock had hit the leg of my down suit and had torn a 20-centimetre (eight-inch) hole in it. But it had miraculously missed my leg, which would otherwise almost certainly have been shattered. The rock had hurtled down like a rocket and I knew how lucky I had been. But I had another problem. My suit was losing feathers like a punctured balloon loses air. I reached for my ice axe where I had stuck a section of duct tape for emergencies. But I couldn't get it to work. The tape came off but the glue remained on the ice axe. In the end, I tied a piece around my leg but it was a hopeless case. Besides, I had far more important things to worry about.

By now the wind was howling and snow was whipping everywhere. There also seemed to be a commotion ahead of us. The line of Indians had stopped and they all seemed to be gathered around a ledge discussing something. Slowly the word trickled back. The team of fixing Sherpas had turned around and were heading down. The wind was just too strong, even for the Sherpas. There would be no fixed ropes above The Balcony.

I stopped next to Sean and Robin. Up until now my head had been turned at an angle away from the wind. But as I moved it to talk to the others, I caught a full blast of wind and in an instant my right eyelid froze shut. Try as I might, I could not open my eye. At first I was stumped, then I was alarmed.

I had never had a frozen eye before and wasn't sure what the consequences would be. I took my hand out of my mitt and held my palm against my eye for about 30 seconds. When I took my hand away my eyelid had thawed. I was fine. But I also realized that people would die unless we turned around. We were in one of the gullies heading up to The Balcony at a 40-degree angle. It was steep and rocky in sections. With so many people about, it was also dangerous. We needed to make decisions, and fast. Around us the storm was picking up, making it difficult to see anything. Below, the line of head-torches was slowly fading into the gloom. We could no longer see Lhotse or any part of the South Col. Pretty soon we would no longer be able to see anything.

This was not a subjective thing. I wasn't thinking about 14 years of my life and my dream. This was about now. Turn around or die. Simple.

Up until this point we hadn't spoken to each other because the conditions made talking difficult. Now we had no other choice but to figure out what to do next. 'What do you guys think?' I asked.

'It's not that bad,' replied Sean.

'It's bad enough and it's only going to get worse. Besides, there aren't any fixed ropes above The Balcony and, even if it stays like this, it's just going to be too risky.'

In my gut I knew we had to turn around but I wanted to hear what the others thought.

'Alex, what do you think?' Robin was cowering next to me, sheltering in his down suit.

'I think we should call it.'

The others agreed. In a way we were all relieved.

'Robin,' I shouted, 'do you know where the others are?'

'I think David is a short way back.'

'And the others?'

'Don't know. Haven't seen them.'

I wasn't too concerned about the others being somewhere behind us because I know that, as the situation worsened, they would probably turn around and head back. If not, we would see them on the way down.

We now had another goal: to get safely down the mountain. We turned around and headed back. Slowly over the next few hours every one of those 100 people did the smart thing and turned around. They all lived, although some got severe frostbite. By the time we got back to camp it was past one am, but we were all right. We dived into the tents and saw out a windy night. In the morning it was still howling and we made a decision to head further down. The death zone was not a place to hang around when you had just been beaten. The tent was a mess. Oxygen cylinders lay about caked in ice and snow. A thick layer of wind-blown snow covered our sleeping bags. And we were running out of oxygen.

Over the next two days we retraced our steps down the Lhotse Face, through the icefall and finally into Base Camp. We were dejected, tired, windbeaten and, above all, I was heartbroken. I just knew deep down that it was over.

In the afternoon the climbing team sat around in the mess tent. Just us, nothing else but our thoughts and feelings. It was an emotional couple of hours. We had to try to decide what to do with the information we had. The forecasts looked even worse than they had on our summit day, and that was supposed to have been a good day. It was now clear that there was no single forecast that we could rely on. To top it off, the Indian team confirmed that the monsoon had started and was heading towards the Himalayas. Oh yes, and we were beat, really beat. We would need rest, lots of it, if we were to try again.

Some of the guys were keen to give it another bash and some of them weren't sure. Robin and Sean Wisedale wanted to rest for a few days and then maybe go back up. David and Deshun were beat and definitely didn't want to try again. Sean Disney was tired and said he could only go back if he could have about a week's rest. And as for me, well, I was somewhere in the middle. The emotional part of me wanted to go back up but the logical part said no. There just wasn't enough working in our favour and, the longer we spent trying, the weaker we would become, increasing the risks for all of us.

Someone suggested we anonymously write our final decision on a piece of paper and then pull it out of a hat. I didn't like that idea because up until now we had been open and honest about everything.

'No, I don't think we should do that,' agreed Deshun. 'Let's just talk about it.'

'Guys, I'm definitely not going back up. It's over for me.' David had made up his mind.

This was a team decision and I felt we needed to make it as a team. Finally, we agreed it was over. There just wasn't enough on our side for us to stay. It was time to go home. Tears filled my eyes as the support crew came back into the mess tent and heard the news.

Once you have made that final decision, there is almost a sense of relief that it's over. You know that, no matter what happens, you will not be going through that icefall again.

But the next day was tough for all of us. We heard the news that the Indians had left a small team high up on the mountain and, along with two of the Irish, they had successfully summited. The weather conditions had remained very poor but they had pressed on and succeeded. I guess that, ultimately, they were just stronger than we were. It was an incredible achievement but, in a selfish way, it was awful for us to hear the cheers going up in the camp next to us. Those cheers could just as easily have been for us, but we had missed out. Fate had played us the wrong hand.

As frustrating as things were on that last day, there was still some light at the end of the tunnel. We were going home. It was like a long campaign at war had finally come to an end and we had survived. There was a bustle around camp as we pulled down our tents and started packing things away. This had been home for almost 10 weeks and soon it would be just another pile of rocks.

I walked over to my 'pet' rock and emptied my pee bottle for the last time. Every morning and every night I had stood on this very rock. At the start of the expedition only two or three rocks had been exposed from the ice around my toilet. Now there were hundreds of them. The ice was gone. In a strange kind of way I had stood day in and day out and watched the rocks slowly appearing, one by one. They were confirmation that time was moving, that we were acclimatizing, that summit day was approaching, and I guess near the end, that the time to go home would soon be upon us. Now, all too soon, we were there.

I turned and looked at the icefall for one last time. In my mind I imagined hiking in to Base Camp at some point in the future with my son on my shoulders helping me to find my pet rock, or the spot where we had camped. I would put him down in a safe place and let him run about for a while. Then I would point out the Khumbu Icefall, Nuptse, Lhotse, and the West Buttress. And, when he asked where the top was, I would be relieved that we couldn't see it from Base Camp because I knew he would ask what it was like. How high was it? How cold was it? And those were questions I couldn't answer and I wouldn't want to disappoint him.

But right now the sweet voice of Brit was calling me home. There were fish in my tank that needed feeding and I'd been told that the garden was looking neglected. There were movies to be watched and pizzas to be eaten, and my bike was longing to feel the smoothness of tar rushing by under its wheels at 40 kilometres (25 miles) an hour. Yup, it was time to go home. I turned away and took the first step of the rest of my life.

'Tragedy is the death of the soul, not the body.'

– Reinhold Messner

A Sherpa climbing through the icefall.

The prayer walls scattered around the valley on the way to Base Camp remind us of our mortality.

The morning after we packed up Base Camp we ordered a helicopter. It was scheduled to arrive sometime around lunch and would save us the 70-kilometre (43-mile) hike out to Lukla. Soon after lunch we realized the helicopter wasn't coming and we were told that bad weather had prevented it from taking off lower down the mountain. After a quick discussion the team was divided on what to do. Four of us – myself included – decided we would walk out, not wanting to risk hanging around Base Camp indefinitely. Lawrence Seeff, Sean and Mark Disney and I set off after lunch and headed down the valley. The rest of the team decided they would rather wait for the helicopter. The next morning we arrived at Lukla shortly before the helicopter landed with the rest of the team. When I asked why Sean Wisedale wasn't there, I was told that he had decided to stay on the mountain and try for the summit one more time. A week later he joined an American commercial expedition and summited on 30 May 2003.

Epilogue

How do I even begin to tell you how I felt when the decision was made not to try again? In a word, devastated. It is not an easy thing to spend almost half your life working towards a goal, and then in a few minutes to bring the journey to an end. But that is what journeys are all about. Somewhere in your life they start, and somewhere in your life they will end. And between those points you will feel everything that life is about. The joy of looking back and thinking of the crazy people who shared that journey. The thrill of standing on top. The fear as you take that first step. The relief as you take the last. The agony of being so close and the wonder of being so far. The goosebumps when you remember what it was like and the tears when you think about what could have been. Yup, that is life. The ups and downs, and the long flat bits in between. The cold places, the warm places. The dreams, the desires and, of course, the reality. This is everything that we are and everything that we could be.

The morning after we made the decision I sent an e-mail to a close friend: 'Hi there, Thank you so much for the kind words. My heart aches as I write this for it has been an emotional few hours filled with tears, anger and confusion. Forgive me if it sounds philosophical but I had to put my thoughts down, so here goes.

'We are broken, in every sense of the word. You probably know by now that we have decided to end the expedition. We have been battered for so long that in our hearts the only place of sanity left was home. I am not sure if I told you but I had made a promise to God and to Brit that this would be my last attempt. Last night I lay in my tent thinking about destiny and dreams, trying to make sense of it all. I couldn't. I just cried and thought of all the years and all the people who have believed in us. I realized that only when you completely turn your back on something can it end, and something else begin. I am now in the twilight of my Seven Summits journey and the hues of what it is about are still strong around me: the risk, the uncertainty, the people, the emotions. But soon it will be night, and the Seven Summits will be a memory I can read about or look at in photographs.

'And yet therein lies the hope, the true hope that for me makes heroes. For I know soon will dawn a day filled with the faint edges of a new dream, a new journey, and a new life. So my hope now is to hold on for that first glimpse, whatever it may be just shining over the horizon, signalling a new start. I hurt for the people who believe their faith has been betrayed, for those are the people we climb and live for. Don't ever believe for a minute this is a selfish sport. We climb, we hurt, we suffer for others. We spend an eternity in the darkest of hours searching for that one shred of hope, so that they might say 'well done'. But I know, too, that they will find the strength to deal with our loss, and that somewhere on each of their roads a day will start differently and bring something new.

'I have realized also that we are only some of the heroes. The real heroes are the people at home: the wives, the husbands, the loved ones, whoever they might be. Without us knowing, they plant the seed of hope in our darkest hours, and it is that seed that, when we take the first step of risk, grows into strength and courage and grace and all the things that allow us to be people of destiny.

'So my sadness will end. Twilight is a time of aching and of healing. Night will bring rest. And day? Well, wherever you are now just go outside and stare. Look across at the horizon, at the sky and the colours. What do you see? Hope and possibility. It is a day of destiny.'

Acknowledgements

Thanks to: Eva and Gordon Harris, my Mom and Dad, for somehow getting it right and instilling in me the things that really count. Sharon, Mark and Debbie, my siblings, for putting up with me and all my 'terror'. The lads at Adventure Dynamics, Sean Disney and David Ker, and the other lads, Robin Walshaw, Anton Erasmus, Michael Hodges, Stephan Meigh, Michael Aldous, Sean Wisedale and Mark Campbell for being part of this journey. To Joby Ogwyn and Jaime Vinals, thank you for those special moments on Vinson. All my sponsors: Suzanne Stevens and the Discovery Health marketing team – you made it happen! Eleanor Scott and the Sportron team, for keeping me fit and healthy. Tom Mynhardt from Makro for the years of support – thanks, *boytjie*! And then of course what must be the coolest team around: the guys from Oakley, David Hyam, Seth Hulley, Cuan Petersen and Charne Heunis. Not only have you guys got a fantastic product, but the level of friendship and integrity you display is astounding. Keep it up! To the team at the Sports Science Institute: Tim Noakes, Justin Durandt and Stephan du Toit, thanks for giving me an understanding of my body I never thought was possible. To Susan Landau and Amanda Patterson from The Writer's Circle for the writing skills. Thank you for putting the pen in my hand. Laine Barnard and Eight Seconds, thanks for funding those thousands of kilometres of racing. The team at Struik: Dominique le Roux for believing in the idea; Michelle Coburn, my editor, and Sian Marshall – thanks for keeping me behind my computer screen for hours! The guys from the Mountain Club of South Africa: Cliff Murch, Greg Devine, Darryl Margetts, Neil Griffin and Russ Dodding for being there in those formative years. To Lawrence Seeff, Roger Pearce and Franco Sianni for being both friends and mentors. And then finally, I must give thanks to God and my Lord and Saviour, Jesus Christ, for the unending grace, the love and the sense of purpose that come with being a child of yours. Any glory in this journey belongs to you!